Dedication

To Corrie Dutton and Ricardo Gonzalez, who we met in 2017 when they were rising 2L law students at Tulane Law School. They embody the spirit of this project in their adventure, approach, kindness, patience, and fearlessness. This project and our lives are richer for the time you devoted to us and our project.

Acknowledgments

To Roxane Cerda for her amazing editing, kindness, and eye, which magically transformed this manuscript into the book that it is. To the whole team at C&T, including April Mostek, Gailen Runge, Sophia Scardaci, and Zinnia Heinzmann. And to Nancy Jewell, who got this all started, and thanks to Amy Barrett-Daffin, for believing in the *Just Wanna®* series.

To those who taught us writing. To Sid's teachers at the New Orleans Center of Creative Arts: Anya Groner, Tia Clark, Andy Young, Anne Gisleson, and Lara Naughton, who shaped who they are as a writer, and, of course, to Yvette Cuccia, the woman who always cheers on our little community of teenaged artists. To Paul Elitzik, Anya Davidson, and Jenny Magnus, Sid's advisors and professors at the School of the Art Institute of Chicago, who have helped navigate the next stages of writing and life. And to Sid's 5th grade English teacher Kimberly Lichtenberger, thank you for making writing a constant presence in life. For Elizabeth, it was Robert Wohl (1937–2021), her dissertation chair, and especially Sarita Steinberg Townsend (1940–2008), who read everything Elizabeth wrote many times over.

The last six years have been a big journey, and we've made many friends along the way. This book could not have been written without tremendous support and insight. To our more than 400 Just Wanna Quilt podcast guests and our over 4000-strong Quilting Army on Facebook, who shared their stories with us, we are so very grateful. Thank you to all of the companies,

quilters, crafters, and legal professionals that have supported our work, especially Mary Fons, Scott Fortunoff, Willow Olson, Patricia Fellows, Brandy Karl, Eric Goldman, Norma Smith, Joel Feldman, Pam Heller, David Gantz, Tula Pink, Jill Repp, Joel Sellers, Janice Sayas, Rachel Arrison, Whitney Chatmon, Andi Barney, Pam Weeks, Judy Walker, Chris Reed, Katie Dye, Brian Frye, Bob Ruggiero, Mickey Krueger, Amanda Murphy, Mary Yetta, Ryan Noormohamed, Marianne Fons, Cheryl Sleboda Whited, and Edith Gross, among many others. And special thanks to the law students, faculty, and administration at Tulane University. The work has been supported by a number of Tulane University grants including the Jill H. and Avram A. Glazer Professor of Social Entrepreneurship, the Lepage Faculty Fellowship, the Paul R. Verkuil Faculty Research Fund, and the Newcomb Institute Faculty Fellowship. And finally, to the volunteers who have helped us with testing the book and to Kelly Connelly at Markify.

And to Ron Gard, of course, who lives and teaches entrepreneurship every day; we love our life with you; to Ina Gard, who gives her support to us every day, as a grandmother, mother-in-law and friend; to Robert Townsend, who lived the entrepreneurial legal life; and finally, to Skyler Yetta, an honorary Gard who always makes his own road in life in the best and weirdest ways. And to Remy and Patrick, who contribute in their own cat way, and never missed a Zoom meeting. But not to Rocky and Abigail, because (our) dachshunds just don't understand trademarks at all.

CONTENTS

Introduction

Just Wanna Trademark for Makers is a legal resource for the busy, creative entrepreneur. Registering a trademark is one of the key anchors of a business venture, just like opening a bank account. It protects the naming of the business, services, or goods that a business sells. The questions are (1) can that trademark be legally protected, and (2) have you infringed on someone's brand by choosing that trademark?

This book advocates for you to apply for a federally-registered trademark with the United States Patent and Trademark Office (USPTO). For a long time, for many small entrepreneurs or start-ups, trying to register your trademark seemed like an impossible task: expensive and intimidating, something to put off for another time. The Internet has made the trademark application process more accessible, but in doing so, also a bit confusing. For the busy entrepreneur, how do you know what you need to do, and how do you do it cost-effectively?

Crafters are a DIY-kind of community. So, why not get real and teach you how trademark really works and help you understand the application process like a pro? That way, you can make informed decisions about your branding and business. You can hire an attorney, use available trademark legal services, or do it yourself. But you will understand the language, the *physics* of trademark.

We are a team: a law professor and an artist/crafter/writer. Together, we tackle the questions surrounding entrepreneurship for start-ups and businesses. Elizabeth Townsend Gard (she/her) is a law professor at Tulane University Law School, where she specializes in copyrights, trademarks, and entrepreneurship (and she loves to quilt). She is also the host of the *Just Wanna Quilt* podcast, which explores the culture and legal side of the quilting

and craft industry. Sidne K. Gard (they/them) is an artist, writer, and crafter. Currently, they are an undergraduate Distinguished Scholar at the School of the Art Institute of Chicago. They are also a managing editor and the entertainment editor for *F Newsmagazine*.

Elizabeth and Sidne at a photoshoot for *Quiltfolk* magazine in the first year of the project • *Photo by Melanie Zacek for Quiltfolk © 2018*

Together, we set out on a journey to understand and communicate the key legal elements of businesses to creatives who are also entrepreneurs. *Just Wanna Trademark for Makers* is the result of that work. We explain and translate key terms for you and walk you through the process.

Over the last five years, Elizabeth has interviewed more than 500 people about their relationship to sewing, crafts, and intellectual property for the podcast *Just Wanna Quilt*. Industry leaders, regular quilters, celebrities, lawyers, law professors, and many entrepreneurs have come to talk to her about their experiences. This project began as an exploration of the business of quilting, but it quickly expanded to the craft and art industries and those who love to make. Some were entrepreneurs. Others were hobbyists. And as we learned from them, we saw that their questions and experiences were the same, whether they were knitters selling on Etsy or someone starting a tech company. That's how this book series, *Just Wanna for Makers*, began.

The *Just Wanna Quilt* podcast launched on February 5, 2018, and it focuses on the intersection of quilting and crafts and the law. People tell their stories and then, in the last fifteen minutes of each episode, discuss any intellectual property issues they have faced in making their art.

One of the key areas that people often need information about is trademark law. Trademarks are the core identity of any business. But for many, hiring a trademark attorney seems out of reach. We are meeting you where you are, hoping to provide a resource that will let you take control of the choices in your business development.

Along the way, on our *Just Wanna* journey, we have met a lot of people who were looking for information about applying for a trademark, and we have met wonderful entrepreneurs fulfilling their dreams. We've watched their businesses grow, and we are happy to play a small part in their trademark journey.

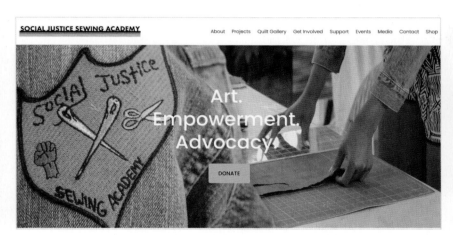
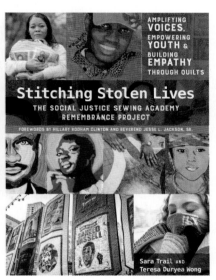

Sara Trail started the Social Justice Sewing Academy, which has grown into a movement of expression and craft.

One such entrepreneur is Sara Trail, who created the Social Justice Sewing Academy (SJSA) in 2017 with the idea that access to textile art could be an agent of social change. Sara's non-profit brings youth workshops into schools, prisons, and community centers, where young artists can express their experiences in cloth. Their work has been shown in museums across the country. Now, they have a number of projects, including *The Remembrance Project*, honoring victims of violence; the *Memorial Quilt Project*, to celebrate lives lost; and co-authored a book, *Stitching Stolen Lives: The Social Justice Sewing Academy Remembrance Project*, C&T Publishing. Early in our project, we also tutored Sara and SJSA in the basics of trademark so that they could file a federal trademark application with the USPTO to protect the name and brand that they were building. Elizabeth still remembers walking through the application one night on the phone. And so, the idea of this book was born.

Another group is the Quilted Twins, twin sisters, Rachel Woodard and Becky Tillman Petersen, who have a tendency to jump in big to whatever they do. Becky lives in Poland, and we still can't figure out how she makes so many quilts, most of which she donates as part of her endless charity work. Rachel owns a quilt shop in Florida, with a large online presence. They have applied for and received three trademarks, one for printed sewing and quilting patterns, another for fabrics for textile use, and a third for a retail store featuring fabrics and quilting products, all under the Quilted Twins brand.

Quilted Twins

The Quilted Twins span the Atlantic Ocean. With a business that is part quilt patterns and part quilt shop, these two are unstoppable.

These are just two of the many stories and people we have come to know. We look forward to hearing about your journey, and we hope you find this book helpful.

Teddie Bernard is a comic artist who is on this trademark journey with us. Teddie's comic *Bad Parable* tells the story of a set of anthropomorphic characters confronting the difficulties of the times we live in. He has graciously agreed to have his characters go on this *Just Wanna Trademark for Makers* journey with us. We have a feeling that what Teddie and his band of characters think about the process may reflect your own thoughts, and so we welcome them to the narrative To see more of *Bad Parable* and Teddie's other comics, go to teddiebernard.net.

BEV the beaver

BEV IS A COOKIE ENTREPRENEUR AND CHILL GUY.

KAT the cat

KAT IS A BIT CYNICAL BUT SUPPORTIVE OF HER FRIENDS.

YELLO the mouse

YELLO LOVES EATING COOKIES.

TEDDIE the cartoonist

TEDDIE WRITES THE COMIC STRIP "BAD PARABLE."

How to Use This Book

This book is designed to help you apply for a trademark and then maintain and use it. We take you through learning about trademarks, getting ready to file a trademark application, and responding to common issues that might arise with your trademark application.

We suggest you jump in and work through this book section by section:

PART I: WHAT IS YOUR MARK? explains what makes a strong trademark and how to think about what you might want to apply to register. From learning about the various types of marks to troubleshooting potential issues, you'll work through all the steps to finalize your desired mark. You will also learn about the *International Classification* system, which tells the world just exactly what your trademark applies to.

PART II: CAN YOU USE THIS MARK? takes you through searches and checks to be sure that your mark is viable and available. In the process, you'll learn how to search the USPTO trademark records to find out whether there are any conflicts with your idea for a mark.

PART III: THE APPLICATION takes you through the application process, step by step.

PART IV: YOUR TRADEMARK looks at what happens once you have your trademark certificate, including how to maintain your trademark; what happens if someone infringes on your trademark; and what others can legally do with your trademark, even without your permission.

Icons Used in This Book

A couple helpful icons are designed to make it easier for you to use this book. When you see these symbols, you'll know what to do.

 Lawyer time icon alerts you that the question or issue at hand may be more complicated than a DIY solution. You are not required to hire an attorney when you encounter something sticky, but we tell you when it may be a wise decision.

 **Online resources icon** provides additional resources on the Web may be helpful in understanding a particular topic.

The Big Trademark Application List and Weblinks Document

Finally, we want to introduce you to the Big Trademark Application List (page 135) and the weblinks document. We have compiled the many steps you will follow into a form that you can fill out as you work through this book so you will be ready when it is time to apply for your trademark. We want you to copy, download, and use this list. Don't let the size of the Big List be intimidating. You will learn along the way that many items will not not apply to your particular situation, and you'll get to **skip them!** The Big List also allows you to double-check that you are prepared, whether filling out the application or chatting with an attorney.

Weblinks are sometimes long and difficult to type accurately. To make it easier for you to quickly find the page you need we've provided a list of links found in *Just Wanna Trademark for Makers*.

To access the document through the tiny url, type the web address provided into your browser window. To access the document through the QR code, open the camera app on your phone, aim the camera at the QR code, and click the link that pops up on the screen.

tinyurl.com/11564-patterns-download

Before you begin working your way through the book, open up this document and keep it handy on your computer. When you find a webpage that you want to visit, scroll down and find the corresponding chapter title. Under each chapter title, you'll find a listing of the direct weblinks for each site discussed in the book. Simply click on the link and avoid lots of extra typing.

Web addresses can also change from time to time. We will update the web addresses in this document when notified of a change to any website addresses found in *Just Wanna Trademark for Makers*.

Ready? Let's Dive In!

We are going to take you step-by-step in understanding trademark and preparing the materials for your application. Get a snack. Grab some coffee. And let's do this!

PART I
What Is Your Mark?

The task is to get your trademark application successfully through the United States Patent and Trademark Office (USPTO) process, from submitting the application, to the review process, and finally, accepted as a federally-registered trademark. Our goal is to get you up to speed on how trademark works—the physics of the system—so that you can be in the mindset of the trademark examiner, the person at the USPTO who will be reviewing your application. To do this, we begin with some basic trademark concepts and vocabulary.

Part I starts with an overview of the types of trademarks and covers some questions people usually have before they dive in. Then, before we do anything else, we walk you through the steps in deciding the type of mark you want to register.

1 **Learn about trademarks.** Learn some basic terms and concepts of trademark so you understand the legal language surrounding trademark and how trademark fits within the larger field of intellectual property.

2 **Choose a mark.** Find out about words, designs, smells, sounds, symbols, motions, color-only marks, phrases, and domain names to determine which is best for your good/services.

3 **Evaluate the strength of the mark.** Identify the type of mark (inherently distinctive or merely descriptive) and make sure that it is not generic.

4 **Check statutory exceptions.** Confirm that no weird statutory limitations might muck up your application.

5 **Choose the category and International Class.** Lastly, select the right category and International Class (sometimes referred to as class) for your mark.

That's the first part! Let's get started.

Trademark Basics

This book is a step-by-step guide through each part of the USPTO trademark application process, as well as from thinking of a trademark for a product, business, or service to expanding the trademark for your products and services and protecting that registered trademark. Think of us as friends (and not your lawyers) helping you along the way.

Obtaining a federal trademark registration is not terribly hard—there are just some steps to get through. You can do it. You can understand it. But we'll also help you identify when it might be a good idea to hire a lawyer because it is a bit more complicated. If you believe that your mark is complicated or you have a large investment at stake, don't hesitate to hire a trademark attorney. And if you have first read this book, you can have more sophisticated conversations with your attorney and be better able to explain what you want because you will understand the ecosystem, the language, and the process. It might even lower

Obtaining a federal trademark registration is not terribly hard—there are just some steps to get through. You can do it.

your attorney's fees because they won't have to take so much time explaining things to you!

This book may seem big and intimidating, but we'll guide you along the way. Sometimes, though, something specific will come up that doesn't apply to your mark, such as using a flag in your logo. We've included all kinds of situations that might occur, with signposts that tell you when you can skip a part. That's why the book is so big! So, don't be intimidated by its length.

You'll likely need a couple of evenings to read through this book, learn about trademarks, and then start to apply the lessons to your own situation. We'll help you along the way. And then, you might need a little bit of time, maybe an hour or so, to fill out the application. And then, you'll wait for the USPTO's response, which often takes *months*, but it is worth it. So, let's learn more about exactly what a federal trademark is and why (or whether) you should apply for one.

What Is a Trademark?

We all see trademarks every day—the Nike swoosh, the McDonald's arches, the Starbucks mermaid, and many more. Large and small companies alike protect their brands, in part by registering their trademarks with the USPTO. Trademarks have become part of our everyday world: They help us recognize and differentiate between the goods and services of companies. Trademarks can become an asset for your business.

When trademark specialists refer to the mark itself, they use all caps: JUST WANNA QUILT, MCDONALD'S, BEYOND BOURBON STREET, or JUKI. These are all trademarks, and we know that we are referring to the mark because it is capitalized. We follow this standard for the remainder of the book.

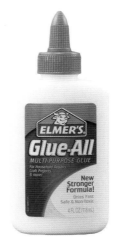

Do Your Trademark Homework

You have a band. You have an Etsy shop. You are writing a comic. You have a non-profit focused on supporting cosplay. You are growing your food truck business. You want to start a quilting and sewing business. No matter what type of business venture you are starting, a trademark protects your brand. You obtain it for specific purposes: to use for education and entertainment, to make rope, or to provide computer repair services, for example. Can you identify what each of the following marks might be for?

You are spending a lot of time building your business. What if all of that effort in making your brand strong goes away? Someone else could register the name before you, or maybe someone else is already using it. By doing your trademark homework now, you can be confident in knowing you are building your business without worry.

Businesses that have registered trademarks for their goods or services with the USPTO

Or, maybe you've been around a long time and just haven't gotten around to applying for a federal trademark. We see many companies that have not registered for federal trademark protection, but applying for a trademark is trending, mostly because of the pressure of the Internet. Amazon requires some vendors to have registered trademarks to sell on their platform, and many social media platforms also require proof of a registered trademark if you complain about someone fraudulently using your logo or other elements of your brand (see Infringing Use, page 188). Lastly, you cannot use the registered symbol (®) unless you have registered your mark with the USPTO. You can use the trademark (™) or service mark (℠) symbols without a registered mark, but they don't carry any legal weight (see Using the Registered Symbol, page 182).

Common Questions

1. Doesn't it cost too much to apply for a trademark with the USPTO? The government fee for the trademark application starts at $250.

2. Doesn't the application take a long time to complete? Nope! We suggest that you read this book, follow the instructions to prepare your application, and then file. None of those actions should take you long at all. You may have to respond to some questions from the USPTO in a couple of months. You can also hire an attorney if that makes you feel more comfortable.

3. Do I really need a trademark certificate from the USPTO? Well, do you have a website identity that is important to you? Have you invested in people knowing about your products, services, or business? Would you care if a competitor started to use your logo, your branding, or your name? In the world of the Internet, securing a federal trademark has become a key business element, whether you are a non-profit, a start-up, an Etsy shop, or an established business. We see well-established brands that are now being required to register their mark for the first time and sometimes finding out that they actually cannot because someone else already has.

If you are feeling hesitant, it's okay. We've worked with a lot of creative entrepreneurs over the years, and we get it.

The law stuff can seem intimidating, impossible, or like something to put off until another day, but the information is actually empowering. It isn't scary or impossible to understand, and it's something to face sooner rather than later.

Our philosophy is simple: Register your trademark ASAP, whether you are preparing to start to use your mark or have been using it for quite a while. As you are creating the name of your product, service, or business, think about trademarks and then register yours as soon as you can.

Which Trademark Is Best?

This book walks you through applying for a federal trademark, but you have other choices, including common law, state trademarks, and trademarks filed outside the United States.

The concept of marking your goods with something that distinguishes them from someone else's has been around for a long time, even as far back as the Roman Empire.

Édouard Manet, *A Bar at the Folies-Bergère* (1882)

The Bass label pictured in the Manet painting is said to be the first registered trademark in the United Kingdom, and so important to the brand that the company renamed itself Bass Trademark No. 1.

The modern trademark system grew from the early days of industrialization, when goods started to move on railroad systems across the country and ships around the world and were no longer local. Some of these marks and products are still famous today.

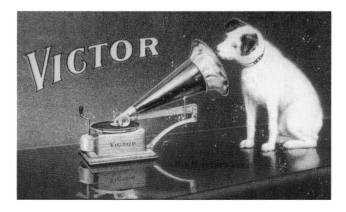

The painting of Nipper, the world-famous RCA Victor Dog listening to a phonograph, is one of the most wildly successful brand examples and was registered as a trademark on July 10, 1900.

"HIS MASTER'S VOICE"

This trademark and the trademarked word "Victrola" identify all our products. Look under the lid! Look on the label!

VICTOR TALKING MACHINE CO., Camden, N. J.

With the advent of highways, people learned that Orange's Hot Dogs in Texas was different from the one in New Jersey, and now the Internet has made goods and services available worldwide. As the world expands, so, too, does the need to protect your trademark.

These nineteenth- and twentieth-century brands knew how important a trademark was for their business. Not all brands rose to the level of a national brand; many remained local. But now, because of the Internet, we are all national (even international), in many ways. Anyone can find us. That's why federal registration has become so important in the digital age.

A 1917 photograph of a woman sewing on a Singer sewing machine, Library of Congress, loc.gov/item/2005696171/

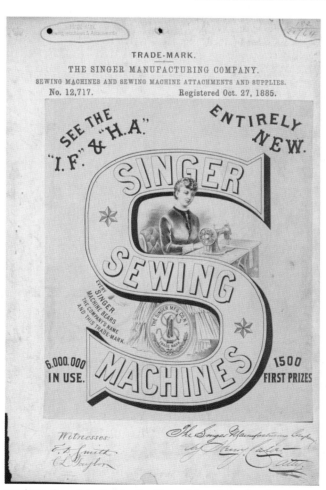

Trademark registration by the Singer Manufacturing Company for S brand Sewing Machines and Sewing Machine Attachments and Supplies. Photograph. Retrieved from the Library of Congress, loc.gov/item/2022674772/

Although we work through how to register your trademark at the federal level in this book, there are, in fact, **three overlapping protections** of trademarks, as well as trademark systems outside the U.S. Let's take a look.

Common Law Trademarks

Once you start to use a trademark, you have priority of that use in your small area—the city or the county where it is known. You don't have to do anything. This is the easiest version to attain but offers the least protection. If another company using that same mark with the same type of business moves into your city, you may be able to stop them from using that mark for their business.

For example, you have a local business called CAT LADY QUILTS. You make quilts for cats. Then, someone else starts a quilt shop called LADY CAT QUILTS in your town. This similarity is confusing to your local community, and especially to your customers (see Likelihood of Confusion or Dilution, page 25).

You, called the *senior* mark holder, may be able to stop this second *junior* user from using the name if it would be confusing to customers, but only in your small area.

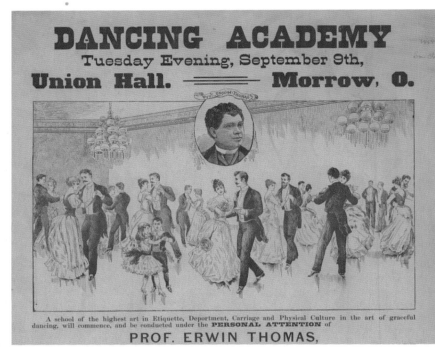

Dancing Academy Union Hall, Morrow, O., Tuesday evening, September 9th. Ohio, 1884. [or 1890] Photograph, loc.gov/item/2005694436/

State Trademarks

A state trademark means that you have dominion over your mark for your type of business throughout the state. You can file a trademark registration with your state, which is usually not that expensive but, interestingly, requires the same steps as applying for a federal trademark. State trademarks traditionally provided enough protection because most businesses weren't crossing state lines and remained local. The state trademark offered a territory sufficient to protect and grow a brand, but then the Internet happened.

As a placeholder, some attorneys recommend that a new company register with the state because it is usually half the price of a federal application and fairly easy to complete. The problem with doing this is that most of the trademark search services that people use to determine whether a mark is already taken do not check state trademarks, which leaves you vulnerable outside your state. If you are thinking about registering in your state, why not just register federally? If you do choose to register a state trademark, you will still want to work your way through this book, as you will follow the same steps and present the same information that you would if you were applying for a federal trademark (see Filing a State Trademark Application, page 173).

Federal Trademarks

Federal trademarks give you priority over the whole country. Most businesses are now on the Internet and have a social media presence, which means that they need protection throughout the United States.

We advocate for federal registration because, by *not* filing for a federal trademark, others can. Let's say LADY CAT QUILTS (the junior user in our previous example) filed for the federal trademark, even though CAT LADY QUILTS was the first to use the mark. CAT LADY QUILTS (senior user) would only be able to use that MARK in that city or, if they filed for a state trademark, in that state, even though they had the name first. The lack of protection would box in CAT LADY QUILTS. But if CAT LADY QUILTS had filed for the federal trademark first, they would be able to stop LADY CAT QUILTS throughout the country and even prevent LADY CAT QUILTS from filing a federal trademark because it would be confusingly similar. That is the power of federal trademark registration. LADY CAT QUILTS wouldn't be able to use the MARK, even for a quilt shop in the same town. A federal trademark gives you a superpower.

WHAT IS THE LANHAM ACT?

Current federal trademark law was enacted by Congress in 1947 (with lots of revisions through the years) and is based on the Commerce Clause in the U.S. Constitution. To read the exact text jump to the Constitution (page 198). We also have federal case law, and some parts of the law vary, depending on what jurisdiction you are in. We talk more about this in Likelihood of Confusion or Dilution (page 25). When the law was just a bill, it was referred to by its author's name, Representative Fritz Lanham, and the name stuck. So, if you hear people talking about the "Lanham Act," you will know that they mean the current federal trademark act.

Texas Congressman Fritz Lanham (1880–1950) began serving in Congress in 1919 and was the lead author of our modern trademark law, known as the "Lanham Act," which was signed into law in 1946 by President Harry Truman.

International Trademarks

If you plan to do business in other countries, you should think about registering your trademark in those countries. The U.S. trademark only applies in the United States. However, by registering with the USPTO, you'll get a nice advantage of an earlier filing date when you file promptly in other countries. We discuss this topic more in Trademarks Outside the U.S. (page 174).

You and the USPTO

The USPTO is where you file for a federal trademark. You fill out an online application, which is then reviewed by a USPTO trademark examining attorney, who may send you a letter (called an Office Action) or even call you to ask for clarification on your application. Then, your trademark is either rejected or *published for opposition* (so that the world has a chance to object). If it passes that phase, then you receive a registration certificate. This book walks you through all these steps.

EVEN UNCLE SAM REGISTERS
Even the USPTO has registered at the USPTO! See the ® by its logo? Only registered trademarks are allowed to include the registered symbol. For more information, see Using the Registered Symbol (page 182).

Reg. No. 4,747,039
Registered June 2, 2015
Int. Cls.: 23 and 26

TRADEMARK
PRINCIPAL REGISTER

AURIFIL S.R.L. (ITALY LIMITED LIABILITY COMPANY)
VIA S. MARIA VALLE, 3/A
MILANO, ITALY I-20123

FOR: YARNS AND THREADS FOR TEXTILE USE, IN CLASS 23 (U.S. CL. 43).

FIRST USE 1-0-2008; IN COMMERCE 1-0-2008.

FOR: ARTIFICIAL FLOWERS; BUTTONS FOR CLOTHING; HOOKS AND EYES; LACES AND EMBROIDERY; NEEDLES, ORNAMENTAL NOVELTY BUTTONS; RIBBONS AND BRAID, SEQUINS, IN CLASS 26 (U.S. CLS. 37, 39, 40, 42 AND 50).

FIRST USE 1-0-2008; IN COMMERCE 1-0-2008.

THE MARK CONSISTS OF THE STYLIZED WORD "AURIFIL" ENCLOSED IN A RECTANGULAR BORDER WITH CURVED CORNERS AND A SMALLER RECTANGLE TO THE LEFT AND RIGHT.

THE WORDING "AURIFIL" HAS NO MEANING IN A FOREIGN LANGUAGE.

SER. NO. 86-402,910, FILED 9-23-2014.

ROBIN MITTLER, EXAMINING ATTORNEY

Director of the United States
Patent and Trademark Office

What You Get

A certificate! Sadly, soon just a digital one rather than one that comes in the mail. But there is more! In addition to your shiny new certificate, you'll have the ability to:

- **Rule the world.** Well, okay, you get to claim ownership of a trademark in a specific class nationwide, except where someone was previously using it locally or in a particular state, where they can continue to use it.

- **Give notice to everyone that you own the mark.** You can let them know by including a registered mark ® on your products, services, and/or company. That tells the world the trademark has been registered with the USPTO.

- **Strengthen your position.** After five years, your trademark becomes stronger, "incontestable," so if someone challenges your use, you are in a better position to win.

- **Claim ownership.** A trademark gives you the legal presumption that you are the owner.

- **Gain priority.** Promptly file an application for the same trademark in other countries through the Madrid Protocol system, and you'll get to use your earlier U.S. application date. Learn more in the Madrid Protocol (page 175).

- **Keep imposters out.** Register your registered trademark with the U.S. Customs Office to keep infringing works out of the country.

- **Collect larger damages.** In a trademark lawsuit, you are more likely to collect larger damages if your mark is federally registered.

- **Better defend your trademark.** If someone starts using your trademark, and you send a cease-and-desist letter, the act has more strength and substance, and the other user is more likely to stop infringing because you have a federal trademark. This includes the ability to file a notice-and-takedown with social media platforms if someone is infringing on your trademark. Some platforms require registration numbers to do so.

FILING FEES

Filing a federal trademark starts at $250. For a full list of prices, head to the USPTO website at USPTO.gov > trademarks > trademark fees.

Do You Need a Lawyer to File an Application?

Lawyers in Term, Library of Congress Prints and Photographs Division, loc.gov/pictures/resource/cph.3a24171/

Even though many people fear lawyers, they can be very helpful. Trademark lawyers are awesome, but you don't necessarily need to hire a lawyer to file a trademark application with the USPTO. In many instances, you can do it yourself with a little guidance, and the USPTO allows regular, non-lawyer people to file applications.

Hire a lawyer if that makes you feel more comfortable, if you have a complicated situation, or if a lot of money is riding on the outcome. If you do choose to hire an attorney, this book will help you prepare for conversations with them.

Word of mouth is often the best way to find a lawyer. Find people who do what you do and ask them who their lawyer is. You can also check with your state's bar association and search for local attorneys based on practice areas. You can also search USPTO records to find out which attorneys were used by your favorite craft company! We teach you how to do this in USPTO TESS Search Strategies (page 80).

When interviewing a lawyer, make sure to ask about their experience in your field (for example, crafts) and their experience in filing trademarks.

Pro Bono Programs

Many law schools in the United States have pro bono trademark clinics that provide free or low-cost trademark assistance, but you still have to pay the U.S. government filing fees. You have to apply for these programs, and there is often a delay in availability because classes must be in session. Each program's requirements and number of clients it takes on each semester vary. You can find the current list of programs on the USPTO website. Just head to USPTO.gov > Learning and Resources > Patent and Trademark Practitioners > Law School Clinic Certification Program.

Volunteer Lawyers

There are also volunteer organizations that help artists. Most notably, Lawyers for the Creative Arts (law-arts.org) hosts a directory of these programs. Check out its For Artists/ National VLA Directory to find volunteer programs in your area.

FREE ASSISTANCE

The USPTO also has the Trademark Assistance Center, especially good for first-time filers. See Uspto.gov > learning and resources > support centers > trademark assistance center.

Online Professional Services

When you look on the Internet, you will find a lot of people or businesses offering to help you search for and file a trademark. It's important to do your homework before working with someone.

Sometimes, the service is only providing access to the free government trademark search, just wrapped in a pretty package. Check to see whether it is offering anything beyond a federal trademark search, which you'll learn how to do on your own with this book. We will teach you how to do this. See, Step 7: Searching the USPTO Trademark Records (page 79).

Don't be afraid to speak up, ask questions, and advocate for yourself.

Some services include a full search, including common law and state trademarks, which is great. One example is Markify, See Professional Search Services, page 197. However, they usually do not offer a full analysis of the search they conduct or interpret the data. You still have to do that on your own or hire an attorney.

But whatever you do, remember, you know your business best, and your knowledge is important in this process. Don't be afraid to speak up, ask questions, and advocate for yourself. This book gives you the language to do that, should you need to.

Not Everyone Needs a Federal Trademark

Not everyone or even every company files for federal trademark protection. Here are a few reasons why:

- You are only selling a few things, or the name of the company doesn't matter. Think of some sellers on Etsy, where store recognition is not really their focus.

- Business practices in your field have not tended to require registered trademarks. Many licensing deals do not require a brand to be federally registered. This includes many fabric companies working with branded fabric designers. But be aware that social media platforms are increasingly requiring proof of a federal trademark when there is a trademark dispute.

- You are not selling anything. Trademarks only apply to goods or services in commerce, which we discuss more in Use in Commerce and Intent to Use (page 24). So, if you are merely recording where your cat moves his favorite toy every day, that won't do. However, if you are also selling cat toys or offering lessons on how to train your cat, you may need to consider applying.

Our friend Gigi Baay and her family make honey and give it as gifts. They even have a lovely logo. But they are not planning to sell the honey or place it in commerce, so there is no need for them to file an application for a trademark.

- If you are crafting for your family, for example, or you have a small quilt repair business where people hire you through word of mouth to fix their quilts, you don't need a trademark.

Speaking Trademark

Now that you've learned why you might want a trademark, it's time to learning some basic trademark concepts. The language of trademarks isn't terribly hard. The idea behind it is that certain symbols, words, or other markers indicate who owns or is responsible for a particular good or service. Legal words communicate these ideas and explain when something counts as a mark and when it doesn't. Let's begin with some basic trademark concepts.

Mark

We use the legal term *mark* to identify goods or services.

> **Trademark** refers to goods. Goods can include toys, fruit, chemicals, purses—anything that is sold in commerce.

> **Service marks** refer to services—that is, things that people do, such as accounting and performing. Music and entertainment, museums, and websites also come under service marks, as do retail shops.

We get into more details shortly, but understand that when you see the word *mark*, it is filling in for both goods and services, and the same is sadly true of the term *trademark*. We use the term "trademark" both generally and also specifically for goods.

Geek Squad is an example of a service mark for computer installation and repair.

Source Identifiers

A trademark must be a *source identifier* for a product or service. Trademarks are most effective when consumers see your mark and choose your goods or services because they identify it as the one they want. They help customers/consumers find products faster (reducing the search cost) and remember what they like and don't like.

As a customer, you know you want a certain type of potato chip because of a name, logo, or other identifying characteristic. Which one do you prefer?

Goodwill

Goodwill is what you think about a particular version of a good or service because you identify the trademark and have feelings about it. Goodwill connects to source identifiers. The goodwill you have toward certain source identifiers is why you buy one product over another or why you know to recommend Service A over its competitor, Service B.

Companies build up goodwill surrounding their trademark through advertising, marketing, and word of mouth. As the trademark becomes known, the goodwill attached to it can become worth a great deal of money and an intellectual property asset of the company.

> **GOODWILL ISN'T ALWAYS GOOD**
> *Goodwill* doesn't mean that consumers must think good things about your products—goodwill is whatever they think of when they see your product. For example, maybe consumers know to avoid buying a certain type of rotary cutter when they see a particular logo.

Failure to Function as a Mark

You know that trademarks must function as a source identifier. Your trademark must identify your goods and/or services. If your trademark doesn't do this, the USPTO will not grant you your trademark due to *failure to function as a mark*. You know the brand of potato chips examples on the previous page because of the logo, the name/packaging. The mark functions to identify the good. There are two additional ways to think about this.

First, let's say a company wants to protect a particular product or claim a particular product as a source identifier. Think of the original Coca-Cola bottle. When you see it, you know it is Coke.

The bottle functions as a mark because it functions as a source identifier. But not every company succeeds in having their product function as a source identifier. Let's say a company wants to protect a specific fabric pattern, but the general public doesn't identify that fabric pattern as being a specific brand. Jenny from Ohio can't identify that this leaf print cotton fabric's source is Pretend Fabric Company the way she can identify the company behind a Coca-Cola bottle.

A second way something fails to function as a mark is if it is a phrase or design that no one would connect to a particular good or service or is merely informational or *ornamentational* (decorative).

Some real examples include:

- WORST MOVIE EVER!
  (refused registration for a parody website)

- I lOVE YOU (refused registration to Peace Love World Live, LLC for bracelets)

- DRIVE SAFELY (refused registration to Volvo for
  the phrase)

Trademarks are often included on labels, tags, and other means of letting the public know the mark of a particular good or service. When you see a Starbucks product, you know that it is from Starbucks because of the name and logo on the outside. The name and logo, in that instance, function as a mark.

Your use must function as a mark, which means that it has to be a source identifier. Even if you have been selling something with the mark, the mark must be used to identify the source of the producer and not be merely ornamental. For instance, Tulane University has started using a half shield as part of its website designs, but it is not a trademark. Unless the school started using it aggressively, no one would see that half shield and think "Tulane."

The Tulane University full shield is registered with the USPTO, but the half shield is not.

Use in Commerce and Intent to Use

As we've discussed, you use your trademark as a source identifier to build goodwill. Pretty simple so far, right? Logos, colors, branding, and all that jazz are key elements to your trademark, and your mark will shape people's perception of your product.

Trademark is a system about selling goods and services. That's what *in commerce* means. Some examples:

- Selling on Etsy? In commerce.

- Selling at your local church or school? Also in commerce.

- Giving a quilt to your friend? Not in commerce.

- Your cousin telling you, "Hey, I'll pay you $200 for that quilt"? Yes, in commerce, technically.

- Starting a business selling those quilts after your cousin suggests it? More in commerce.

- Deciding to start a website, forming an LLC, and naming the business? *Really* in commerce.

But what about goods and services that aren't purchasable, such as podcasts, tv shows, and other things that you engage with, even though you haven't purchased them directly? Not everything has to be purchased in the traditional sense for it to be in commerce. We talk more about what qualifies in Use in Commerce Requirements (page 128).

People often want to reserve a mark before their goods or services are ready. In that case, you can apply for an *intent-to-use* mark, which gives you time to get your goods or services into commerce.

If you are worried about someone starting to use your intended mark, but your business isn't quite ready to launch, then you should file an intent to use application.

With an intent-to-use mark, you apply for the mark, but it will not be issued until you have submitted a complete application showing use in commerce to the USPTO. For more information, see Use in Commerce and Intent-to-Use Applications (page 129).

Trade Dress

Sometimes, the public will recognize your product or service because of the uniforms your employees wear, the box your product comes in, or the look of the shop they enter. All of that—the look, the packaging, the colors, and even how the store or restaurant is set up—is called *trade dress*. Like trademarks, trade dress must function as a source identifier to qualify for protection. You'll learn more in Nontraditional Mark Searches (page 122) and Registering Trade Dress (page 153).

One of our favorite examples is Pinkbox Doughnuts, which has a full Intellectual Property page on its website, including diagrams, of what it identifies as its trade dress; see pinkboxdoughnuts.com/trademark.

Consumer Confusion and Dilution

In many ways, the main function of a trademark is clarity and identification. You have to have a viable mark (which, as we've seen, means a source identifier that functions as a mark in commerce). You must also make sure that your intended mark does not conflict with someone else's mark for a similar product or service. If your intended mark is likely to be too easily confused with another mark, then your application will be turned down due to the *likelihood of confusion*. *Dilution* is when a mark is so famous and well-known, it gets extra protection so people don't mess with it, either by naming their product something similar or by trying to tarnish the mark. If you really want to get a head start, see Likelihood of Confusion or Dilution (page 73).

International Classes of Marks

Remember that marks can be either goods or services. When you apply for a trademark, you apply for a specific class that falls under one or the other. This helps the trademark examining attorney and the world better identify whether there is a likelihood of confusion between one use of a mark and another. We discuss this more in Step 5: International Classes (page 58).

There's no likelihood of confusion between Delta Faucet Company and Delta Airlines because they are in different classes. You wouldn't go to Delta Faucet for a plane ticket, and you wouldn't call Delta Airlines asking about prices on faucets. There's no overlap, despite the similar names.

What this means is that you get a property right not on the whole word or mark but on a particular kind of use. We devote a lot of time to helping you understand and choose your International Class. It can seem daunting, but in some ways, that is one of the fun parts.

The Principal and the Secondary Registers

If your application is approved, the USPTO registers your mark on the Principal Register. *Principal* means that the mark is fully registered. If your application needs additional steps, it goes onto the Secondary Register until it can proceed further. *Secondary* means that you still have to do something to show that it functions as a mark (which can take years) or that you have filed an intent-to-use application and the USPTO is now waiting for you to transform it into a use-in-commerce application.

Specimen

When you file your application, you must upload a PDF of your *specimen*, an image of you using the mark in commerce. This could be a website, a physical display, an image of a podcast app with episodes, or packaging and/or tags with the goods included, among other possibilities (see Step 8: Preparing Your Specimen, page 128).

A Trademark Is a Form of Intellectual Property

Trademark sits within a legal field called *intellectual property* that includes not only trademarks but also copyrights, patents, trade secrets, and rights of publicity. Each category has its own requirements and potentially protects different aspects of your business.

Here is a breakdown of these categories, their legal basis, protections, and how you would acquire each type of intellectual property.

	Trademark/ Trade Dress	Patents	Copyrights	Trade Secrets	Rights of Publicity
What It Protects	Source identifiers of products, services, and packaging	Inventions	Creative works, including photographs, books, films, art, and software	Business information deliberately kept secret	Persona of individuals for privacy and for commercial exploitation
Legal Basis	Federal, state, and local protections	Federal	Federal	Federal and state	State (laws vary state to state)
How to Acquire These Rights	Federal: apply at the USPTO State: apply to the state Local: common law use only	Apply at the USPTO	Rights arise automatically upon fixation*, but you can register at the U.S. Copyright Office for stronger protection	Protected, as long as it's kept secret	Varies depending on the state, but usually they just exist

Fixation is a technical term of copyright, which means that you have fixed your creative work in a tangible medium of expression—a book, film, photograph, digital art, and so forth.

A product or service can potentially be covered by more than one area of intellectual property. Think of an iPhone. The iPhone encompasses a lot of different types of intellectual property:

- The iPhone logo and name are protected by federal trademarks.

- The hardware has patents on it.

- The software is protected by copyright and patent law.

- Apple definitely has trade secrets about the manufacturing process and other business issues.

- Steve Jobs's right of publicity, even after his death, continues legally for a long time.

- The Apple store and the packaging your phone comes in is protected as trade dress.

- Apple protects the design of some of its store windows through a design patent.

As recently as October 2022, the USPTO granted Apple 2,285 new patents, including design patents for the iPhone 14 Pro Camera Configuration and the animation used in the Touch ID setup. Apple also has many trademarks related to the iPhone. You will learn more about what kinds of trademarks you can file throughout the rest of the book. But all this is to say that one object can include many components of intellectual property protection.

An image can also be protected by copyright and by trademark. You can have an image registered with the U.S. Copyright Office and use that image as a source identifier that is registered as a trademark with the USPTO.

Consider labels. Those could be copyrighted. The name and logo on the label may be trademarks, and the look and feel of the label may be trade dress. There's a lot of overlap between different types of intellectual property.

The USPTO's Trademark Examining Attorney

The *trademark examining attorney* is the person who reviews and analyzes your trademark application. These individuals have graduated from law school and then completed a special training program with the USPTO. Their job is to serve as gatekeepers, making sure that your proposed mark is a source identifier that functions as a mark that has been used in commerce and will not cause the public any likelihood of confusion with any other marks. See? You understand that sentence!

For you to have a successful trademark application, your mark has to be viable, and it has to be able to survive a number of hurdles. We help you try to anticipate any issues the Trademark Examining Attorney might find and either fix them (for example, change the mark you are using) or be prepared to explain why they aren't a problem. That's why it is important to understand the basic concepts of trademarks and carefully prepare your federal trademark application.

Is Every Application Accepted Automatically?

No, many applications are rejected. Here are the most common reasons why:

- **Likelihood of confusion.** Your mark is confusingly similar to one already registered. We help you check for that in Likelihood of Confusion or Dilution (page 73).

- **Doesn't serve as a trademark.** The mark fails to function as a source identifier. We walk you through ensuring that your mark qualifies in Step 2: Choose Your Mark (page 29).

- **Doesn't qualify as a trademark.** It isn't used in commerce and is not distinctive enough for the general public to identify it as a mark. We help you make sure that this is not an issue in Step 3: Check the Strength of the Mark (page 34) and Step 4: Confirm There Are No Disqualifying Statutory Exceptions (page 52).

- **Missed important deadlines.** If you miss a deadline from the USPTO, your application or registered mark is deemed abandoned. We help you be sure that you avoid this pitfall in Office Actions (page 155).

- **Your application is missing something.** The USPTO gives you a chance to fix mistakes, but you actually have to fix them, see Office Actions (page 155).

The philosophy of this book is to try to anticipate all of these things and more. We want to make sure that your application is in the best shape possible *because* you have done and thought through all the elements that the USPTO trademark examining attorney will be looking at. There are no guarantees, of course, but we can help you avoid making the most common mistakes that trip people up.

MORE PITFALL EXAMPLES
The USPTO has an overview of typical pitfalls at uspto.gov/trademarks/additional-guidance-and-resources/possible-grounds-refusal-mark.

The next chapters take you through the process of assessing the viability of the mark you have chosen. Let's pretend that this process is a video game. You have to start on a path, complete a lot of tasks, and pass several levels. Sometimes, you reach a dead end and have to start again, but sometimes, you find treasures along the way. The process of figuring out the viability of a mark, whether you already have the name or logo or are searching for one, has similar steps. You've completed the first step by learning the basics of trademarks. Now it's time for your next quest: **choosing your mark**.

Choose Your *Mark*

In this chapter, you will decide what will serve as your mark (for example, a word, logo, or other) and whether it is classified as a good or service. Whether you already have a mark or are still searching for that perfect word or logo, let's walk through the steps to make sure that your application(s) won't have any potential problems. If you are deciding between a number of options, follow along with each of them to decide whether they are trademark contenders.

> *Marks can be many things as long as they serve as a source identifier for goods or services.*

Anything can serve as a mark, but some things need to go through more hoops. Word and design marks are the most common, but there are also only color, sound, motion, smell, slogans, phrases, and domain names (specifically used as a trademark).

A Word or Words

You can register a word or words as a source identifier, which is called a *word mark*. Many companies use word marks, even when they have a logo. This means that you can change the logo, color, or physical appearance, but the word itself is still protected. A lot of companies begin with a word mark and add a design mark later, and some companies register a word mark and a design mark at the same time.

For example, Wefty Needles registered the word mark WEFTY. Its domain name is weftyneedle.com, and its site has a beautiful logo using *Wefty*, but it chose to file an application for a word mark.

The word *Wefty* is registered, even if the company changes the color, font, and other elements of the logo, but it did not secure the design elements, only the word.

The work mark WEFTY is registered, but the design elements of the logo are not.

A Design, Including Logos

Design marks include logos and other graphics that can include a word mark or stand on their own without the name of the product or service. If this is your choice, we walk you through Design Mark Searches (page 116) and Mark Information (page 142).

If the design is really important to your identity, register it. There are also instances when a design mark will help your mark be more distinctive, and thus more registrable, which we cover in more depth in Step 3: Check the Strength of the Mark (page 35). However, once you have secured your design mark, you cannot change your logo or design without having to reapply for trademark protection, which takes time and money.

Many companies opt to register a design mark in black and white, so they can change the color without having to reapply. Interestingly, this is often the case even when the company uses a dominant color.

From top to bottom, Olfa and Michael's Made by You, two examples of design marks that can be made in any color

Less Common Types of Marks

A Color by Itself

Do you know what to expect when you are handed a small blue Tiffany box or when the brown UPS truck rolls down the street? If the public recognizes color alone as a source identifier of your goods or service, you can get a trademark on it, called an *only color mark*.

But that doesn't give an owner total dominion over that color. The law does not allow Tiffany to control that particular color blue from all uses. It only controls the color for its specific class of products.

Many companies use color as a source identifier, even if they don't always officially register the color. AccuQuilt uses green for its packaging and plastic covers for its fabric die-cutting system.

Sentro, a circular machine knitting tool, uses a dusty pink for its packaging and the knitting machines themselves. They are very distinctive. But the company has registered only a design mark for SENTRO, without color.

Sentro packaging and even machines feature a dusty rose color.

The packaging and use of the color start to have meaning when consumers identify the specific color with the source of the product. And the USPTO says that that gets protection once consumers identify that secondary meaning with the color, which usually requires five years of use. For a deeper discussion on color marks, jump to Nontraditional Marks That Are Only Color, Sound, or Smell (page 42).

Companies do not necessarily have to register their use of color to have protection with the USPTO. That protection is called *unregistered trade dress*, which we explore in more detail in Unregistered Trade Dress (page 154). But just because you use a color doesn't mean that you have exclusive rights to use it, even on the products you create. Many companies use and identify themselves with hot pink. We know the companies, but we don't

necessarily think that they are the only ones to use that color for that class of goods or services. To claim color as a sole source identifier, you have to do more work than merely use the color.

THINKING OF REGISTERING ONLY A COLOR?

It is not easy to have a color on its own act as a source identifier. You have to prove to the USPTO that the public sees that color and thinks of it as a source identifier for your product or service. If you are planning to do this, we strongly suggest that you find a trademark lawyer specializing in color registration.

Sound, Motion, or Smell

Many people know the sound Netflix makes when it loads or NBC's three-note chime. There's a whole documentary on the four-note theme used by the Disney Channel! Sound marks are less common than word or design marks, for sure, but you still can register a sound, as long as it is a source identifier and functions as a mark.

There are also motion marks, such as the animated Microsoft Windows logo. Another example is the Disney castle animation at the beginning of its movies. These sorts of short movies or animations help us identify the source.

Even a scent can stand in as a trademark, as long as it is a source identifier and the smell is not a functional component of the goods or services. A strawberry-scented toothbrush can be registered because the strawberry scent does not add to the functionality of the toothbrush. Scent marks are

even rarer than sound marks. (See Less Common Applications, page 151).

THINKING OF REGISTERING A SCENT, MOTION, OR SOUND?

You guessed it: We encourage you to find a trademark lawyer with experience filing these less common types of marks. In Part III, we walk you through nonvisual applications, but these atypical applications can get complicated, so you may want to hire an expert, not just any trademark attorney. You often have to appeal the initial decision of the USPTO, which really does require expertise.

A Slogan or Phrase

Slogans are a little weird. Sometimes they are registered. Sometimes they aren't.

SHINGRIX PROTECTS and SHINGLES DOESN'T CARE are source identifiers for a particular version of the shingles vaccine and are registered at the USPTO. But there are a number of limitations on slogans or phrases:

Direct quotes, passages, or citations from religious texts, including the Bible, the Koran, the Torah, and the Diamond Sutra, cannot be registered because consumers will not see them as a source identifier. They are seen as mere indicators of religious affiliation and therefore fail to function as a mark.

Nothing that the general public just commonly says because that wouldn't serve as a source identifier for your goods or services. This includes such phrases as "Happy Halloween" and "How is it going?"

But when such phrases are combined with a design mark or other words, they become registrable. "Black Lives Matter" is not a registrable phrase on its own because it doesn't serve as a source identifier for goods or services. But adding a design element and being tied to specific goods and/or services makes the same phrase registrable.

Three examples of adding materials to make common phrases registrable as a mark using the phrase "Black Lives Matter"

Donald Trump was able to register MAKE AMERICA GREAT AGAIN for seven classes, including stickers, clothing, buttons, political campaign services, online journals, and online social networking. Trump controls the phrase, and, in truth, it is a source identifier and functions as a mark for his brand.

Celebrities and Phrases

In 2013, Paris Hilton attempted to trademark her phrase "That's hot." She did so under the category of alcoholic beverages. Eventually, the application was abandoned. But even in this instance, Paris Hilton couldn't apply for the phrase generally; it had to be related to a good or service.

Taylor Swift registered THIS SICK BEAT, a phrase from her album *1989*. She also applied for other phrases. She was doing this for merchandise opportunities. Her registration doesn't keep people from saying the phrase, but it keeps people from using it for merchandise, particularly on the surviving marks. Swift is not the only pop star to register key phrases *identified with them*. What it comes down to is whether the phrases can serve as a source identifier. It can get a little tricky to answer.

Pop singer Lizzo has applied to register the phrase "100% that bitch." It is still in process as of 2023. Lizzo already has a word mark for LIZZO and has also applied for the mark BIG GRRRLS.

A Domain Name as a Mark

You do not usually have to register your domain name separately as a mark, but some companies register their name and their domain name. Amazon has AMAZON and AMAZON.COM as registered marks.

NOTE

If you are not using the *.com*, then you can't add it. For instance, ricRACK, a sewing and textile recycling and repurposing store in New Orleans, uses the domain name ricracknola.com, even though its name is ricRACK. It could not register ricrack.com, as it is being used by a different company.

DECIDING WHETHER TO REGISTER YOUR MARK AND YOUR DOMAIN NAME?

That's a decision for you and your attorney. It is a strategy. We return to domain names when we talk about generic marks; see Generic (page 40). Many believe that you do not need to register your domain name, only your word mark. But maybe it is your source identifier. In this case, you might want to register it. This is a legal decision, so an expert trademark attorney who understands online businesses and identities would be really good to seek out.

Less Common Categories of Marks

We've been discussing the various types of marks, but we must also discuss the categories. Trademarks and service marks are the predominant categories. But you should know about three others.

Certification Marks

Part of our trademark world includes what are called Standard Setting Organizations (SSOs). They use trademarks to communicate to consumers that a product or service complies with a set of standards. One kind of mark used for this is the *certification mark*. These provide a shorthand to the public that something has been approved—for safety, for use of particular resources, for appropriateness, and so forth.

You likely encounter these more frequently than you think. For example, you take your kid to a PG movie because the Motion Picture Association of America has marked it that way with a certification mark. (It has actually registered the trademark for the rating system as well as for each of the different ratings: G, PG, PG-13, R, and NC-17). Or maybe you decide to buy a particular vacuum cleaner because it has the *Good Housekeeping* Seal of Approval.

There are a number of kinds of certification marks:

- The quality of a good (Example: Kosher marks, wool, *Good Housekeeping* Seal of Approval)

- Regional area of a product (Example: GROWN IN IDAHO)

- Made by a particular group (Example: union-made)

Good Housekeeping has a number of certification marks, including the two above.

To have a certification mark, you must have **a process in place** for certification. There are a number of rules:

- The certifying organization can't sell the products/services it certifies.

- Certifying organizations must restrict the use of the mark to only certified goods and services that meet the required standards.

- Certifying organizations cannot discriminately refuse to certify.

As an alternative, we see certifying organizations using traditional trademarks or service marks and then using licensing for quality control. There is less fuss about meeting the USPTO trademark applications for certification marks.

Collective (Membership) Trademarks

A *collective mark* is a source identifier used by members of a cooperative, association, or other collective group or organization. Collective marks are different from certification marks. You can be a member of your own club, which you can't be with certification marks. Examples include AAA for membership with the American Automobile Association and FTD for members of the Florists' Transworld Delivery association. Collective marks carry with them proof that you have members, and those members are identified by the mark.

Just because you have a member group does not mean that you have to register as a collective mark. One example is the Craft Industry Alliance, which is registered not as a collective membership but as business networking and continuing education services under a service mark. Registering as a service mark means that you have fewer hurdles to undergo because as a collective mark, you have to prove that you have members who use the mark to identify themselves as part of the collective. For more, see Less Common Applications (page 151).

House Marks

A *house mark*, sometimes called a *corporate mark*, is the least common of all the categories of marks, so much so that most people don't even know it exists! House marks do not identify particular goods or services. Instead, they identify the provider of a wide variety of goods or services, with the goods or services often identified with separate marks. We see these used mostly in the chemical, pharmaceutical, publishing, and food industries.

The application would include "a house mark for ...." You would still identify the goods and services where the mark appears, but it is recognized that the house mark is seen across different goods and services as a second mark. You must demonstrate in your application that it is used as a house mark.

De facto house marks are companies that are using trademarks or service marks as house marks but

have not registered them as such. Many companies do this. Many use International Class 35 and/or 42 to do this.

Fewer than 400 house marks have been filed, and many have been canceled or abandoned. It is not a well-used part of the trademark system.

TIME FOR HELP

If you do want to file a certification mark, collective mark, or house mark, we encourage you to find a trademark attorney with expertise in successfully maneuvering these through the process; these are not easy marks to obtain, and you have to cross many hurdles to satisfy the USPTO examining attorneys.

Check the *Strength* of the Mark

To be registered, a mark must be *distinctive*, which is another way to say that your mark must be strong enough to serve as a source identifier. This is a legal term and a requirement you have to meet. If the public doesn't recognize your mark as a mark, then it is not functioning as a mark. The USPTO wants to make sure that every mark it grants functions correctly. The office doesn't want people to register nonfunctioning, nondistinctive, or merely ornamental marks.

Distinctiveness comes in two flavors:

Inherently distinctive marks. These marks are unique from the beginning, and once you are successfully through the application process, you can use the registered mark. The public can get to know your brand, and you are on your way.

Acquired distinctiveness. With this type of distinctiveness, you have to prove to the trademark examiner that the public has recognized your mark as a source identifier for at least five years. Some things you could pick require this extra step, such as using only your surname or only a color (with no design or words). It's a lot more time, work, and money, so you want to really consider whether it's worth the effort to have a mark that requires acquired distinctiveness. Alternatively, you may have been using a merely descriptive mark for years, and it has already acquired distinctiveness!

Let's look at each type of distinctiveness in more detail.

Inherently Distinctive

In the world of trademarks, there's a hierarchy: the stronger the mark, the better. We are going to start with the strongest types of marks and work our way down to generic marks, which are not protected.

Arbitrary

When Steve Jobs named his new computer company APPLE, the choice was random and arbitrary. His biographer, Walter Isaacson, explains that he had come back from an apple orchard and the name seemed "fun, spirited and not intimidating." Other arbitrary names include BANANA for tires and AMAZON for well … Amazon! Another is STARBUCKS, which comes from Herman Melville's novel *Moby-Dick*. That's random. The thing with arbitrary distinctiveness is just that—they are not last names or something related to the product/service. They are just arbitrary. They get one of the strongest protections.

XYRON for a crafts company is a good example. *Xyron*, according to *Urban Dictionary*, is an "all or nothing person." This is an arbitrary name for a company that makes adhesives and other supplies for simplifying the crafting process. Can you think of other marks that are arbitrary?

Fanciful

In this context, *fanciful* refers to a made-up word. These marks get strong protection, too. We know many examples, including Xerox, Exxon, Kodak, Pepsi, and Clorox. A lot of drug names are fanciful, such as Zoloft. If the word doesn't exist in a dictionary, it's fanciful. If it is a foreign word, it is not fanciful.

VIVIVA is an example in the arts and craft industry. This is just a jumble of letters and not something that is translatable. This company creates watercolor color sheets for painting. The founders made up the name from their grandmother's name, whose initials were Vi Vi Va. And so, Viviva was born. To read the story of this name in their own words, jump to vivivacolors.com > story.

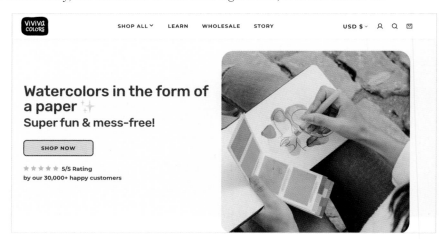

SEPHORA, the well-known makeup company, is a blend of two words, one Greek, *sephos* for "pretty," and the second *Zipporah*, the wife of Moses in the Bible, known for her beauty. Putting them together created a fanciful name.

Founded in 1932, LEGO is another combination word, coming from the Danish phrase *"leg godt"*, meaning "play well." To read the origin story of the LEGO name, visit lego.com/en-us/history/articles/b-the-beginning-of-the-lego-group.

Suggestive

Marks that describe or conjure images of the product or service are *suggestive*. Some common examples are

- COPPERTONE for sunscreen

- PAGE A DAY for calendars

- EHARMONY for a dating company

- THE NORTH FACE for outdoor gear

- BIG TWIST for yarn

- THE WARM COMPANY for quilt batting

If your mark is arbitrary, fanciful, or suggestive, you are golden. If, however, the mark does not qualify as fanciful, arbitrary, or suggestive, you have two potential paths: one to trademark protection and one to no protection. We talk more about suggestive marks shortly when we compare them to our next category, merely descriptive marks that require secondary meaning.

Acquired Distinctiveness

Acquired distinctiveness, which is often called *merely descriptive with secondary meaning*, is a category of trademarks where you have to prove that the public identifies your mark as a source identifier; it doesn't happen automatically. You must show that for five years, the public has identified your mark as connected to your goods and/or services and that your mark serves as a source identifier.

> *If the mark describes at least one significant function, attribute, or property of the goods or service, it may be found to be merely descriptive.*

Although it is ideal to avoid the time, expense, and uncertainty of proving acquired distinctiveness, there are instances when you will have to. In some cases, you have already been using the merely descriptive mark for five or more years, so you will have to prove only that it has acquired distinctiveness in the mind of the public.

Many companies have done so, including the following:

- **PARK 'N FLY** is the classic example. What do you do? You park your car at the airport and fly away. The courts found that after five years, PARK N FLY had acquired secondary meaning: The consumer perceived it as a specific brand and mark.

- **WOODWORKER'S SUPPLY** was designated as merely descriptive, requiring secondary meaning. The company had to prove that consumers identified its store with its mark. It did this by using examples of its catalogs and advertisements.

- **BULK APOTHECARY** was also found to be merely descriptive for soap but was able to acquire secondary meaning.

- **LONE STAR CANDLE SUPPLY** was found to be merely descriptive for a candle company in Texas. This did not mean that it could not register their trademark; it just meant that it was required to prove secondary meaning to obtain the trademark.

My Mark May Be Merely Descriptive!

That's okay! Don't panic. You can still register your mark; you just need to prove that your mark has a secondary meaning. Let's talk about how that works.

The USPTO accepts three types of evidence to show that secondary meaning has been achieved:

- **Other registrations.** This means prior registration of the same mark for goods or services that are similar to those in the pending application. So, if you already have a registration on similar goods and services, that helps.

- **For at least five years.** This is a verified statement of use by the applicant in a substantially exclusive and continuous way in commerce for at least five years before the date on which the claim of distinctiveness is being made.

- **Other evidence of acquired distinctiveness.** This can be advertisements and other elements that show that the general public recognizes your mark as a source identifier of your goods and/or services.

We look at this more closely when we go through the application process. (See Additional Statements About the Mark, page 145).

Substantially Exclusive and Continuous

For at least five years—you will hear that a lot. You must have at least five years of "substantially exclusive and continuous use." Others might also be using the mark, but their use must be either inconsequential or infringing on your use.

Suggestive Versus Merely Descriptive

The line between suggestive (inherently distinctive) and merely descriptive (requiring secondary meaning) is not always clear. Courts often flip-flop on whether something is suggestive or descriptive. It's a hard call. Is BLOC LOC merely descriptive or suggestive? It's a ruler that locks fabric into place. The USPTO issued a trademark on the Principal Register, indicating that it did not think that it was merely descriptive. So, what truly is the difference between suggestive and merely descriptive? It is the idea of the imaginative leap.

The Imaginative Leap

The *imaginative leap* is a key concept in trademark, especially when thinking about whether something is inherently distinctive or merely descriptive. You need to make a "mental leap" to get to suggestive (and therefore inherently distinctive). If a mark imparts information directly, such as PARK 'N FLY (you park your car and fly away), it is descriptive. If a mark stands for an idea that requires some operation of the imagination to connect it with goods or services, such as THE WARM COMPANY, it is suggestive.

It isn't always easy to discern what requires an imaginative or mental leap to know what the product/service is. Let's look at some examples. Which of these do you think are suggestive (immediate protection) or merely descriptive (requiring secondary meaning)?

24 HOUR FITNESS

CROSSFIT

XTREME LASHES

COASTAL WINE

24 HOUR FITNESS was found to be descriptive, so it required secondary meaning. However, CROSSFIT was suggestive and thus could acquire protection. XTREME LASHES, a mark for artificially elongated lashes, was found to be suggestive. But COASTAL WINE, which is wine made on a coast, was merely descriptive and required secondary meaning.

So, how do you know whether your mark is suggestive or merely descriptive? Wait to see what the trademark examining attorney says, and have a good response prepared to explain why the mark is suggestive and not merely descriptive. If the examining attorney still finds that it is merely descriptive, it just means that you will have to show secondary meaning by the public. It isn't a disaster, just something to think about. You can also add stylization or register a design mark (logo), which may help establish the word mark as suggestive and not merely descriptive.

How will you know? The examining attorney will make a decision, and if you disagree, you can try to persuade them. But our goal here is to get you prepared for your application.

Dictionary Definition

The USPTO examining attorney will also be heading to the dictionary to determine whether the term you use corresponds to the thing you are trying to identify. If the dictionary definition of the word corresponds to what the service/product is or does, that is going to be seen as merely descriptive. This includes foreign translations and words that sound alike. You can't get away with weird spellings to avoid being found merely descriptive.

 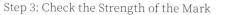

Generic

Generic is the last category in our spectrum of strength of the mark, and it is the weakest. Generic marks do not get protection. They never qualify for distinctiveness, whether inherently or acquired through secondary meaning. You don't want to choose a trademark that is generic. There are two types of generic marks: born generic and becoming generic.

Born Generic

APPLE for apples is a no-go. It's just too generic. But this doesn't mean that you can't name your company a generic term. Doing so can help people easily find you. Choosing a generic mark just means that you can't get federal trademark protection. Sometimes, even though it is not supposed to happen, a generic mark is categorized as merely descriptive in narrow situations. But this is not something to count on.

In April 2022, a company filed for a trademark for ENGLISH PAPER PIECING. English paper piecing is a quilting technique, a common term in quilting. A company wanted to use it as a mark *for English paper piecing.* The USPTO recognized that it was merely descriptive and sent an office action:

> Here, applicant has applied to register the mark ENGLISH PAPER PIECING for use in connection with "Paper products, namely, patterned paper

for use in paper piecing templates; Pre-cut papers for use in paper piecing templates" in Class 16. In this case, ENGLISH PAPER PIECING refers to the process of using paper pieces in a specific style of quilting. See the attached evidence from Homemade Emily Jane, The Spruce Crafts, American Patchwork & Quilting. Specifically, this process involves "precut paper templates," and applicant provides this specific type of paper, particularly "pre-cut" papers for use in paper piecing. Furthermore, applicant's own specimen indicates that the precut papers are hexagonal in shape, something that is specific to the English paper piecing process. *See applicant's specimen and the attached Internet evidence.* Thus, the applied-for mark merely defines the function of applicant's paper goods, which is to be used in the English paper piecing process of quilting. Non-Final Office Action, December 28, 2022

Becoming Generic (Genericide)

Sometimes, marks start out as protectable, but over time become generic. *Genericide* happens when the public starts to identify the name and the product as being the same thing. Some famous examples are ESCALATOR, ASPIRIN, DRY ICE, FLIP PHONE, HEROIN, CELLOPHANE, LINOLEUM, LAUNDROMAT, and VIDEOTAPE. These marks became generic for two reasons.

First, they did not separate the thing from the source of the thing. This was true of ESCALATOR. A company named the moving steps ESCALATOR, so what else was the public supposed to call them? There wasn't a brand of ESCALATOR, simply the object. Same with MURPHY BED.

Another example is the mark RISO. *Riso* is a type of printing that  uses a specific machine to layer ink, one color at a time, onto the same page. It is a technique and a type of machine. Riso has a word mark and a number of design marks for machines, toner cartridges, printers, and paper goods, among other International Classes (ICs). It included in the registration the English translation of *Riso* as "an ideal." Do you see the potential problem? If a competitor starts to make Riso machines, could it then become generic? Just because you create a new type of technique, method, or machine does not mean that you can prevent others from using the mark through trademark, see Permissible Uses (page 186).

Another way marks can become generic is if the public uses the mark as a generic term so much that it loses its trademark. The company Xerox takes out ads to tell the public they are photocopying on a Xerox machine, not "xeroxing." (What about "Googling," you ask? That's a weird one. It is so famous that somehow it has escaped this destiny.)

MODA, a fabric company, has registered the term JELLY ROLL to describe a roll of 2½″ strips of fabric. This is part of its naming of different precut fabrics for what it calls its Bake Shop. But then the idea of a "Jelly Roll" became so popular that people started using the term for their own versions of 2½″ strips of fabric rolled into a circle. Moda is working hard to *police their mark*—that is, to make sure that others do not use "Jelly Roll" to describe a roll of

2½″ strips. We share more about protecting your mark in Police Your Mark (page 183). The company does that so that its mark does not become generic. Will its efforts succeed in the end? Only time will tell.

IF YOU THINK YOUR MARK IS GENERIC

If you have found that your mark is generic, this might be a good time to try a different term, if you are not already using the mark. If you already are using the mark, you might consider a combo of a design and word mark. This may also be the time to hire an attorney, especially if you are determined to pursue something that borders generic and merely descriptive.

Generic + .com

There have been recent exceptions to the generic rule. You know that generic terms are not protectable. However, in 2020, the U.S. Supreme Court in the *Booking.com* case addressed the question of whether generic.com marks were registrable. These are marks that would be generic but have *.com* added to the end of them. Were they still generic, or were they now distinctive enough for registration? The Court said that it depended on whether the public perceived it as

a source identifier or as a generic term. In the case of Booking.com, it was considered merely descriptive (not generic). It had acquired secondary meaning. Thus, the company was able to have a federally protected mark. Just adding *.com* doesn't automatically make a mark not generic; it has to act and be perceived by the public as a source identifier. You still have to prove the mark has secondary meaning.

Strategic Generic Filing

There is another way to think about generic marks. If you have the time and money and you want to make sure that a word, phrase, or design is not used by others, you can try to register the mark to obtain a generic ruling from the USPTO. LeBron James registered TACO TUESDAY, not with the idea of locking that up so no one could use it but to preclude others from claiming it and to get confirmation from the USPTO that, indeed, it is a generic phrase. People do this with patents too, filing the patent application so that others cannot try to patent the work and to get confirmation that it is not patentable. It's a strange but sometimes useful way of ensuring that certain generic marks stay generic and usable for everyone.

Special Areas to Check

Regardless of how clever they seem, some marks still need to obtain secondary meaning, or they may have specific elements to consider. This does not mean that they are not registrable.

These include:

- Non-traditional marks, including only color, smell, or sound

- Some names

- Some geographical names

- Naughty words and cannabis

You can skip this section if none of these descriptions applies to your mark. If you are using a mark that falls into one of these categories, make sure to read through the relevant section(s).

Nontraditional Marks That Are Only Color, Sound, or Smell

The USPTO allows for the registration of nontraditional marks, but marks that are only color, sound, or smell **always require secondary meaning**. These can get complicated and often require a lawyer who specializes in this type of registration. We talk more about them in Less Common Applications (page 151).

Names and Titles

Names are a bit fickle. The thing to remember is that a name must serve as a source identifier and function as a trademark. There are a lot of rules when it comes to names.

If you are using a name for your mark, you should read through the next section, which covers:

- Only a surname
- First + surname
- Name, portrait, or signature of a living individual
- Well-known individuals
- Famous deceased persons
- Historical persons or historical places
- Living and deceased U.S. presidents
- Performing groups
- Character names
- Names of artists used on original works
- Titles of single expressive works versus series of works
- Newspaper columns and sections

This section is a bit long, but the short take is this: A name has to be seen by the public as a source identifier, and if it is not, it requires **secondary meaning.** What counts automatically as inherently distinctive varies, but as you work through this section, you will start to understand the USPTO's logic. **If you're not registering a name-based mark, skip ahead.**

Merely a Surname

If you are using only a surname without anything else, the USPTO requires secondary meaning. The idea is simple: You don't want someone to lock up a surname so that no one else can use it.

The first question to answer is does the public perceive the mark as a surname? A number of factors have been identified to assess whether the public views a surname as a mark:

- **Degree of the surname's rarity.** If the public would not identify it as a surname, it has a greater chance of success in overcoming the problem of being "merely a surname." BAIK as a surname was rare enough to survive surname refusal. But if its significance is primarily as a surname, it will be refused, even if it is rare. (The USPTO looks to media and publicity related to the name to determine whether it is rare.)

- **Whether the applicant is connected to the surname.** If the applicant's name is the same as the mark, this provides strong evidence that it is merely a surname, and it has a good chance of being blocked from registration.

- **Whether a surname has a nonsurname meaning.** Sometimes, this is through dictionary definitions or widespread usage of the term as other than a surname. SAVA had a non-surname meaning and so was able to be registered and protected.

- **Whether the surname feels/seems like a surname.** Will it be perceived as a surname? The more it is perceived as a surname, the less likely the chance of protection without secondary meaning.

- **Making it possessive** by adding an apostrophe + *s* does not clear it from being merely a surname.

- **Making it into a domain name** does not change its status. You still need secondary meaning to register it. JOHNSON is not protectable, nor is JOHNSON.COM, unless the owner proves secondary meaning.

The following are not considered merely a surname. There's something more than the name, and that's enough to get over the hurdle of requiring secondary meaning. Here are some examples:

- **Effect of the fonts/appearance on a design mark** that distinguishes the mark as more than merely a surname.

- **Surname + other words.** The USPTO prefers when a name is combined with something else. The added words can't be generic or merely descriptive. This is an important point. What must be added has to be inherently distinctive: arbitrary, fanciful, or suggestive. Otherwise, the applicant will have to prove secondary meaning.

- **What about double surnames?** They don't count as merely surnames! For example, SCHAUB-LORENZ does not count as merely a surname, because it is distinctive from the two surnames individually. Thus, it can be protected as a mark.

- **What about a surname plus initials?** It depends on consumer perspective, but this would likely be perceived as a personal name + a surname and so move from the "merely a surname" category. Examples include M. C. ESCHER, P. T. BARNUM, and T. S. ELIOT. Single initials, however, are often found to still be "merely a surname."

> *If you are able to prove at least five years of "substantially exclusive and continuous use" (or previous applications or other proof), you'll overcome the merely a surname problem.*

HAVEL'S is a good example of products/services using a surname. When the company registered the mark, it had to confirm that it was a surname and that it had acquired secondary meaning for longer than five years.

First Names + Surnames

What if you are using your first and last name? So, here's where it gets interesting. The USPTO will register first and last names as an inherently distinctive mark, with no secondary meaning required—but common law (if you don't register them) doesn't! How crazy is that?

Name, Portrait, or Signature of a Living Individual

Just because your mark includes a living individual doesn't mean that you can't use it. You just have to include a statement from the living individual with your application that provides their permission for you to use their name, signature, or portrait. If the name is a first name, stage name, surname, nickname, or title, the examining attorney will evaluate whether consent is needed and whether the relevant public would perceive the name as identifying a particular individual.

If the name, portrait, and/or signature in your mark identifies and/or depicts a particular living individual, you must provide one of the following statements:

"The **name** shown in the mark identifies a living individual whose consent to register is made of record." Or

"The **signature** shown in the mark identifies a living individual whose consent to register is made of record." Or

"The **portrait** or likeness shown in the mark identifies a living individual whose consent to register is made of record."

In addition to the statement, you must also include consent from the living individual, personally signed by the individual and using the following language:

"I consent to the use and registration by _ of my **name** as a trademark and/or service mark with the USPTO." Or

"I consent to the use and registration by _ of the **signature** of my name as a trademark and/or service mark with the USPTO." Or

"I consent to the use and registration by _ of my **portrait** or likeness as a trademark and/or service mark with the USPTO."

NOT the Name, Portrait, or Signature of a Living Individual

If the name, portrait, and/or signature in your mark does not identify or depict a particular living individual, you must provide the following statement:

"The **name** shown in the mark does not identify a particular living individual."

"The **signature** shown in the mark does not identify a particular living individual."

"The **portrait or likeness** shown in the mark does not identify a particular living individual."

MORE THAN JUST A NAME

For a deeper dive into how the USPTO handles the names and likenesses of living individuals, visit uspto.gov/trademarks/laws/inquiry-regarding-nameportraitsignature-particular-living-individual-mark.

When Jenny McLean originally registered TULA PINK, the USPTO responded (in what is called an Office Action, page 155), asking whether the mark was the name of a living individual. She responded that it was a nickname and that she approved the use of the name as a mark.

Kat Von D, a famous tattoo artist, has registered many trademarks using her name on products and services. As part of the process, she has included the statement: "The Name Katherine von Drachenberg, aka 'KAT VON D,' identifies a living individual whose consent is on record."

An example of one of Kat Von D's trademarks

Amanda Murphy, a fabric, tools, and pattern designer, registered her name with her initials as part of the design mark. Her mark was inherently distinctive. As part of the registration process, Amanda confirmed that the mark was the name of a living individual.

June Tailor had to confirm that the name was not of a living individual. June had passed on before the trademark was registered. The record states: "The name shown in the mark does not identify a living individual."

June Tailor, Inc.

In many ways, this requirement of consent from a living individual nods to the right of publicity, another area of intellectual property, which prohibits the commercial exploitation of someone's name, likeness, voice, and so forth without their consent.

Right of publicity is covered by state laws, but the USPTO also acts as a gatekeeper to make sure that people are not registering living individuals' names and likenesses without their consent. One weird part is that the right of publicity generally lasts for 70 or more years after the death of the individual, but the USPTO does not have the same requirement. Only living individuals are protected under this area of the trademark law.

Angie Wood Creations, a family business in Canada that makes wooden watches, had to confirm that Angie Wood was not a living individual. Olive & June, an online spa and nail company, was asked by the examiner to confirm that neither name identified a living individual. The business is actually named after the owner's great-grandmother and grandmother.

Well-Known Individuals

Well-known individuals, including celebrities and world-famous political figures, can register their names *without having a connection to goods or services*. Odd, right? It's long-standing. This can include their first name, surname, shortened name, pseudonym, stage name, title, and/or nickname. An example is PRINCESS KATE for Kate Middleton. So, you can't register DOLLY PARTON, unless you have permission from Dolly Parton. That makes a lot of sense. But Dolly Parton doesn't have to have registered goods or services to keep others from using her name. That makes sense, too.

But some well-known celebrities do register their name as a mark and do identify a particular good and/or service. Meryl Streep registered her name, MERYL STREEP, to prevent others from misusing it. Many news stories describe celebrities registering their children's names. These are usually intent-to-use marks, where eventually they will have to have a use in commerce or they will run out of extensions. We see that Jay-Z and Beyoncé, through their company, BGK, registered their twins' names RUMI CARTER and SIR CARTER as intent-to-use marks in 2017. They filed extensions through 2021, and then the marks were abandoned. Then, they registered them again in 2021, restarting the trademark application process.

If the mark includes the name of a famous deceased person, the examining attorney may double-check to make sure that they are actually deceased, and the applicant may be required to include a statement that the mark does not include a living individual. But beware: Just because someone is deceased doesn't mean that other parts of the law don't prevent you from using that name. Again, right of publicity protects the name, likeness, and other aspects of a person, even after their death, from unauthorized commercial use. Right of publicity varies from state to state.

PUBLICITY RIGHTS BY STATE

To see an overview of publicity rights by state, check out Jennifer Rothman's Right of Publicity Roadmap at rightofpublicityroadmap.com.

Living and Deceased U.S. Presidents

You cannot use the name, portrait, or signature of a living president of the United States without their consent, and if they are deceased, you still must get consent during the *life of the widow*. After that, you are free to use the name, portrait, or signature on a mark! So, as of 2023, you can use Ronald Reagan and George Bush without asking permission, but you can't use Jimmy Carter without consent, because his wife is still alive. When Jimmy Sias tried to register JIMMY CARTER for headphones, his trademark application was refused.

Bands and Performing Groups

Whether you are recording an album or are just starting to go on tour, you can register the name of a band or performing group. Register as a service mark, as long as it is on a series of sound recordings, and the name is the source identifier for those recordings. For instance, the Ramones registered the mark RAMONES for prerecorded vinyl records.

You can also register the name for merchandise, a key way performing groups make money. For example, the band My Chemical Romance has seven trademarks, including three that are in process. They hold trademarks for jewelry; backpacks, wallets, and other bags; printed posters, blank writing journals, stickers, and writing instruments; toys; a website featuring information regarding performances and music; clothing, headwear, messenger bags, and clothing accessories; music publishing services, and production of music videos; clothing, including T-shirts, sweatshirts, jackets, ties, and belts; and (what they are known for) musical sound recordings, musical video recordings, and other audiovisual recordings. Unlike an individual celebrity, the name of the performing group is tied to a good or service to be registered. It is not merely "My Chemical Romance" but tied to many things to gain protection. They are protecting the source—My Chemical Romance—rather than the source of the T-shirt (for example, Hanes).

Character Names

What if you have a character that is central to your business and you want to register it? We see a lot of variety in how characters are registered. The creators of STEVEN UNIVERSE, a cartoon series, registered this mark for the show fifteen times for a variety of goods and services, just like My Chemical Romance did. But they did not register the individual characters from the television show.

But then, let's look at American Girl dolls. This company has a whole page on its website devoted to trademarks, letting the public know that it has registered nearly every one of its dolls' names (americangirl.com/pages/trademarks). What is interesting is that in this case, the company is registering first names and then first + last names. In the applications, we also see this disclaimer: "The name(s), portrait(s), and/or signature(s) shown in the mark does not identify a particular living individual."

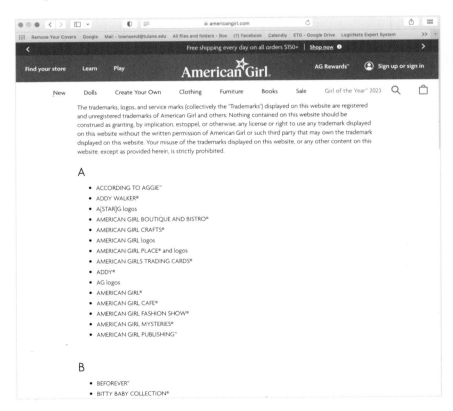

Titles of Single Expressive Works Versus Series of Works

The title of a single expressive work cannot be registered. This includes a book, song, movie, or video game. But computer software, computer games, coloring books, and activity books are not included—these can be registered as single titles. Weird, right?

Title for a series of works? Yep, that's okay. We registered JUST WANNA for a series of books. And you can use a portion of a title. Other examples include THE LITTLE ENGINE, and then you can add to it—That Went to the Fair, Goes to School, or other things. The FOR DUMMIES series and THE COMPLETE IDIOT'S GUIDE marks are other examples.

Service marks for entertainment services including the title of a series of motion pictures or television programs are also registerable. Examples from television are the medical drama GREY'S ANATOMY, the children's program BLUEY, and the British drama CALL THE MIDWIFE. For movies, this includes the INDIANA JONES, with more than 40 registrations. For continuing series, including TV, movies, live performances, podcasts, and radio programs, the mark can be registered as entertainment services or educational services. But not all do register. The popular podcast *Welcome to Night Vale,* for instance, has not.

The title of a play, musical, or opera is not registrable because it is considered a single creative work.

But if the content changes with each issue, then the work is *not* considered a single creative work. This includes magazines, newsletters, comics, and printed classroom materials because the content of these works changes with each issue. Second editions do not count as content changes.

A Clever Lawyer

Hamilton the musical, including its iconic design mark, is registered with marks for the website, the retail store, paper goods (including souvenir programs), downloadable music, and clothing, among other things. We expect that, right? But the mark for the theatrical show was also registered. *What?* Didn't we just say that's not allowed? So, how is *Hamilton* the musical registered as a trademark?

When the mark was applied for, the applicant received an office action stating that it could not be registered because it was the title of a single work. The trademark examiner wrote,

> "Single creative works include works in which the content does not change significantly from one performance to another, such as a theatrical play, musical, or opera. TMEP §1202.08(a); see In re Posthuma, 45 USPQ2d at 2013–14 (citing In re Scholastic, Inc., 23 USPQ2d 1774, 1776 (TTAB 1992)). Here, the specimen shows the mark on the cover of a theater program. A consumer viewing applicant's specimen, in the context of the recited services, i.e., at the theater or with knowledge that the relevant services are the provision of a theatrical performance, would understand the mark as the title of the theatrical performance described in the program rather than the source of the recited services. Put plainly, the mark, as used on the specimen of record, shows what the services are, not who

provides the services. This determination is supported by the recitation of services ("entertainment services in the nature of a theatrical performance of a musical play") that references a singular musical play as opposed to a series."

So, what happened next? Well, the lawyers wrote an amazing response. That's why you *hire lawyers* when things could get complicated. What did they say? They argued that titles, like so much of what we have already seen, should be allowed to be registered upon showing a secondary meaning or acquired distinctiveness. Moreover, they suggested that the mark was used in a commercial setting on programs, the marquee outside the theater, posters, and other spaces. "All of these uses promote Applicant and its production and make clear that Applicant's mark is a brand that communicates to consumers a single source for Applicant's goods and services. As a result of this widespread use and great fame, there is no question that consumers perceive Applicant's mark as a trademark."

Alternatively, the lawyers argued that they would disclaim the title and use only the design mark we have all come to know. Then, the image and not the words would be registered. They also argued that the mark was more than merely the words, but words and design. Finally, the lawyers noted that other musicals had been registered *as a source identifier for the musical*, including *Rent, My Fair Lady,* and *Shrek the Musical*. In the end, registration was granted! If you are planning to do something that may be rejected or is risky in other ways, hire a clever attorney.

Names of Artists Used on Original Works

An artist can register their name or pseudonym affixed to original works, even when they have not created a series of artworks. Art includes paintings, murals, sculptures, jewelry, and other kinds of works. This was decided in the case *In re Wood*, 217 USPQ 1345, 19500 (TTAB 1983). The court playfully stated, "[l]est we be accused of painting with too broad a brush, we hold only that an artist's name affixed to an original work of art may be registered as a mark." The same, however, is not true of authors. When you affix your name to a book, you cannot register that as a mark.

Newspaper Columns and Sections

We've left the least applicable and the most complicated category for last. **If you are not involved in applying for a newspaper column or section, skip this.**

The USPTO has specific rules about newspaper columns and whether the name of the column, rather than the author, is registrable. Columns are normally not considered separate "goods" unless they are sold, syndicated, or offered for syndication separate and apart from the larger publication in which they appear.

Here are the basic rules:

- **Syndicated columns.** Syndicated columns and sections that are separately sold, syndicated, or offered for syndication constitute goods in trade and are registrable.

- **Nonsyndicated Columns with Separate Recognition.** If a nonsyndicated column or section has acquired separate recognition and distinctiveness, it can be registered, but the applicant bears the burden of establishing through evidence of promotion, long use, advertising expenditures, and breadth of distribution or sales that the public has come to recognize the proposed mark as an indicator of source.

- **Columns or Sections of Online Publications.** These are registrable because they can be directly accessed and can exist independently of any single publication. They must be nondownloadable.

Marks with Geography

In terms of trademark, *geographic terms* mean any terms referring to a place, such as the West Coast, Texas, Smoky Mountains, or Harlem. A geographic location may be any term or nickname identifying a country, city, state, continent, locality, region, area, or street.

Many marks include geographic terms and names of places: the New England Quilt Museum, for instance, or American Girl dolls. Geographic terms as marks can become complicated and may require secondary meaning to be registered. We have to look at geographically descriptive terms and primarily geographically deceptively misdescriptive marks (yes, that's what it's called). **If you are not using a geographic term, you can skip this section.**

Geographically Descriptive Terms

Geographic terms that are merely descriptive and describe a place **require secondary meaning**. A three-part test determines whether a mark is merely geographically descriptive. A mark will be refused registration if it is *primarily geographically descriptive* until it has secondary meaning if:

- The primary significance of the mark is a generally known geographic location,

- Purchasers would be likely to think that the goods or services originate in the geographic placed identified in the mark, and

- The mark identifies the geographic origin of the goods or services.

For example, CAROLINA APPAREL for clothes sold in North Carolina was flagged by the trademark examining attorney as geographically descriptive, but the company responded that it had been using the mark for five years and so had gained the secondary meaning it needed to be registered.

Many marks are registered that have geographically descriptive terms, so don't despair if this is your situation. You may also have additional terms that help. And then sometimes, the application goes through even though it is for a geographically descriptive term, especially if it is in a design mark.

But wait! Will you always have to prove secondary meaning? Nope, just if the trademark examining attorney requests it. Let's look at Missouri Star Quilt Company, which has a descriptive term within its name. It is located in Missouri. When we look, we find that the trademark examining attorney did not have a problem with the name at all. Now, the company did register a design mark, and not just Missouri Star Quilt Company. That may have made it easier, as the design mark makes the name more distinctive. But the company didn't have to prove secondary meaning. It was just registered!

The New England Quilt Museum has a registered trademark that was issued in 2013. When it applied, it got an office action saying that the mark was merely descriptive—it is a quilt museum in New England. The museum responded that it had acquired distinctiveness for use over more than five years. The trademark examining attorney accepted the response, and so the mark was registered. This is the case with many businesses.

Primarily Geographically Deceptively Misdescriptive Mark

A second kind of geographic mark will always be refused: *Primarily geographically deceptively misdescriptive marks* are marks that attempt to deceive consumers regarding the geographic origin of the goods or services. These are ineligible for registration, even with secondary meaning. Here are the elements to determine whether a mark is considered primarily geographically deceptively misdescriptive:

- The primary significance of the mark is a generally known geographic location,

- Purchasers would be likely to think that the goods or services originate in the geographic place identified in the mark,

- The goods or services do not originate in the place identified in the mark, and

- The misrepresentation would be a material factor in a significant portion of the relevant consumers' decision to buy the goods or use the services.

USING A GEOGRAPHIC TERM AS A MARK?

If you are thinking of using a geographic mark, you might consider hiring an attorney to help you through the process. You may hit some bumps—but then again, you may not. If you have been using your mark for longer than five years or your mark includes a design, you may have already established secondary meaning.

Don't Despair

Don't panic if you have a geographic word as part of your mark. Plenty of geographic marks have been registered with the USPTO. *Plenty.* Registering a mark with a geographic word requires additional steps, but the steps are simple. Recognize that you will likely need secondary meaning to register it. If you have been using it for more than five years, that is really good! You will have to indicate that to the examining attorney, but it should serve to establish secondary meaning. Just because your mark has a geographic term does not mean that it can't be registered. You just might have to do an extra step. That's the takeaway here.

Geographical Indicators

There is one additional area: specific terms that relate to goods coming from a particular geographic location. These are terms that are specially protected by the trademark system, both in the U.S. and around the world, and are called *geographical indicators* (GIs). These are protected as certification marks, with required standards. Examples include IDAHO (for potatoes from Idaho), WASHINGTON (for apples), and FLORIDA (for citrus). We also know famous ones from around the world, including SWISS MADE (for watches made in Switzerland).

DEEP DIVE INTO GEOGRAPHICAL WORDS

For more on GIs, check out the guidance from the USPTO, uspto.gov/ip-policy/trademark-policy/geographical-indications-gi-protection

Naughty Words

Scandalous, immoral, and naughty words used to be denied registration, but first in 2017, and then in 2019, the U.S. Supreme Court ruled that restriction in the law was unconstitutional based on the First Amendment.

Section 2(a) of the Lanham Act barred registration of immoral or scandalous materials, often referred to as the "scandalousness provision." The Supreme Court ruled on the scandalousness provision in 2019 in *Iancu v. Brunetti*. In that case, Erik Brunetti, an artist, started a clothing line with the trademark FUCT, which he said stood for "Friends You Can't Trust." The USPTO found the mark had "decidedly negative sexual connotations." Brunetti didn't give up, took the issue to court, and went all the way to the U.S. Supreme Court, which found the scandalousness provision unconstitutional under the First Amendment.

You can use naughty words—that is immoral, disparaging, or scandalous materials—as part of your mark! You still have to meet all the requirements (inherently distinctive or merely descriptive with secondary meaning), but they are no longer off limits.

Cannabis-Related Trademarks

Some states are now legalizing marijuana, but as of 2023, the federal government still has not. In 2019, Congress deleted *hemp* from the Controlled Substances Act definition of marijuana, and the USPTO released updated guidance. You can now get federal trademarks on hemp-derived and cannabis plants that contain no more than 0.3 THC goods and services, but you must meet certain conditions. The use must be lawful under federal (and not state) law. This means no registration of marijuana-based goods and services because they are federally illegal.

Confirm There Are No *Disqualifying* Statutory Exceptions

The next step is to make sure that no statutory exceptions will prevent your mark from being registered. The USPTO has explicitly said that a few things cannot be used as a mark. Most of these likely do not apply to your mark, but just in case, you should run through them. There is a list of specific words that are off-limits *by law*. You should check that list. Marks that have anything related to the government are also not allowed. Let's take a quick look and make sure that there are no problems.

> *The USPTO has explicitly said that a few things cannot be used as a mark.*

Words and Designs Deemed Off-Limits by Statute

Parts of the federal law protect specific names, terms, initials, acronyms, and marks. These are words that were specifically made off-limits by Congress. Some are the names of organizations. Certain government agencies and instrumentalities are also protected from others' registering their names, logos, and the like. Before you proceed any further, be sure to check the current full list of protected items.

To give you an idea of the types of things on the restricted list, here are some examples:

- 4-H Club or 4-H Clubs
- The American National Theater and Academy
- American Symphony Orchestra League
- American Veterans
- Big Brothers—Big Sisters of America
- CIA [Central Intelligence Agency]
- F.B.I. [Federal Bureau of Investigation]
- Federal (when used "as part of the business or firm name of a person, corporation, partnership, business trust, association or other business entity engaged in the banking, loan, building and loan, brokerage, factorage, insurance, indemnity, savings or trust business")
- Peace Corps
- Postal Service
- Woodsy Owl

The list of off-limits words is too long to include here, and it continues to grow over time. For the full list of words and designs that are off-limits by statute, go to tmep.uspto.gov/RDMS/TMEP/current#/current/TMEP-Cd1e1.html.

You cannot register these as marks.

Spotlight on "Olympics" and Knitting

In the realm of words that are off-limits, the word *Olympic* is particularly notorious. The International Olympic Committee (IOC) has been a fierce enforcer of its trademarks, especially the use of the word OLYMPIC. Many countries, including the United States, have passed laws to protect the brand, and this is required of a host country of the games.

The Nairobi Treaty on the Protection of the Olympic Symbol protects the mark from misuse by others: "All States party to the Nairobi Treaty are under the obligation to protect the Olympic symbol—five interlaced rings—against use for commercial purposes (in advertisements, on goods, as a mark, etc.) without the authorization of the International Olympic Committee." That's the whole treaty, and it's been signed by 54 member countries.

The Special Olympics has a relationship with the IOC that allows it to use the term, with the agreement that it does not register the mark. No marks, except those owned by the IOC, have been registered with the use of OLYMPIC in the title.

An odd event between the Olympics and Raverly happened during the 2012 Summer Olympics. Ravelry, one of the largest online knitting communities, thought that it would have some fun by hosting the "Ravelympics." This did not sit well with the U.S. Olympic Committee (USOC), which polices the name very seriously, and so it sent a cease-and-desist letter to Ravelry for its use of *lympics* for its games that included such events as "scarf hockey" and "sweater triathlon." Unlike other groups that have gotten the same cease-and-desist letter (such as the Redneck Olympics), the Ravelry members responded on Facebook, on the U.S. Olympic Team's Facebook page and Twitter account. The USOC ended up *apologizing twice* to the knitters. The media picked up the story: Don't mess with knitters and their pointy things. But, in the end, Ravelry did not continue its Ravelry Olympics.

Government and Official Stuff

In this section, we are looking at flags, famous spaces, government entities, and national symbols. **If you don't have any of these things in your mark, skip ahead to Step 5: International Classes** (page 58).

Flags

Flags, insignia, or coats of arms of any state, municipality, or foreign nation are not registerable, at least if they serve as any of these things on their own. For example, you can't use a national flag for your logo.

The USPTO gives examples of MARKS that should be refused:

You can see why these would not be good: They use the goodwill of Texas and the United States as their own symbol. These types of content may be allowed if the use is merely suggestive of a flag, coat of arms, or insignia, or if it is the flag of a former country, state, or municipality (for example, the flag of East Germany or Yugoslavia). However, former flags of existing countries will be refused, including the original flag of the United States representing the thirteen colonies.

If you want to include a flag in your design mark, consider incorporating it in a different way.

Stylized and incomplete flags are not refused registration, including:

- When it is used to form letters, numbers, or a design
- When the flag is substantially obscured by words or design
- When the design is not in the normal shape of a flag
- When the flag appears in colors different from the normal colors
- When a significant feature is missing or changed

Here are some examples:

Yarnify is a yarn shop in Chicago that has registered two marks in two separate applications. In 2016, it registered a word mark. We've seen an evolution in its logo, which started out mimicking the Chicago flag and now has progressed to something else. Yarnify did not register the first logo, and it would likely have been refused. However, the second logo would likely be accepted. Can you see why?

The first logo plays
on the Chicago flag.

The Chicago flag

The new logo does not resemble
the Chicago flag.

Government Entities and National Symbols

The U.S. Postal Service, the Los Angeles Police Department, and the U.S. Army, along with other government and national entities, can register their marks. These include monuments, statues, and buildings associated with the government. However, these are not registrable when they falsely suggest a connection. Anyone who isn't representing these organizations can't swoop in and register the mark before them.

This includes the bald eagle, the Statue of Liberty, "Uncle Sam," the heraldry and shield designs of government offices, and certain uses of *U.S.* The national symbols of foreign countries are also not registrable. For example, you won't be allowed to register the hammer and sickle of the former USSR.

The name of a country is not considered a national symbol but may be considered a "false connection" under certain circumstances. Marks may be refused registration for false suggestion of a connection.

International Classes

Marks fall under two main categories: goods or services.

Each of these is divided into different classes (think of these as topics). When you apply for a trademark, you choose the class in which your trademark fits. There are 45 classes. Goods are Classes 1–34, and services are Classes 35–45. For example, we registered the JUST WANNA QUILT podcast as Class 41 for entertainment. It is time to determine which class(es) you are going to select for your mark. We sometimes use the shorthand IC, for International Class, when we are talking about them (for example, IC 041).

Each class has been carefully designed and is used throughout the world as a way to understand what the mark protects. For example, Class 1, chemicals, is the same in the United States as it is in South Africa, Argentina, France, and so on. Everyone then has a common language to understand the property right (that is, which class) of a mark.

The Nice Classification (NCL) was created in 1957 to classify goods and services in the registration of marks. It is now updated annually. You can find many versions online, but the official version is housed at the World Intellectual Property Organization (WIPO).

OFFICIAL INTERNATIONAL CLASSES LIST

To see the full list of classes published by WIPO, go to wipo.int/classifications/nice/nclpub/en/fr. What is beautiful about this resource is that it gives you examples and also explains what is *not* included in each class. This is a must-use resource.

Let's look at an example of an entry—in this case, Class 2.

On the left-hand side of the screen, you can click on any class of goods and services. In this case, we clicked on 2, Chemicals. The main portion of the screen displays a description, paints, varnishes, and so forth. This is followed by the "Explanatory Note," which describes what the class includes and does not include. Here, we see that dyestuffs for clothing is included in this category, but it does not include cosmetic dyes. Notice that after cosmetic dyes, it points you to the proper class. When you scroll down, you will see that the entry also includes a list of reference numbers that detail what is included in the class.

We are going through commonly used classes in arts and craft businesses, but you can also browse the list yourself, or even search by using key terms to find the class that best relates to your goods or services. Click on the Search tab at the top of the screen and enter your search term. As an example, we searched for "thread."

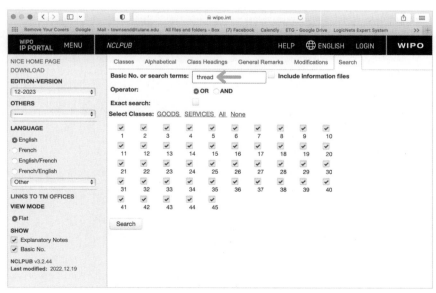

Our search returned 41 results ranging from surgical thread to screw-thread cutters, among many others. We found what we were looking for—yarns and threads for textile use—in Class 23.

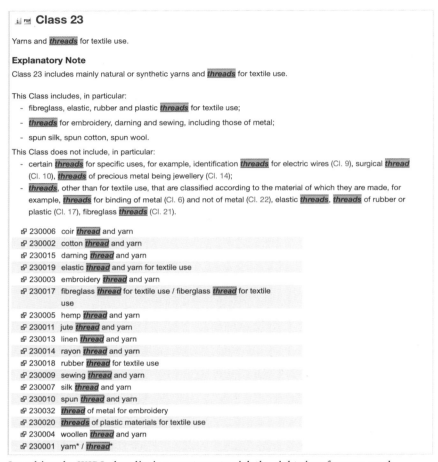

Searching the WIPO class list is a great way to pick the right class for your mark.

Class-Choosing Strategies

Choosing from among all the different classes can seem pretty confusing. Sometimes, it's hard to narrow down exactly which class your trademark fits into.

If you have tried searching the WIPO list and are still unsure, here are some ways of thinking about it to help determine which class is right for you:

- Some register the structure like an online retail store.

- Some register the goods or services sold in that store.

- Some do both.

What should you do? That really depends on the goal of the products and services. In Part II, we look at a lot more examples of what other companies have done. So, if you're feeling lost, look there. To get started, let's take a look at the most common categories we see used with arts and crafts.

Most Common Classes of Marks

Trademark divides the world into goods or services. Goods are just that: items people can purchase. Services are just that: something done for someone. A service can have goods: McDonald's has goods (fast food) and provides service (restaurant services). But those are two separate categories—the company would have registered the service and the goods that it wanted to protect by trademark.

If you have an online or a brick-and-mortar store, then you are registering the act of having a retail store, and not the specific goods. These are found under *Services* rather than the Goods heading.

Goods Classes

Let's look at some of the ICs as related to crafts, art, sewing, and quilting.

Class 2: Paints, including dyestuffs for clothing and colorants for foodstuffs and beverages. This includes VIVIVA, which uses IC 002 for watercolor paints.

Class 3: Nonmedicated cosmetics and toiletries, perfumes, essential oils, nail art stickers, and, strangely, sandpaper. For instance, the makeup company Tarte has TARTE registered in IC 003, and Bain Amour Bath & Body Company has registered aftershave, body creams, and other nonmedicated creams in IC 003.

Class 4: Industrial oils and greases, wax, candles, and wicks for lighting. RED ROCK CANDLE CO is a word mark registered in IC 004 for scented candles. Bain Amour Bath & Body Company has also registered a word mark not only in IC 003 but in IC 004, for candles and wax melts.

Class 7: Machines, machine tools, power-operated tools, and so forth, including 3-D printers, but not hand tools, and certain special machines. APQS has registered its sewing and quilting machines in IC 007, as has Baby Lock and Gammill. AccuQuilt registered in IC 007 quilting supplies and accessories—namely, cutting machines for quilting and craft use and dies for use with the aforementioned cutting machines.

Class 8: Hand tools, cutlery, razors, side arms, except firearms. Havel's Sewing has registered in this class for hand-operated sewing tools— namely, scissors, buttonhole cutters, fabric control tools, laying tools, tweezers, needles, and seam rippers. Olfa has also registered its hand-operated cutting instruments in Class 8.

Class 9: Electrical and scientific apparatus, including magnets, optical, weighing, recording discs, cash registers, calculating machines, computers, software, and safety gear. CRAFTOPTICS has registered its magnifying oculars for nonmedical purposes, especially crafts, in Class 9. The Imaginator, a 3-D printer for crafters, is in Class 9. Creative Grids, which makes lots of rulers, is registered in Class 9. Electric Quilt Company has applied for a word mark in Class 9 (computer software for use in designing quilts on personal computers).

Class 14: Jewelry, including precious metals, goods in precious metals not included in other classes, and (in general) jewelry, clocks, and watches. The Thread Cutterz (a ring that has a blade for cutting thread) is registered in Class 14. Angie Wood Creations, which creates handmade wooden watches, has also filed in Class 14. It focused on the watch aspect and not the wood.

Class 16: Paper goods and printed matter. This is a big category for crafters and quilters. Class 16 can include paper and cardboard, printed matter, bookbinding material, photographs, stationery and office requisites (except furniture), drawing materials and materials for artists, paintbrushes, instructional and teaching materials, plastic sheets, films, and bags for wrapping packaging, and printers' type and printing blocks. Office machines like typewriters are included, as are painting supplies, like palettes and paint rollers. Goods made of paper, from containers to figurines of papier-mâché, are included, along with framed and unframed lithographs, paintings, and watercolors. Note that paints are not included. PrismaColor felt-tip markers, for instance, are registered in Class 16. Olfa and Accuquilt Go! are also in this category. C&T Publishing (books) also uses this category, as does American Patchwork & Quilting. Quilter's Select uses this category for heat-fusible sheets and paper stabilizers for embroidery.

International Quilt Festival is registered in this category for printed publications and flyers. Orange Dot Quilts has also registered printed patterns in IC 016.

Class 17: Rubber goods, packing, and insulating materials. Mistyfuse uses Class 17 for its fabric-like web of fusible adhesive.

Class 18: Leather goods, travel goods but not including clothing, laptop bags, or golf bags without wheels. For instance, BACAES, backpacks for pets, cosmetic bags, and other bags, are registered in Class 18. The company ByAnnie uses this class for leather labels.

Class 20: Furniture and articles not otherwise classified. Handi Quilter has registered adjustable tables and frames in this class.

Class 21: House or kitchen utensils and containers. Naomi Singer, an individual who does business as Modern Mud, has registered a word mark MODERN MUD for ceramic sculptures, vases, vessels, bowls, plates and pots, and planters for flowers and plants in Class 21. Here is the specimen photograph.

Class 22: Cordage and fibers. Quilter's Select uses this category for cotton batting, as does The Warm Company.

Class 23: Yards and threads for textile use. Superior Threads, Aurifil, Wonderfil, and Sulky all use Class 23.

Class 24: Textiles and substitutes for textiles; household linen, curtains of textile or plastic. Quilter's Select uses this category for embroidery stabilizing fabric for appliqué. Michael Miller Fabrics uses Class 24 for fabrics for textile use, as do The Blank Quilting Corporation, FreeSpirit Fabrics, Tula Pink, American Made Brand, Camelot Fabrics, Cherrywood Fabrics, and more. At the right is one of the specimen photographs for FreeSpirit Fabrics.

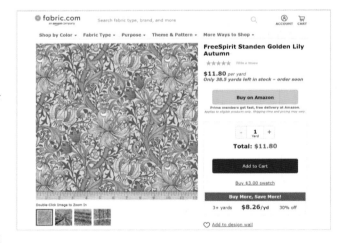

Class 25: Clothing, footwear, and headwear for human beings, including costumes. Doll clothes and clothes for animals are not included. (IC 028 is for doll clothes, and IC 018 is for clothing for animals of all kinds.)

Class 26: Fancy goods; lace, braid and embroidery, haberdashery ribbons and bows; buttons, hooks and eyes, pins and needles; artificial flowers; hair decorations; false hair. Organ Needle Co. has registered its needles in Class 26, as has Groz-Beckert.

Class 28: Games, toys, playthings, video game apparatus, gymnastic and sporting articles, carnival masks, action figures, amusement and novelty items, dolls, and decorations for Christmas trees. MONSTER HIGH is a word mark in Class 28 for dolls.

Service Classes

Let's look at some of the classes related to services, and in particular those that are most commonly used by creatives.

Class 35: Services involving business management, operation, organization, and administration of a commercial or industrial enterprise, as well as advertising, marketing, and promotional services. The Modern Quilt Guild and Quilts of Valor are registered in Class 35. Sewing Machines Plus, Rockler, We Are Knitters, and the Daily Charme are all registered in IC 035 as online retailers. Amazon is also registered in Class 35, among others. IC 035 can be used for brick-and-mortar stores as well. Joann's has 035 for its online and retail stores as well as other registered marks. Consulting services for businesses are also included in this class.

Class 39: Travel, including travel arrangements, packaging and storage of goods, and general transport. World of Quilts Travel is registered in Class 39.

Class 40: Treatment of materials. The Warm Company, a batting company, has registered its service of treating materials in this class.

Class 41: Education and entertainment education; providing of training; entertainment; sporting and cultural activities. Class 41 is a big one for creatives. It includes education; podcasts; websites; photography; exhibitions; publications of books and texts; news reporting services; film direction and production services; cultural, educational, or entertainment services provided by amusement parks, circuses, zoos, art galleries, and museums; training of animals; sports and fitness training services; online gaming services; ticket reservation and booking services; rental of artwork; calligraphy services; coaching; arranging and conducting concerts; arranging and conducting conferences; organization of cosplay entertainment events; film distribution; gambling services; lending library services; the production of music; and much more. Bernina has a Class 41 registration. QuiltCon is registered in Class 41 for organizing events in the field of quilting for cultural or educational purposes. Podcasts are registered in this category, including JUST WANNA QUILT. Educational websites are also registered in this class. The Social Justice Sewing Academy is registered in this category as well, for educational services in the nature of workshops that foster participatory art as a vehicle for personal transformation, community cohesion, and social change in schools.

Class 42: Scientific and technological services. Alexander Henry Fabrics, strangely, is registered in Class 42: retail and wholesale store services in the field of fabrics. (What makes this strange is that it seems like it should be in Class 24.) Hoffman California Fabrics is registered in Class 42 as well as in Class 24 (textiles). This indicates that Hoffman California Fabrics provides a service of printing fabric rather than just the fabric itself.

Class 43: Food and drink services, temporary bed and board, campgrounds, animal boarding, daycare, and reservation services for travelers.

Class 45: Legal services; security services; personal and social services rendered by others to meet the needs of individuals; services related to social events, including escort services, matrimonial agencies, and funeral services; babysitting; clothing rental; copyright management; detective agencies; dog-walking services; firefighting; house sitting; and tarot card reading services for others.

Specific Areas and International Classes

Let's take a look at some specific areas that may be important to you when choosing your class. These include some less common situations, such as trademarking kits and gift baskets, classes used by museums, and virtual goods.

Kits and Items Sold as Units

If you are registering a kit or gift basket as a good, you can include in the kit or basket goods of different classes without registering them as separate classes, but this is only true within the United States. Kits are classified in two ways.

If the items in the kit will be used to make a single object, then the unit is classified by the item the kit will be made into.

A kit created around a theme, or whatever object is most dominant, controls the class. If a number of the items are in the same class, that would dominate. The USPTO gives the example of a nail care kit with nail polish (IC 003), nail files (IC 008), nail polish remover (IC 003), instructions (IC 016), and false nails (IC 003). IC 003 it is. You include all the elements in the description. The identification must include the type of kit and the main goods; the kit must not include services or computer software.

A doll and a book, for example, can be a kit if they are sold as a unit. You have to include in your description that it will be "sold as a unit" and make sure to put whatever object is the dominant class first. This does not work for services, only for goods.

Museums

The International Quilt Museum registered two marks, IC 016 (printed materials) and IC 041 (museum services) as a word mark. In 2007, the National Quilt Museum filed for an IC 041 word mark, which has been renewed. The Art Institute of Chicago and the Field Museum of Natural History have each registered a word mark in IC 041, education and entertainment services. The Field Museum also uses IC 042, "Scientific research; habitat development and preservation services, namely, monitoring, testing, analyzing  ecological success in the field of environmentally sensitive habitat conservation and preservation of native plants and wildlife," and EXPEDITIONS@ FIELDMUSEUM for IC 038 (online video broadcasting). It has also registered a design mark for its "Sue," the very special T. rex at the museum, in IC 025 (T-shirts). Now, of course, it has a gift shop full of Field Museum specialness, including even small-batch whiskey, but it didn't do additional trademark registrations.

Virtual Goods, Cryptocurrency, and NFTs

More and more, artists are using new technologies to support their work. We also see entrepreneurs creating businesses based on virtual goods and other digital items. Some artist communities are using non-fungible tokens (NFTs) as a way to support each others' art.

PART 1: WHAT IS YOUR MARK?

> ### ARTISTS AND VIRTUAL CURRENCY
> For more on the artist response to NFTs, see Sidne K. Gard, The Artist's Underground of NFTs, Fnewsmagazine, October 10, 2022, fnewsmagazine.com/2022/10/the-artistic-underground-of-nfts.

New technologies present interesting questions for the law. Here, for a trademark, we have to sort out what is functional from what is a source identifier, and to do that, we have to distinguish the underlying concepts and technology with goods and/or services. The USPTO has put out guidelines for registering uses of these new technologies.

Virtual Goods: These are digital objects for use in online virtual worlds, including avatars. These can be registered in Class 9 (downloadable virtual goods), Class 35 (online retail store selling virtual goods), Class 41 (entertainment services—namely, providing virtual objects for use in virtual environments), and Class 42 (computer programming of virtual goods).

Cryptocurrency: Cryptocurrency, including bitcoins, is a form of exchange tracked on a blockchain. The USPTO does not recognize it as a good or service, but you can register related items: Class 9 (for cryptocurrency hardware wallets), Class 36 (for cryptocurrency exchange services), Class 42 (rental of computer hardware for cryptocurrency mining or for storage of cryptocurrency), and Class 45 (providing legal information in the field of cryptocurrency).

Blockchain: Blockchain is a way of keeping track of transactions in a digital, distributed, and encrypted way. The USPTO does not recognize this as a good or service; it is usually a feature of a good or service or a way of rendering the service. You can register blockchain-related goods and services in Class 9 (downloadable software for blockchain-based inventory management), Class 35 (for example, for maintaining patient records by using blockchain), and Class 42 (providing user authentication service by using blockchain).

Non-fungible tokens (NFTs): NFTs are a piece of data connected to a digital or physical item, something like a digital baseball card. Each uses blockchain technology, and owners are given a certificate of authenticity. The USPTO does not identify NFTs as a good or a service, but, you can register them in Class 9 (downloadable image files containing trading cards authenticated by non-fungible tokens), Class 25 (for example, sneakers authenticated by non-fungible tokens), and Class 35 (online marketplace for downloadable digital art files authenticated by non-fungible tokens).

MORE ON THE VIRTUAL WORLD
If you want a deeper dive into how the USPTO is handing new technologies, check out its PowerPoint presentation on the topic at uspto.gov/sites/default/files/documents/TM-Newer-Technologies-webinar.pdf.

Selecting Multiple Classes

You can select more than one class in which to register your mark. When you submit an application to more than one class, list the IC numbers in consecutive numerical order. For each class selected, you must submit a filing fee, verify the dates of use of the mark, and submit a specimen and a verified statement. Let's look at a couple of examples.

Olive & June is a spa turned online shop that also has merchandise. Founded in 2013 in Beverly Hills, California, Olive & June provides nail salon–quality nails at home for an approachable price (a service) and merchandise (goods). It has registered six trademark applications. They are registered in Class 8 (emery boards, nail clippers, and nail files), Class 3 (cosmetic masks, lotions, nail art stickers, and so forth), Class 30 (tea), and Class 25 (footwear), and the company has design marks, O&J and Olive and Jane, in Class 44 (day spa services). We talk more about adding additional classes in Changing or Expanding Your Trademark (page 193).

We Are Knitters has registered as a word mark WE ARE KNITTERS for yarn (Class 23); hand-knitting needles, sewing kits, and sewing needles (Class 26); and an online retail store (Class 35). We've seen 35 a lot.

Crochetville has four classes for the word mark CROCHETVILLE: digital materials—namely, patterns and pdf files featuring crochet, fiber arts, and mixed medium; and downloadable documents in the field of crochet, fiber arts, and mixed media provided via a website (Class 9); online retail store (Class 35); online forum for companies to showcase, display, demonstrate and promote new and innovative ideas, products, and services in the convention or meeting management area (Class 38); and educational services—namely, providing online instruction in the field of crochet, fiber arts, and mixed media via an online website; and online journals—namely, blogs featuring crochet, fiber arts, and mixed media (Class 41).

ByAnnie has registered BYA in four classes: Class 18 (leather labels), Class 26 (hardware for handbags—namely, zipper pulls and handle couplers; zippers), Class 35 (online retail store featuring sewing supplies, patterns, and tools), and Class 40 (providing information regarding sewing).

U.S.-Only Designations for Collective and Certification Marks

We have already discussed collective and certification marks. The U.S. has three specific non-Nice classifications for the categories of marks that don't fall under the umbrella of either goods or services.

They are:

- **Class A:** certification marks for goods
- **Class B:** certification marks for services
- **Class 200:** collective membership marks

Choosing Your Description

The description of the mark is just that—it describes what your mark covers in your chosen class. For example, you choose Class 23, for thread. You then need to choose a description, such as thread, sail thread, wood thread, or maybe even gold thread jewelry. You will have a bunch of choices, which you will find in the Trademark ID Manual (the official title is the Acceptable Identification of Goods and Services Manual). We look at descriptions in more depth shortly, but for now, what you are looking for is a description that matches the goods or services that you want to register.

You will need to use the Trademark ID Manual to choose your class and accompanying description. It includes all the different descriptions of International Classes the USPTO has already accepted.

Go to uspto.gov > Trademarks > Tools & links > More tools & links > Apply for a trademark > Select goods & services in ID Manual.

Once there:

1. Search the term of whatever type of product or service your mark is related to.

2. Sort the results and decide which suits your mark best.

You will see that the different terms will relate to a particular International Class. Be aware of this. If you want to protect a retail store but choose fabric (Class 24), that will affect the enforceability of your mark.

For example, we entered *thread* and got 212 results. Most were Class 23 (yarns and threads for textile use), but there was also Class 10 (surgical thread), Class 9 (thread counters), Class 9 (thread snips), and even Class 14 (gold thread jewelry). You will encounter this list as part of the application process when you choose your class(es) and have to add a description.

Trademark ID Manual homescreen

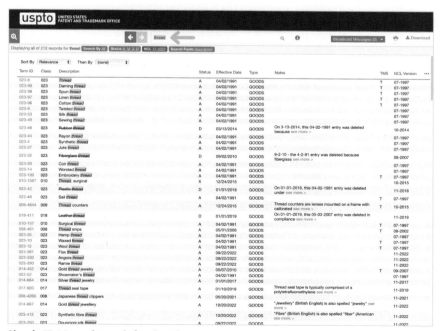

Simple ID Manual search for *thread*

Some Helpful Search Information

You will notice a column titled "Status."

Each of these letters means something:

- A: Added to the ID manual

- M: Modified since original addition

- X: Example

- D: Deleted and usually crossed out (if you click on the Term ID, it will explain why it was deleted)

Brackets: [Information that doesn't have to be included in the description, but if you want to include it, you will remove the brackets.]

"Chow mein [meat-, fish-, or vegetable-based]."

In the application, you could write, "Chow mein, meat-, fish-, or vegetable-based."

Curly Brackets: Some entries allow you to add additional detail to the description that is connected to your goods and services. When you can do this, the USPTO indicates it with {curly brackets}. You can then modify it within the application process.

| 026-6 | 026 | Needlepoint kits, consisting of {indicate the components, e.g., needles, *thread*, patterns} | A | 04/02/1991 | GOODS |

Descriptions containing brackets allow you to customize the description.

In the screenshot above, you can see the description, "Needlepoint kits, consisting of {indicate the components, e.g., needles, thread, patterns}". So, here, you could write "Needlepoint kits, consisting of needles, fabric, pattern, and cookies."

Compare this to the following static description you **cannot** change because it does not have curly brackets: "Sewing kits comprised of needles, thimbles, scissors, and thread, sold as a unit." If you do not include thimbles in your sewing kit, you cannot use this description. Does this make sense?

Broad or Specific Description?

Whether you choose a broad or a specific description is up to you. If you choose a broad one, it covers more. *Thread* would include all kinds of thread. Shoemaker's thread is much more specific. You might need a specific description when you are distinguishing your mark from another good or service mark.

Have you figured out a couple that you like? Jot down the:

- **Search term**

- **Term ID** (the ID that goes with that description, so you can find it again)

- **International Class**

- **Description**

- **Status**

- **And whether it is a good or service**

You've learned so much and you will need this information for your application. Let's go to the Big Trademark Application list, page 135.

You should be able to fill in:

- **Mark**

- **Strength of the Mark**

- **No statutory Problems**

- **International Class**

- **Description of the Mark**

That's it! You've chosen your mark, checked its strength and any limitations, and determined its class and description. Ready to see whether you can actually *use it*? Don't fret. We know that sounds scary, but you have to make sure that there are no conflicts with goods or products already out there. On to Part II!

BAD PARABLE

PART II
Check Your Mark

You know what mark you want to use, and you've done your homework. You know what category it is, how strong it is, and what kind of mark you want to pursue: word, design, or other. You are likely madly in love with your mark. Now, you have to find out whether you can use it! Don't despair. We walk you through all the steps, including how to start over, if needed.

In this part, you will:

- **Find out how to do a trademark clearance**, including checking for common law uses, making sure that there is no likelihood of confusion, and completing other basic tasks.

- **Learn how to search for and read a United States Patent and Trademark Office (USPTO) trademark record**, so you can confirm that the mark you are interested in is available, including a design search and nontraditional marks search.

- **Learn how to use the World Intellectual Property Organization's (WIPO's) Global Brand Database** to do a worldwide, country-by-country search of your mark.

- **Prepare your specimen** for the application, checking to make sure that you have met all the requirements for *in use*, including specifics for goods versus services.

This is the research part. Let's dig in!

Out-in-the-World *Check*

Check by Searching

The first thing you're going to want to do is to find out whether others are using the mark. You can then decide what you want to do with the knowledge. We do additional searches shortly, but you'll want to start with some general sleuthing. This step can be done before Part 1, but for our purposes, we've put it here. Once you get a sense of how trademark works, you can do the steps in any order that you want. This is just one method of learning the steps.

In conducting an out-in-the-world search, you are checking for any uses of the mark you hope to use that are already in use by others. These other uses may or may not be registered. Remember common law and state trademarks? Simply put, we're trying to find anything that might be problematic by doing a search out in the world. This helps us catch common law marks as well as state marks that might be in use. A general search is not perfect, but it is a great place to start. You can also hire someone to do a comprehensive search; for more, see Full Clearance Searches (page 114).

Domain Names

This is easy: Check to find out whether anyone is already using the domain name. Does someone already own and use your desired domain name? What do they do with it? Is it in the same field your use would be?

Finding someone already using your intended mark as a domain name doesn't preclude using it as your mark, but you should do further research to make sure that your product is not in the same field. This search will also tell you what competition might already be using the mark. We look more at fields and classes soon, but this search will also give you information about other uses, even if they are not similar to or in competition with your use.

Obtaining the domain name is *not* the same as getting the trademark. Here is what the USPTO writes: "Registration of a domain name with a domain name registrar does not give you any trademark rights." *GoDaddy* is an easy place to check whether anyone is using your domain name. Other domain name search sites also work. Do you have a couple of ideas for your domain name? Go find out whether those URLs are available.

You can purchase the domain name if it is available. It helps alert others that the name is already, or will soon be, in use. Even if you do not end up using the domain name, this will keep others from claiming it.

Google

Search things similar to your potential mark in different ways, spellings, and word combinations to make sure that others are not using the name or something similar. Obviously, you can use other Internet search engines, but we have found Google to be the most thorough. The USPTO trademark examining attorneys also do a Google search, so why not see what they will see? If you are using an image, you can also do a reverse image search on Google.

The examining attorney will also do a reverse image search on Google and other search engines. They are looking to make sure that your design image is not fake, stolen, or already used by someone else, even if it is not registered.

Dictionaries

Online dictionaries can be very useful in helping you see whether the word you are using is merely descriptive of the good or service. If the mark matches the dictionary definition, then it will be deemed generic. This is also true if it is a foreign translation. Also, make sure that the name doesn't mean something you don't expect. Times change, and so do meanings and connotations. What are you looking for? If your mark is merely descriptive, that will be flagged by the examining attorney, and you may have to prove secondary meaning. If the definition is a generic word for what you do, that's really a problem.

Wikipedia

See what Wikipedia says about the proposed mark. The examining attorney might also do this. You are looking for others' use of the mark that might cause a likelihood of confusion. For a refresher, see Likelihood of Confusion or Dilution (page 73) and also find out whether the mark is merely descriptive or generic.

Trade Sources and News Stories

If you are in a particular trade, check industry resources to find out whether the name is in use. You can use Thomasnet.com or superpages.com to search for industry products, news, and information. These are not perfect tools, but they are free, and you can see what pops up for your suggested name.

In 2018, we attended International Quilt Festival and we went to Quilt Market in 2019 to see what was going on in the field and also to host a booth on legal help. Quilts, Inc. also puts out an exhibitor list, a good example of a trade resource.

News stories related to trademarks also sometimes come up. You may be able to find examples in a search engine or in more specialized databases, such as LexisNexis. Also, remember, common phrases in the news are generally not registerable as a source identifier of goods/services; see A Slogan or Phrase (page 32).

Be Creative

If you are creating a podcast, search iTunes to find out whether another show is named similarly. If you are creating candies, search for a list of candies. Be creative. You are in detective mode. Know your market. Know what might be conflicting.

Did you find anything troubling? If not, you have reached the next level of inquiry. If you did, stop and consider whether this is the right mark for you. If it already has too many problems, start again and think through another mark. That's part of the video game quality of determining a mark for your goods and/or services.

Likelihood of Confusion or Dilution

The likelihood of confusion is the test for trademark infringement, but it is wise to use this to understand whether the name/mark you have chosen might cause confusion or bring the wrath of another company upon you. Dilution is used for famous marks—*only* famous marks—and gives them extra protection. The trademark examining attorney will be doing this same analysis, so it's good for you to do it ahead of time.

Likelihood of Confusion Analysis

Likelihood of confusion is one of the problems that can arise during the examination period.

> *By doing a quick check and becoming aware of whether your mark could be confused with a senior mark, you can save time and money by altering your mark in advance.*

A likelihood of confusion analysis includes the steps below. This test varies, but in general, this process is the way a court reviews for likelihood of confusion between a senior mark (the first user) and a junior mark (the subsequent user).

The scenario is that the holder of a senior mark may be out there and would be upset if you named your goods or services something that would confuse customers. Do some investigating. Do you see anything similar? For instance, we had contemplated using the mark Just Wanna Quilt Con, but we started to worry about QuiltCon and how its organizers would feel about that. This is a good example of something that might cause confusion (or not). We decided it was too close and not to risk it.

It is important to note that you may want to do this analysis with registered and unregistered marks. Just because something is not registered doesn't mean you are in the clear. Mariah Carey applied to register the word mark QUEEN OF CHRISTMAS, but someone objected. The objector also used Queen of Christmas, even though the other use was not registered. If you have found similar marks along the way—registered or not—do the analysis.

To conduct a likelihood of confusion analysis, ask a number of questions. The trademark examining attorney may refer to this as the *du Pont* factors test. The Federal Circuit uses this test for trademark infringement cases, and so it has been adopted by the USPTO.

The test has thirteen points, but the two key elements are the similarities between the two marks and the relatedness of the compared goods and or/services.

Below are the elements of a *du Pont* factors likelihood of confusion analysis:

1. The similarity of the marks in their entireties as to appearance, sound, connotation, and commercial impression. This is considered the most important factor.

2. The similarity and nature of the covered goods and services described in the application or registration.

3. The similarity of established likely-to-continue trade channels.

4. The conditions under which, and buyers to whom, sales are made ("impulse" versus careful sophisticated purchasing).

5. The fame of the prior mark.

6. The number and nature of similar marks in use on similar goods.

7. The nature and extent of actual confusion.

8. The length of time during, and conditions under which, there has been concurrent use without evidence of actual confusion.

9. The variety of goods on which a mark is or is not used.

10. The market interface between the applicant and the owner of the prior mark.

11. The extent to which the applicant has a right to exclude others from the use of its mark.

12. The extent of possible confusion.

13. Is there any other established fact probative of the effect of use?

Let's take a look at some of the key concepts involved in a likelihood of confusion analysis.

Similarity of the Marks

Determining how similar two marks may be is subjective. Sound-alikes, the same word with different spellings, and translations of the same word are included in this category. The more similar the name, word, or design of the mark, the more likely consumers may be confused regarding the association. Look at the mark as a whole—word, design, sound, color, and so forth—and decide how similar (or not) the two marks are. Also, consider such elements as the style of the fonts used and the packaging. It's about the whole look and feel.

Here are some examples that are too similar:

- MAGNAVOX versus MULTIVOX
- PLATINUM PUFF versus PLATINUM PLUS
- ZIRCO versus COZIRC
- MATERNALLY YOURS versus YOUR MATERNITY SHOP

When trying to figure out whether your mark is too similar to another mark, here are some things to keep in mind:

- **Spelling.** Just because you spell a word differently doesn't make it less confusing. The USPTO gives this example: T.MARKEY versus TEE MAQUEE.

- **Translation.** If you use a word in a different language, that doesn't count either: WOLF versus LUPO (Italian).

- **General meaning.** If the words generally mean the same thing, that doesn't work either: CITY WOMAN versus CITY GIRL.

Similarity and Nature of the Goods and/or Services

The more similar the products and services themselves are, with similar marks, the more likely they are to cause confusion. Would a purchaser be confused into thinking they were buying the product from the senior user of the mark? A classic example is GALLO wine and GALLO cheese, where the court found that they were too similar in "sight, sound and meaning." Another famous case that hinged on the similarity of the products or services is McDonald's suing McSleep. The hotel chain could be perceived as related to the fast food company, as they appeared on the highway together, and customers might think that McDonald's had opened a hotel chain.

Similarity of the Established Trade Channels

Are the two products selling to the same customers? Are they products that would be compared or near each other?

Strength of the Senior User's Mark

You are encouraged to assess the strength of the mark already in use. Determine whether the potentially confusing mark is inherently distinctive versus merely descriptive. Remember, arbitrary, fanciful, suggestive, merely descriptive with secondary meaning, and well-known marks get protection. Inherently distinctive marks get stronger protection, and famous marks get the strongest, but merely descriptive without secondary meaning or generic marks do not get protection. If you have found a mark that is strong and likely to be confused with yours, you might want to pivot away from this mark. Your application may get denied. For a refresher on assessing the strength of a mark, refer to Step 3: Check the Strength of the Mark (page 34).

Proximity of the Products and Services

Proximity means how close the products are to each other in the marketplace. Is the name you chose similar to that of related products/services, so a similar customer base might be confused over affiliation? Again, because of the proximity of the services, Just Wanna Quilt Con might have been confused with QuiltCon, and it may have seemed like we were affiliated with that very popular event. If we had been in different sectors, that might not have been true; for instance, ComicCon is not confused with QuiltCon, nor is FashionCon. They must be related goods and/or services to be a problem.

Examples often cited as in the same proximity include:

- T-shirts and pants versus hats

- Banking services versus mortgage lending services

- T-shirts and pants versus online retail store services featuring clothing

Remember the earlier example of DELTA Faucet versus DELTA Air Lines? They're both protected and registrable marks because they share a name but exist in separate realms.

Bridging the Gap

This is our personal favorite. How likely is the senior user to start creating products that the junior user is trying to register? Let's look at SINGER sewing. Singer has a number of word and design marks in Class 7 for its sewing machines. How likely is it that SINGER sewing would branch out to fabric, thread, or scissors? Trademark gives that room to grow to a mark. Pretty cool, yes? In fact, Singer has word or design marks for fabrics (Class 24), electric irons (Class 9), hobby craft kits (Class 28), printed publications (Class 16), thread (Class 23), and dress forms (Class 20).

Companies get to "bridge the gap." They can make names from their trademark and expand on the brand. We're doing that with Just Wanna Quilt. We now have *Just Wanna Trademark* and other books. We're building a brand. So, be careful that you are not trying to trademark within an existing family. See why? You would be playing on the goodwill of the other company, and that's not fair. And trademark is really about preventing unfair competition.

Actual Confusion

Could customers actually confuse your mark with an existing senior mark? Hopefully not. It could be too close to the senior mark, or worse, you could actually be using the senior's mark as your own. We had quilt show organizers swipe our design mark for Just Wanna Quilt and try to use it for their event. This would have caused *actual confusion*.

Sophistication of the Buyers

The less sophisticated your buyers, the more possible their confusion, or so the logic goes.

The level of sophistication is often measured by the price of the products and whether they are considered specialty and niche items. If the goods are expensive, customers are more likely to do the research and really know what they are buying and from which company.

Defendant's Intent

If this were a court case, the court would look to determine whether the junior user *intended* to use the goodwill of the senior mark by using the particular mark. Don't do this. It's rude, and it will cause you a lot of problems.

That's the last step of the likelihood of confusion test. If you perform this analysis before you register a mark, you are less likely to have these issues come up as substantive problems with the trademark examining attorney at the USPTO. And if something substantive *does* come up, you'll be prepared to hire a lawyer and make the arguments as to why there is, in fact, no likelihood of confusion.

Dilution Check

Dilution occurs when a junior mark uses the goodwill of a senior mark, either by *blurring* (it seems too close) or *tarnishing* (giving the mark unflattering associations). If a mark is famous, you can not use that fame for your own. Period. You can't tarnish that brand or blur it with your own.

A recent example of a mark that was found to create likelihood of dilution was JUST DREW IT! for athletic wear, playing off Nike's famous mark JUST DO IT! This was a *pro se* application (someone without an attorney), and so they probably did not understand dilution or the likelihood of confusion. This mark was refused by the examining attorney, and the applicant appealed to the Trademark Trial and Appeal Board (TTAB), which sustained the refusal. (See The Trademark Trial and Appeal Board, page 170). The marks were found to be too close. A sound test revealed that DO and DREW were too similar even though they look different. The TTAB also found that JUST DREW IT! would conjure the famous and well-known mark JUST DO IT! in the minds of consumers and thus constituted dilution of the more established mark.

When does dilution apply? First, the senior mark has to be famous—to everyone, not to a particular niche. It has to be recognized by the general consuming public of the United States as a source identifier for the goods or services at issue. Everyone knows Singer (manufacturer of sewing machines); fewer know Juki, a company that also makes sewing machines; it is not a household brand like Singer.

Dilution would likely only apply to Singer. So, if someone comes along and wants to use the mark SINGER pianos, Singer (sewing machines) may sue for dilution to prevent the public from confusing/blurring the SINGER sewing machine mark with that of SINGER pianos, the junior user. The test to determine whether a mark is famous enough includes (1) duration, extent, and geographic reach of advertising and publicity of the mark; (2) amount, volume, and geographic extent of goods or services offered under the mark; (3) the extent of actual recognition of the mark; and (4) whether the mark was registered under the current or previous trademark laws in the United States.

A dilution test looks a lot like the likelihood of confusion test. Examine the factors and make sure that you do not choose a mark that could be viewed as diluting someone else's brand. There are factors for each kind of dilution.

For dilution by blurring and tarnishment, we look to the following six factors:

- Degree of similarity between the junior mark and the famous mark

- Degree of inherent or acquired distinctiveness of the famous mark

- Extent to which the owner of the famous mark is engaging in substantially exclusive use of the mark

- Degree of recognition of the famous mark

- Whether the user of the junior mark intends to create an association with the famous mark

- Any actual association between the mark and the famous mark

We also have additional elements for dilution by tarnishment:

- Shoddy quality

- Portrayal as unwholesome or in an unsavory context

- Public association of the lack of quality or lack of prestige in the mark with the famous mark's unrelated goods

Actual dilution need not have occurred—the likelihood of dilution may suffice.

If your mark has survived this out-in-the-world search, move on to Step 7. It's time for the next level.

LIKELIHOOD OF CONFUSION OR DILUTION PROBLEM SPOTTED
If you do find a possible likelihood of confusion, this may be a good time to work with an attorney regarding the viability of your mark.

Searching the USPTO Trademark Records

So far, your mark has survived! So next, we're going to search the USPTO Trademark records. Once you are really familiar with trademarks, you may choose to run this search first, but for the sake of learning, we have put it at Step 7.

> *These records provide a wealth of information on how you might structure your own application. You can look up similar companies and see what they used for their International Classes and other elements.*

Again, once you know how to do all of these things, you can do them in any order that you want. In this chapter, we show you how to search the USPTO trademark records, give you some search strategies, and explain how to use the results to inform your own application.

The USPTO keeps a public database of trademark records called the Trademark Electronic Search System (TESS). All of these records are available to the public for free on its website, tess2.uspto.gov. These records include the application, correspondence, and specimens, see Step 8: Preparing Your Specimen (page 128).

THE TESS OFFICIAL HELP PAGE

If you find yourself mid-search and need more information about searching TESS, the USPTO has made a help page at uspto.gov > Trademarks > Search (TESS) > Help. In fact, most search pages feature a small blue help button. Clicking that button will take you to the help page.

The Goal of Your Search

The goal is to confirm that no one is using your desired mark. So, getting the notice to the right is good.

But sometimes, you'll get this notice because of a problem with the search, not because the mark is available. We are going to show you how to employ a bunch of search strategies to make sure that there are no conflicts.

> **TRADEMARK**
>
> **No TESS records were found to match the criteria of your query.**
>
> **Click on the ⇐ BACK button in your browser to return to the previous TESS screen**
>
> Logout
>
> Please logout when you are done to release system resources allocated for you.

If you get this message, read it carefully and try again. Sometimes, you may have done the search improperly. Other times, this means that no one has registered the word or other fields you are searching. But double-check to make sure that this is the case and that you haven't mistyped or forgotten an element of the search, such as a closing parenthesis or other detail.

You also may find others using the mark, and then it becomes a legal decision of whether the trademark examining attorney will find it to cause a likelihood of confusion or dilution, refer back to Likelihood of Confusion or Dilution (page 73). But you can run that analysis yourself, or hire an attorney. And you can make some choices before you submit your application and potentially get an Office Action, for more on this topic see Office Actions (page 155). If you find that a competitor's mark is too close to what you are thinking about, or you realize that the mark you chose is really a dilution of another's mark, then you can change your mark before you pay $250 and go through the heartbreak of a refusal. Recognizing that someone else may not be happy with your choices can save you a lot of time and money.

USPTO TESS Search Strategies

The examining attorney will be using the USPTO database to confirm that the mark is not already registered, is not confusingly similar to another mark, is not a surname or other problematic category, and is not generic or merely descriptive. In a recent video put out by the USPTO, examining attorneys suggested that to be successful in registering a mark, you might perform several increasingly more complicated searches on TESS to ensure that your mark has a better chance of going through.

They (and we) recommend running at least:

- **TESS dictionary search**
- **Basic TESS word search**

Those who are more daring can also run a TESS structured search and free form search.

If you're using a design mark, we suggest that you run a TESS design search.

Let's learn how to do each search. They are actually not that difficult, and even rather fun.

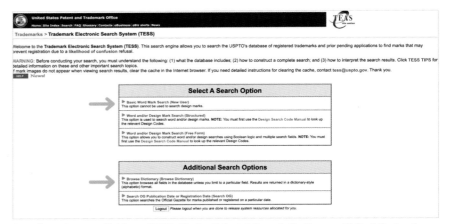

Search options available on TESS. Under Select A Search Option you'll find the basic word mark, structured, and free-form searchs. Under Additional Search Options you can access the dictionary search.

Then, we will look at how you can use TESS to find other helpful information!

To get started, go to **tess2.uspto.gov**. You'll be using this site a lot, so you may want to bookmark it.

Search #1: Dictionary Search

This is one of our favorite tools at the USPTO. It's a quick way to see who else is using the word(s) you are considering. You can even see alternative spellings. It's really useful, helpful, and fun.

This is a good place to begin your search, just to get a sense of how often the words you are using have been used. Always be creative—think of alternative spellings and other ways of envisioning your mark. We will be trying further search strategies shortly. You can also use * at the beginning, middle, or end (or a combination of these) to substitute for multiple possibilities—for example, wan* for wanna and want. We'll talk more about using asterisks and other forms of what is called truncation, but for now, play with the dictionary database and see what you find (for more, see Truncation, page 106).

On the TESS main page, click on the browse dictionary option and enter a search term. We tried "sewtite." Sewtites are magnets you can use for sewing. We wanted to see whether the manufacturer had registered the mark and whether others were also using the term.

We got a number of hits. Notice the asterisk at the end of some of the results. That means that there could be more letters after the asterisk to catch other uses of SEWTITE. If you were doing this search, you would look at all the relevant returns close to SEWTITE, including SEWTITES, SEWTITES*, SEWTITE*, SEWTIT*, and SEWTI*. They are likely the same records, but you want to make sure.

From our search results, let's look at SEWTITES* more closely. If we were trying to register a mark with SEWTITE as part of the mark and it was in the arena of sewing, we might now consider the likelihood of confusion and do further investigation and comparison. Sewtites as a product is not famous enough to have a dilution problem.

First page of search results for "sewtite"

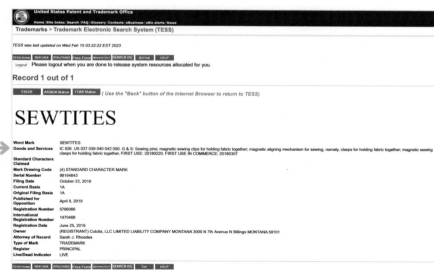

SEWTITES is registered in Class 16, which includes sewing pins and, in this case, magnetic sewing clips.

Search #2: Basic TESS Word Search

Now that we've done a quick dictionary search, let's learn a little more about a basic word mark search. We are going to look up one record to understand what is included and how it works. This is often also called a *dropdead search* because you are matching the exact words. We will expand by varying the word(s) shortly.

Return to the TESS main search options page and choose Basic Word Mark Search. This is the simple way to do a search to make sure that nothing would likely be confused with your mark.

Search Example: DURATIONATOR

In the Search Term field, type DURATIONATOR. We're going to learn about TESS records by using this term. Once you type and enter this term, you should get one record.

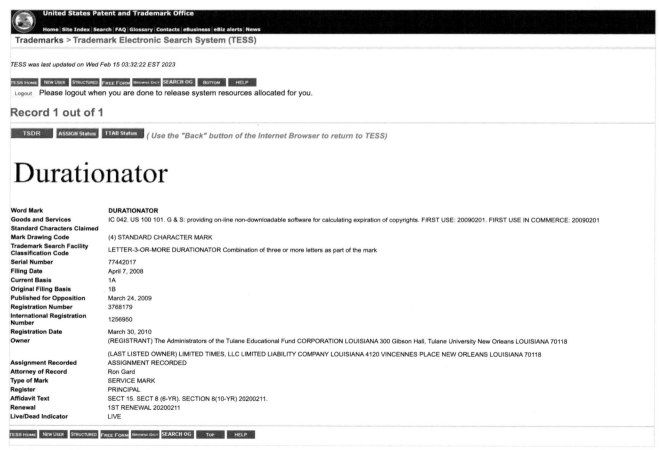

Single record from a search for DURATIONATOR

This record tells us a great deal about the mark. Here are what the fields on this page mean:

Word Mark. You see that DURATIONATOR has a word mark. There is no design mark. You also know that because there are no additional codes or indication that it is not a word mark. Also, design marks tend to be prettier. On the TESS site, all word marks are in the same font in black and white, a clear indicator that this is a word mark.

Standard Characters Claimed. This is blank, which means that only the basic word mark, without stylized or special characters, is claimed. You will not see this category on every entry. For design marks, you will see the Design Search Codes instead (see Design Mark Searches, page 116).

Just Wanna Quilt

Word Mark	JUST WANNA QUILT
Goods and Services	IC 041. US 100 101 107. G & S: Educational and entertainment services, namely, a continuing program about copyright, community, quilting, history, entrepreneurship and crafting accessible by means of audio, video, web-based applications, mobile phone applications, and global computer networks; Entertainment services, namely, providing podcasts in the field of copyright and quilting; Providing a website featuring online training resources, namely, non-downloadable publications in the nature of training manuals, books, magazines in the field of copyright, community, quilting, history, entrepreneurship and crafting; Providing on-line non-downloadable directory publications in the field of copyright, community, quilting, history, entrepreneurship and crafting. FIRST USE: 20171104. FIRST USE IN COMMERCE: 20180206
Standard Characters Claimed	
Mark Drawing Code	(4) STANDARD CHARACTER MARK
Serial Number	88421323
Filing Date	May 8, 2019
Current Basis	1A
Original Filing Basis	1A
Published for Opposition	November 12, 2019
Registration Number	5971280
Registration Date	January 28, 2020

Word mark record for Just Wanna Quilt

Word Mark	JUST WANNA QUILT COMMUNITY COPYRIGHT CREATIVITY
Goods and Services	IC 041. US 100 101 107. G & S: Educational and entertainment services, namely, a continuing program about copyright, community, quilting, history, entrepreneurship, intellectual property, and crafting, accessible by means of audio, video, web-based applications, podcasts, social media groups, mobile phone applications, website, and global computer networks. FIRST USE: 20180202. FIRST USE IN COMMERCE: 20180206
Mark Drawing Code	(3) DESIGN PLUS WORDS, LETTERS, AND/OR NUMBERS
Design Search Code	26.01.13 - Circles, two (not concentric) ; Two circles 26.01.21 - Circles that are totally or partially shaded. 26.09.14 - Squares, three or more ; Three or more squares
Serial Number	90455777
Filing Date	January 8, 2021
Current Basis	1A
Original Filing Basis	1A
Published for Opposition	April 26, 2022
Registration Number	6784598
Registration Date	July 12, 2022

Design mark record for Just Wanna Quilt. Note the differences in the "Standard Characters Claimed" in each record.

Goods and Services. This is where the International Class (IC) is indicated. We look at the first three numbers—in this case, IC 042. We know that this is Class 42. After that, we see a bunch of other numbers, which we can ignore, and then a description, in this case providing online nondownloadable software for calculating the expiration of copyrights. That's the description of the service. You will be writing one of those as part of your application, but the USPTO gives you help to do it.

On this record, you also see on that line "FIRST USE: 20090201 and FIRST USE IN COMMERCE: 20090201." That is also information that you will be providing on your application. The first use and first use in commerce can be the same dates. In this case, it is February 1, 2009.

Mark Drawing Code. (4) Standard Character Mark. The code "4" means that this is *not a design mark*, only a word mark. We will come back to this shortly.

Serial Number. Every application is assigned a serial number, which is NOT the same as the registration number. The serial number for the DURATIONATOR is 77442017.

Filing Date. Here, we see that the filing date is April 7, 2008. That's when the application was filed.

Current Basis. 1A means that the mark is being used in commerce. See Use in Commerce and Intent to Use (page 24).

Original Filing. 1B means that the mark was an intent-to-use application when it was filed. That means that it wasn't already in use and that this was an application in anticipation of use. Once use was proven, the application could be evaluated as an in-use application. See Use in Commerce and Intent to Use (page 24).

Published for Opposition. This is the date on which the mark was published for opposition. Once your application has been through the system, your application is published in the USPTO Gazette for the world to see and comment on to make sure that no one opposes your registration. That's what happened when Mariah Carey's company, Lotion, was trying to register QUEEN OF CHRISTMAS; someone objected. For more, jump to Published for Opposition (page 172).

Registration Number. This tells you that the mark is registered! Exciting! You can also see the registration date just below the registration number. Remember, this is different than the serial number. The registration number for the DURATIONATOR is 3768179. The registration date is March 30, 2010.

Owner. You see the name of the registrant, the one who registered the trademark; in this case, it was the Administrators of the Tulane Educational Fund. And in this case, there is also a company, Limited Times, LLC, listed as the second owner and assigned the mark.

Assignment Recorded. This record notes that an assignment was recorded at the USPTO. An *assignment* means "a change in ownership" (see Transferring Ownership of a Mark, page 193).

Attorney of Record. Ron Gard is listed as the attorney of record. The record always lists the current attorney. You can look at the records to see who the previous attorneys were.

Type of Mark. Here, the type of mark is a service mark. We also know that from the International Class number. Remember, you can have the following type of marks: trademark, service mark, collective mark, collective membership mark, or certification mark.

Register. There are three options for this category: Principal (inherently distinctive), Supplemental (requiring secondary meaning and not yet registered), and *Principal-2(f)*, which means that it was registered on the Principal Register only after it acquired distinctiveness. The "2(f)" refers to a part of the trademark law. To gain Principal-2(f) registration, you have a merely descriptive mark that has acquired distinctiveness with at least five years of use. Your mark could also be registered as Supplemental, meaning that it required secondary meaning to acquire distinctiveness.

Affidavit Text and Renewal. These come later, when you have to confirm that you are still using the mark at five years and every ten years thereafter. For now, you can see that one renewal has already happened (see Maintaining Your Mark, page 183).

Live/Dead Indicator. You will see as we go that trademarks and/or applications are either alive or dead. Dead can be because they were abandoned by the trademark owner at some point in the process or canceled by the USPTO.

Every trademark record looks somewhat like the one for the word mark DURATIONATOR. As we continue, we look at more records and go into more detail about the information found within the records.

Search Example: BERNINA

Now that you know how to read the basic record, let's do a search with more than one record. Return to the main Basic Word Mark Search page and enter Bernina in the search term field. Note: You do not have to type searches in all caps, even though we do that to indicate that it is a word mark when we write about marks.

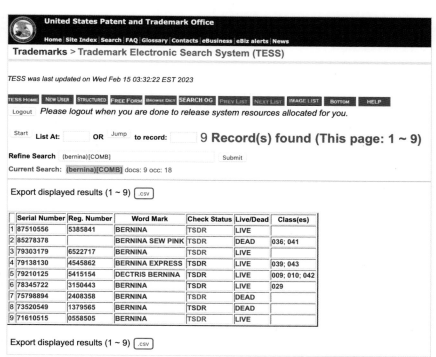

You should see nine BERNINA entries (although there may be more by the time you are searching).

When your search returns more than one record, your screen will display the search results. The search results tell you:

- **Serial number.** Every application is assigned a serial number.

- **Registration number.** One result doesn't have that, and you'll notice that it is dead. That means that someone filed it, but then, for some reason, the registration process was not completed. You can click on "TSDR" (Trademark Status & Document Retrieval) to find out more.

- **Check Status.** There's a Check Status column with the TSDR filled in for each entry. That links you to the records for the application, and you can click on them if you are curious. We'll get to that shortly.

- **Live/Dead.** You see that three are dead. We'll get to that next.

- **Classes.** Some have them listed, and some don't. They all actually do have classes; some are just not listed within the search results.

Live/Dead Marks

Live marks include all applications and registered marks that are still in use. If you see a registration number and "live" that means that the mark has been registered and is still in use. If you see no registration and a serial number plus "live," that means that the application is in process.

There are two kinds of dead marks:

Abandoned marks. Somewhere in the process or during renewal, the owner decided not to go forward with the application. The mark is now abandoned. This can happen for a variety of reasons.

Sometimes, owners over-register intent-to-use marks to protect potential uses. We saw that with Taylor Swift earlier in the book. This is pretty common.

The owner registered five classes, but ended up only using one or two. The owner abandoned the rest.

Another thing that happens is that a business changes, and the owner decides to go in a different direction.

Maybe the mark is not registrable or something happens and someone makes a decision not to go forward.

And, finally, sometimes people forget to do the "next step," whatever that may be— responding to an Office Action, not renewing, and so forth—and the mark becomes abandoned by inaction. That does not mean that the mark is free and clear to use; that same company may have reregistered it under a different application. So, don't assume that "dead" means "available."

Canceled marks. This indicates that the USPTO has taken action. Canceled marks come in many shapes and sizes: Something may become generic, or someone may file a petition of protest, to name two examples.

For our purposes, we want to look at the dead marks to make sure that they are not actually still alive in some other form. The trademark examining attorney likely will not be viewing these records, however. From what we can see, they often limit their searches to what they refer to as "not dead."

Let's look at the search results. To become comfortable using the TESS system, do the searches as you read through the book. We walk you through each of the search results.

Arts and crafts people know Bernina as a sewing machine company. Let's see what the entries show—are they all for sewing machines? Nope! Let's start with the first result.

BERNINA for Hardwood Flooring

Look at the search record and answer the questions below:

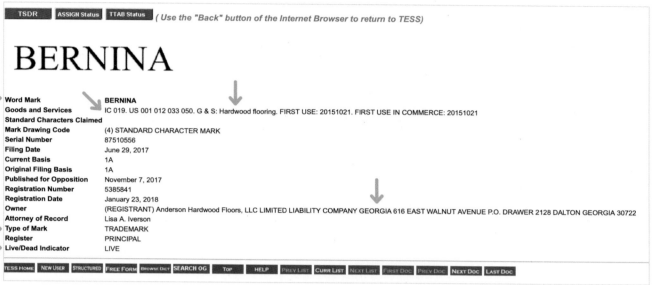

The first record displayed when searching BERNINA is for hardwood flooring.

Is this a word or design mark? Did you say *word*? If so, you are correct. You know this for two reasons. First, it says "Word Mark" and then BERNINA. Also, it has Mark Drawing Code (4) standard character mark, which means "word mark."

Is this a good or service? Look under Type of Mark. Hint: trademark = goods, service mark = service. This record represents a good.

What is the International Class? Did you say Class 19? Correct! You can find this under Goods and Services.

What does the description say? Hint: Look at Goods and Services. The description is next to the International Class number. This BERNINA trademark is for hardwood flooring. Interesting.

What else do you see? We can learn other things from this record. The mark is live. The registrant is from the state of Georgia.

The TSDR Button

What else can you learn from this record? In the upper-left of the screen is a button labeled TSDR. This stands for Trademark Status & Document Retrieval. Click that button.

TSDR button in the upper-left corner

Clicking that button takes you to the TSDR page for this mark. In the middle of the page, you'll see tabs for Status, Documents, and Maintenance. Click on the Documents tab.

The Documents tab is magic! Here, you will find all the documents related to the application, starting with the application form at the bottom. You can click on each of these documents and trace the process and issues that arose with the application. It's detective time. The beauty of the USPTO trademark records is that they include all the applications and correspondence related to every mark. How cool is that? We can learn from others' applications!

All the documents for the BERNINA for hardwood flooring mark

You can see that on June 29, 2017, a new application was submitted. On the same day, a specimen and a drawing were entered into the log. Then, on September 26, 2017, you see a Notation to File, which means that the trademark examining attorney put a note in the file regarding what they searched. Click on that record.

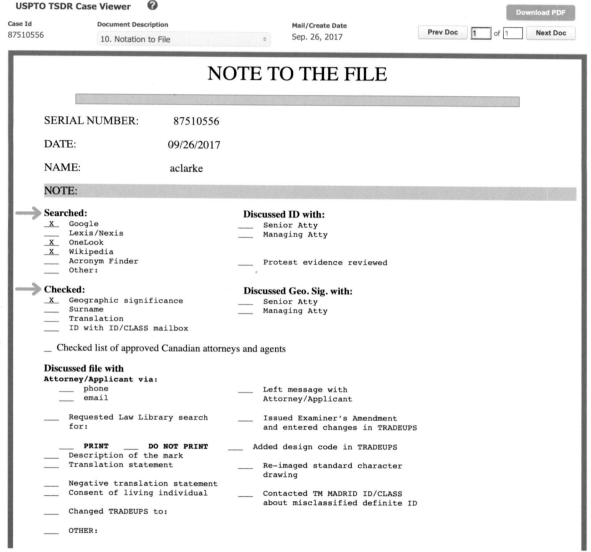

USPTO TSDR Case Viewer ?

Case Id	Document Description	Mail/Create Date			
87510556	10. Notation to File ⇕	Sep. 26, 2017	Prev Doc	1 of 1	Next Doc

Download PDF

NOTE TO THE FILE

SERIAL NUMBER: 87510556

DATE: 09/26/2017

NAME: aclarke

NOTE:

Searched:
- X Google
- ___ Lexis/Nexis
- X OneLook
- X Wikipedia
- ___ Acronym Finder
- ___ Other:

Discussed ID with:
- ___ Senior Atty
- ___ Managing Atty

- ___ Protest evidence reviewed

Checked:
- X Geographic significance
- ___ Surname
- ___ Translation
- ___ ID with ID/CLASS mailbox

Discussed Geo. Sig. with:
- ___ Senior Atty
- ___ Managing Atty

__ Checked list of approved Canadian attorneys and agents

Discussed file with
Attorney/Applicant via:
- ___ phone
- ___ email

- ___ Left message with Attorney/Applicant

- ___ Requested Law Library search for:

- ___ Issued Examiner's Amendment and entered changes in TRADEUPS

- ___ **PRINT** ___ **DO NOT PRINT**
- ___ Description of the mark
- ___ Translation statement

- ___ Added design code in TRADEUPS

- ___ Re-imaged standard character drawing

- ___ Negative translation statement
- ___ Consent of living individual

- ___ Contacted TM MADRID ID/CLASS about misclassified definite ID

- ___ Changed TRADEUPS to:

- ___ OTHER:

The trademark examining attorney's record of searches run

Look at which searches the examining attorney ran. They ran a Google search, a OneLook (dictionary) search, and a Wikipedia search, and then they checked to see whether it had any geographic significance because Bernina is a mountain range in Switzerland.

You can look at all the documents—the application, the specimen, any Office Actions, all of it. You can look up anything that has a registered trademark or an application and see all the goings-on.

Let's look at another record for BERNINA. Click back to return to the main search results page for BERNINA. Select the second search result, BERNINA SEW PINK.

BERNINA SEW PINK for Charitable Fundraising

This is a design and a word mark. Under the word mark are the words BERNINA SEW PINK, but there is also the mark drawing code (3) DESIGN PLUS WORDS, LETTERS AND/OR NUMBERS. That tells us that it is a design with words. You also can tell because there is a design in the upper-left corner instead of the all-black, all-caps standard-font word mark. There are also design search codes that were not present on the first record. We discuss searching for design codes in Design Mark Searches (page 116).

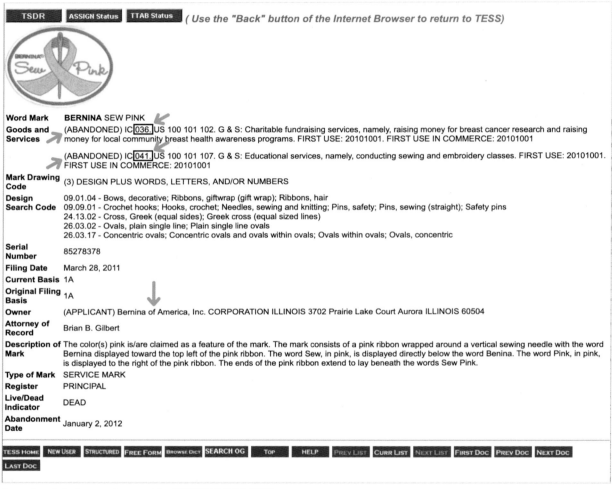

Word Mark	**BERNINA** SEW PINK
Goods and Services	(ABANDONED) IC 036. US 100 101 102. G & S: Charitable fundraising services, namely, raising money for breast cancer research and raising money for local community breast health awareness programs. FIRST USE: 20101001. FIRST USE IN COMMERCE: 20101001
	(ABANDONED) IC 041. US 100 101 107. G & S: Educational services, namely, conducting sewing and embroidery classes. FIRST USE: 20101001. FIRST USE IN COMMERCE: 20101001
Mark Drawing Code	(3) DESIGN PLUS WORDS, LETTERS, AND/OR NUMBERS
Design Search Code	09.01.04 - Bows, decorative; Ribbons, giftwrap (gift wrap); Ribbons, hair 09.09.01 - Crochet hooks; Hooks, crochet; Needles, sewing and knitting; Pins, safety; Pins, sewing (straight); Safety pins 24.13.02 - Cross, Greek (equal sides); Greek cross (equal sized lines) 26.03.02 - Ovals, plain single line; Plain single line ovals 26.03.17 - Concentric ovals; Concentric ovals and ovals within ovals; Ovals within ovals; Ovals, concentric
Serial Number	85278378
Filing Date	March 28, 2011
Current Basis	1A
Original Filing Basis	1A
Owner	(APPLICANT) Bernina of America, Inc. CORPORATION ILLINOIS 3702 Prairie Lake Court Aurora ILLINOIS 60504
Attorney of Record	Brian B. Gilbert
Description of Mark	The color(s) pink is/are claimed as a feature of the mark. The mark consists of a pink ribbon wrapped around a vertical sewing needle with the word Bernina displayed toward the top left of the pink ribbon. The word Sew, in pink, is displayed directly below the word Benina. The word Pink, in pink, is displayed to the right of the pink ribbon. The ends of the pink ribbon extend to lay beneath the words Sew Pink.
Type of Mark	SERVICE MARK
Register	PRINCIPAL
Live/Dead Indicator	DEAD
Abandonment Date	January 2, 2012

A word and design mark record for BERNINA SEW PINK

From the main record page, you can see that the application owner is Bernina of America. That's the sewing machine company. It is for Class 36, charitable fundraising services, and for Class 41, educational services. You can also see that it is abandoned and dead, meaning that Bernina is not using it anymore. We can peek behind the scenes to find out why, using the TSDR records.

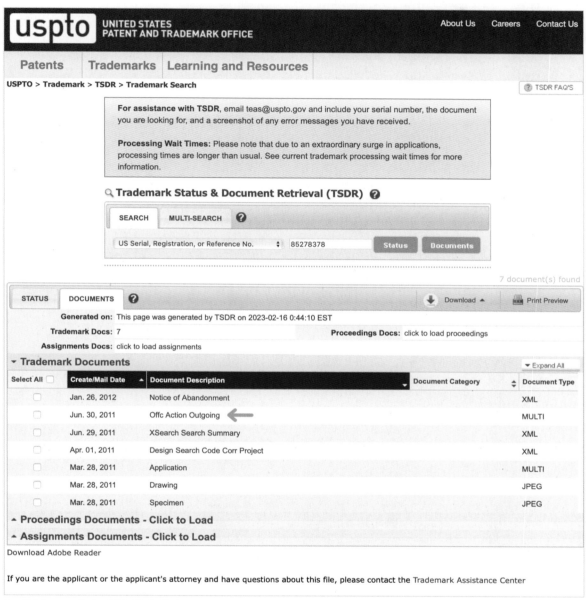

Available records for BERNINA SEW PINK

You can see that the company received an Office Action on June 30, 2011. For more information on the possible responses to an application, jump ahead to Office Actions (page 155). In this case, the Office Action noted that the mark may be confused with other registered marks. Those marks turned out to be other BERNINA marks, so that would not have been an issue in the end. Although the application could have been easily fixed, the company didn't respond, and in not doing so, they abandoned the application. Remember, an applicant might choose to abandon a mark for any number of reasons: Priorities shift, initiatives evolve, or maybe a new application was submitted. Because the TSDR doesn't document a response, it remains a mystery.

UNITED STATES PATENT AND TRADEMARK OFFICE (USPTO)
OFFICE ACTION (OFFICIAL LETTER) ABOUT APPLICANT'S TRADEMARK APPLICATION

APPLICATION SERIAL NO.   85278378

MARK: BERNINA SEW PINK

85278378

CORRESPONDENT ADDRESS:
   BRIAN B. GILBERT
   GOULD & RATNER LLP
   222 N LASALLE ST STE 800
   CHICAGO, IL 60601-1086

CLICK HERE TO RESPOND TO THIS LETTER:
http://www.uspto.gov/trademarks/teas/response_forms.jsp

APPLICANT: Bernina of America, Inc.

CORRESPONDENT'S REFERENCE/DOCKET NO:
   109050.001
CORRESPONDENT E-MAIL ADDRESS:
   trademarks@gouldratner.com

OFFICE ACTION

STRICT DEADLINE TO RESPOND TO THIS LETTER
TO AVOID ABANDONMENT OF APPLICANT'S TRADEMARK APPLICATION, THE USPTO MUST RECEIVE APPLICANT'S COMPLETE RESPONSE TO THIS LETTER **WITHIN 6 MONTHS** OF THE ISSUE/MAILING DATE BELOW.

ISSUE/MAILING DATE: 6/30/2011

Inexpensive The referenced application has been reviewed by the assigned trademark examining attorney. Applicant must respond timely and completely to the issues below. 15 U.S.C. §1062(b); 37 C.F.R. §§2.62, 2.65(a); TMEP §§711, 718.03.

Section 2(d) Refusal – Likelihood of Confusion
Registration of the applied-for mark is refused **for class 41** because of a likelihood of confusion with the marks in U.S. Registration Nos. 0558505 and 1379565. Trademark Act Section 2(d), 15 U.S.C. §1052(d); *see* TMEP §§1207.01 *et seq.* See the enclosed registrations as EXHIBIT A.

Trademark Act Section 2(d) bars registration of an applied-for mark that so resembles a registered mark that it is likely that a potential consumer would be confused or mistaken or deceived as to the source of the services of the applicant and registrant. *See* 15 U.S.C. §1052(d). The court in *In re E. I. du Pont de Nemours & Co.*, 476 F.2d 1357, 177 USPQ 563 (C.C.P.A. 1973) listed the principal factors to be considered when determining whether there is a likelihood of confusion under Section 2(d). *See* TMEP §1207.01. However, not all of the factors are necessarily relevant or of equal weight, and any one factor may be dominant in a given case, depending upon the evidence of record. *In re Majestic Distilling Co.*, 315 F.3d 1311, 1315, 65 USPQ2d 1201, 1204 (Fed. Cir. 2003); *see In re E. I. du Pont*, 476 F.2d at 1361-62, 177 USPQ at 567.

In this case, the following factors are the most relevant: similarity of the marks, similarity of the services, and similarity of trade channels of the services. *See In re Opus One, Inc.*, 60 USPQ2d 1812 (TTAB 2001); *In re Dakin's Miniatures Inc.*, 59 USPQ2d 1593 (TTAB 1999); *In re Azteca Rest. Enters., Inc.*, 50 USPQ2d 1209 (TTAB 1999); TMEP §§1207.01 *et seq.*

Applicant applied to register BERNINA SEW PINK and design for in relevant part "educational services, namely, conducting sewing and embroidery classes."

The registered marks owned by the same registrant are:

   BERNINA, Reg. No. 0558505, for "household and industrial sewing machines and parts thereof."

   BERNINA, Reg. No. 1379565, for "maintenance and repair services for sewing machines of any kind and origin" in class 37 and "educational services, namely, providing courses and seminars concerning sewing and dressmaking" in class 41.

Comparison of the Marks
In a likelihood of confusion determination, the marks are compared for similarities in their appearance, sound, meaning or connotation and commercial impression. *In re E. I. du Pont de Nemours & Co.*, 476 F.2d 1357, 1361, 177 USPQ 563, 567 (C.C.P.A. 1973); TMEP §1207.01(b). Similarity in any one of these elements may be sufficient to find a likelihood of confusion. *In re White Swan Ltd.*, 8 USPQ2d 1534, 1535 (TTAB 1988); *In re Lamson Oil Co.*, 6 USPQ2d 1041, 1043 (TTAB 1987); *see* TMEP §1207.01(b).

The marks are compared in their entireties under a Trademark Act Section 2(d) analysis. *See* TMEP §1207.01(b). Nevertheless, one feature of a mark may be recognized as more significant in creating a commercial impression; greater weight is given to that dominant feature in determining whether the marks are confusingly similar. *See In re Nat'l Data Corp.*, 753 F.2d 1056, 1058, 224

Office Action regarding BERNINA SEW PINK

BERNINA for Sewing Machines

Let's look at another record. Head back to the main search results page. Look at the third result, the one with registration number 6522717. Remember that even if no classes are listed on this main search page, that does not mean that there are no classes.

Refine Search (bernina)[COMB] **Submit**

Current Search: S1: **(bernina)[COMB]** docs: 9 occ: 18

Export displayed results (1 ~ 9) .csv

	Serial Number	Reg. Number	Word Mark	Check Status	Live/Dead	Class(es)
1	87510556	5385841	BERNINA	TSDR	LIVE	
2	85278378		BERNINA SEW PINK	TSDR	DEAD	036; 041
3	79303179	6522717	BERNINA	TSDR	LIVE	
4	79138130	4545862	BERNINA EXPRESS	TSDR	LIVE	039; 043
5	79210125	5415154	DECTRIS BERNINA	TSDR	LIVE	009; 010; 042
6	78345722	3150443	BERNINA	TSDR	LIVE	029
7	75798894	2408358	BERNINA	TSDR	DEAD	
8	73520549	1379565	BERNINA	TSDR	DEAD	
9	71610515	0558505	BERNINA	TSDR	LIVE	

No classes are listed for registration 6522717.

Let's see which class(es) this one is! For crafters, sewers, and quilters, this is the trademark we thought that we would find. What do we learn?

TESS HOME | NEW USER | STRUCTURED | FREE FORM | BROWSE DICT | SEARCH OG | BOTTOM | HELP | PREV LIST | CURR LIST | NEXT LIST | FIRST DOC | PREV DOC | NEXT DOC | LAST DOC

Logout | Please logout when you are done to release system resources allocated for you.

Start | List At: [ ] OR Jump to record: [ ] **Record 3 out of 9**

TSDR | ASSIGN Status | TTAB Status (Use the "Back" button of the Internet Browser to return to TESS)

BERNINA

Word Mark	BERNINA
Goods and Services	IC 007. US 013 019 021 023 024 031 034 035. G & S: Sewing machines of all kinds; motors for sewing machines; knitting and embroidery machines for household and industrial use
Standard Characters Claimed	
Mark Drawing Code	(4) STANDARD CHARACTER MARK
Serial Number	79303179
Filing Date	December 7, 2020
Current Basis	66A
Original Filing Basis	66A
Published for Opposition	August 3, 2021
Registration Number	6522717
International Registration Number	0568285
Registration Date	October 19, 2021
Owner	(REGISTRANT) BERNINA International AG AKTIENGESELLSCHAFT (AG) SWITZERLAND Seestrasse CH-8266 Steckborn SWITZERLAND
Attorney of Record	Larry H. Tronco
Type of Mark	TRADEMARK
Register	PRINCIPAL
Live/Dead Indicator	LIVE

TESS HOME | NEW USER | STRUCTURED | FREE FORM | BROWSE DICT | SEARCH OG | TOP | HELP | PREV LIST | CURR LIST | NEXT LIST | FIRST DOC | PREV DOC | NEXT DOC | LAST DOC

BERNINA is registered for sewing machines of all kinds.

Review the main records page and the TSDR documents for this application. You can see that sewing machines are Class 7, sewing machines of all kinds, motors for sewing machines, knitting, and embroidery machines for household and industrial use.

Here are some additional observations on the main records page:

- We are not going to confuse hardwood floors with sewing machines. Both can exist. They are in different classes, and they are more like DELTA Faucet and DELTA Air Lines.

- This mark is a word mark, and even though the company has been around for a long time, the mark was filed in 2020.

- The fling basis is listed as 66A. We haven't covered that yet, but 66A means that the company is based outside the United States, and because of that, it had to use an attorney to file. To learn more about the filing basis, jump ahead to Basis for Filing (page 149).

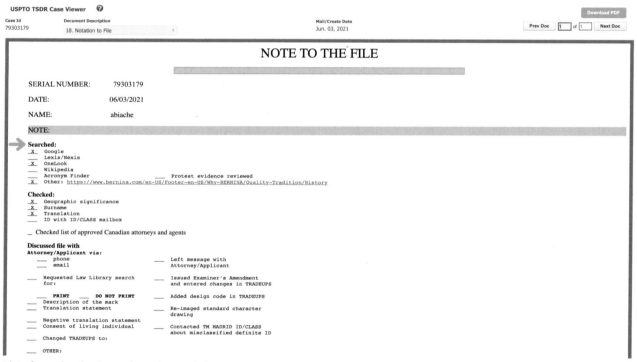

List of searches by the trademark examining attorney

In the TSDR documents, you can see that the examining attorney performed the following searches:

- Google

- OneLook

- Other: the Bernina website

- Geographic Significance

- Surname

- Translation

Let's look at another BERNINA mark. Return to the main search results page and select the fourth result, BERNINA EXPRESS.

BERNINA EXPRESS for Transport Company and Snacks for Traveling

This Bernina is an application for Class 39, escorting travelers by railway vehicles, and Class 43, snacks. This record has all the standard information that you're likely used to reading, but you'll notice that this record has something new, a disclaimer: "NO CLAIM IS MADE TO THE EXCLUSIVE RIGHT TO USE 'EXPRESS' APART FROM THE MARK AS SHOWN." Sometimes, the USPTO trademark examiner will make you *disclaim* that you are not trying to keep others from using part of your name (see Disclaimer Requirement, page 161). Disclaimers are usually for merely descriptive words for which you are not claiming an exclusive right. We had to disclaim the use of "QUILT" in our mark for Just Wanna Quilt.

This record contains a disclaimer for the word *express*.

BERNINA for Household Sewing Machines

We found a second registration for sewing machines for Bernina. This was the original registration from 1951. It was a foreign registration, 44E, which we discuss shortly. And it is alive after all this time. Trademarks last as long as they are in use. It is a word mark and has been renewed five times!

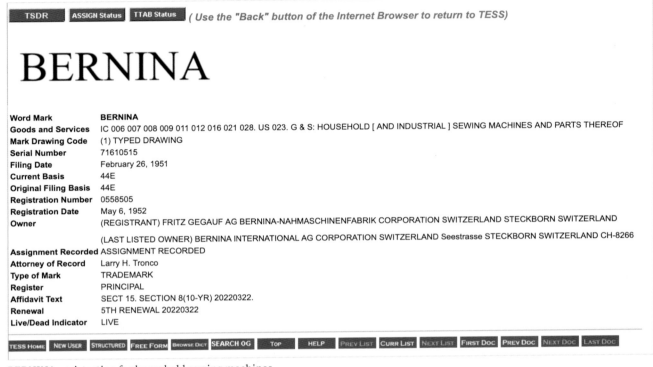

BERNINA registration for household sewing machines

There are other BERNINA marks; our favorite is for "bovine meat." Really? But, you can see that BERNINA the sewing machine company can exist and have multiple live and dead marks and that others can use BERNINA too.

So, if you were trying to register BERNINA, you would now have to do a likelihood of confusion analysis (page 73) for what you want to use the name for and what it is already being used for. If you were hoping to use it for sewing products, that would not be a great idea. But if it was for something else, getting the mark would be a possibility. See how trademark works?

Run Your Own Search!

We hope that you are starting to get the hang of this and feeling more confident. It's not scary. Run some searches of your own and see what you find. Just play. Put your work mark in and see what you find.

If your search term contains an apostrophe, omit it and replace the apostrophe with a space. For example: "Don't" should be "DON T." We look at more in-depth strategies for searching shortly, but take some time to play first. The system can be very fun to use.

A Few More Tools

Now that you are comfortable running and reading a basic search, you can use a few more tools in a basic word mark search. On the screen where you enter your search term, you will see a few options that we've not yet tried. You can search by plural and singular or just singular and by live and dead, or live, or dead. You'll get the broadest results and the most information by leaving these at the default settings of Plural and Singular and Live and Dead, so it is best to leave these as is.

Trademarks > Trademark Electronic Search System (TESS)

TESS was last updated on Wed Feb 15 03:32:22 EST 2023

TESS HOME | STRUCTURED | FREE FORM | BROWSE DICT | SEARCH OG | BOTTOM | HELP

WARNING: AFTER SEARCHING THE USPTO DATABASE, EVEN IF **YOU** THINK THE RESULTS ARE "O.K.," DO **NOT** ASSUME THAT YOUR MARK CAN BE REGISTERED AT THE USPTO. AFTER YOU FILE AN APPLICATION, THE USPTO MUST DO ITS OWN SEARCH AND OTHER REVIEW, AND MIGHT REFUSE TO REGISTER YOUR MARK.

View Search History:

○ Plural and Singular ○ Singular
○ Live and Dead ○ Live ○ Dead

Search Term:

Field:
✓ Combined Word Mark (BI,TI,MP,TL)
Serial or Registration Number
Owner Name and Address
ALL

Result Must Contain:

Submit Query | Clear Query

Logout   *Please logout when you are done to release system resources allocated for you.*

Plural and singular and live and dead are filters that can be applied.

You can also select from a drop-down menu of fields:

- **Combined Word Mark.** This is the default setting. This search includes BI (Basic Index, which includes word marks and pseudo-marks), TI (Translation Index), MP (Mark Punctuated, which includes marks with punctuation characters), and TL (Translation). That's a lot to search for and a great start! You will also see this later written as [comb].

- **Serial or Registration Number.** You get a serial number when you apply and a registration number once your application has gone through the process and been accepted. Once you have the serial or registration number for a record that you want to view, you can use this option to go right to that record.

- **Owner Name and Address.** You can search for an owner (an individual or a company), and you can search with or without the address.

- **ALL.** You can search all of these at once.

One last item to note: The basic word mark search is for searching for word marks, not design marks. However, the search does return some results for design marks, if the word you are searching for is included as part of the mark.

Search #3: Structured Searches

Structured searches allow you to choose two fields and search them together. For example, a search for the word BERNINA and Class 9 would eliminate all other categories, including hardwood flooring and bovine meat. This is especially helpful if you get a lot of search results when running a basic word mark search. Return to the TESS home page and select Word and/or Design Mark Search (Structured).

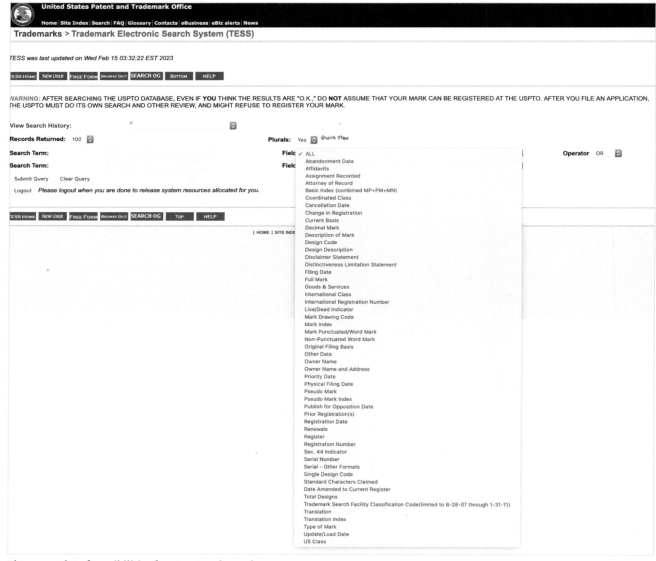

Select A Search Option

▶ **Basic Word Mark Search (New User)**
This option cannot be used to search design marks.

▶ **Word and/or Design Mark Search (Structured)**
This option is used to search word and/or design marks. **NOTE:** You must first use the **Design Search Code Manual** to look up the relevant Design Codes.

▶ **Word and/or Design Mark Search (Free Form)**
This option allows you to construct word and/or design searches using Boolean logic and multiple search fields. **NOTE:** You must first use the **Design Search Code Manual** to look up the relevant Design Codes.

Structured searches combine search items.

Some Useful Fields

There are a lot of possibilities for structured searches.

You have a number of options to select for a field, but if you're wondering which fields are best for you to use, don't worry. Below is a list of some of the most popular (and useful for this purpose) fields and what each of them does.

You can search by:

Attorney of Record. Use this when you are trying to find what a particular attorney has filed to see how successful they have been or what kinds of marks they have handled in the past. This information can be superhelpful when you're considering hiring an attorney. You want someone who has been successful with marks similar to yours. It can also give you ideas of whom to contact. Search for a company that does something similar to you and see who their attorney was/is.

Basic Index. This includes word marks and pseudo-marks. A *pseudo-mark* is something assigned by the trademark examining attorney when your mark has a weird or alternative spelling. XSEW might be assigned CROSS SEW as a pseudo-mark. It is only for search purposes and doesn't extend or change the word mark.

Decimal Mark. A decimal mark allows you to search just for a special character, called a standard character by the USPTO. These include such characters as an exclamation point or an accented letter and can be searched by adding the USPTO code for those characters. For a list of standard characters to use in a decimal mark search, go to uspto.gov/trademarks/standard-character-set.

Design Code. These are the numbers associated with particular design elements (see Design Mark Searches, page 116).

Description. This allows you to search the description for words. For instance, if you are looking for things with the description "gel" or "scent," use this field.

Disclaimer Statement. These are words that are merely descriptive that the USPTO examining attorney has required the applicant to disclaim (attest that the applicant is not trying to keep others from using these words). For more, see Disclaimer Requirement, page 161.

Goods and Services. You can choose whether you're searching for goods or services, which could give you fewer results to wade through.

IC. This can be useful if you're looking for something in a particular Class (see Step 5: International Classes, page 58).

Mark Index. This searches all word marks.

Owner Name. This is one of our favorites. Enter *Disney* as your search term and select the field "owner name." You'll be able to see all the marks owned by Disney. You can do the same for any owner name, whether that is an individual or a company.

Smart Searching

Let's return to the BERNINA example and do a combined search of the mark (Mark Index) and the IC. But first, let's learn about something you probably already know but may not know the name of: Boolean and proximity searching.

If you run a search with the terms BERNINA for Mark Index in one field and then 007 for IC in the second field, and do nothing else, you'll get results for every trademark that includes either Class 7 **or** BERNINA. That's not helpful.

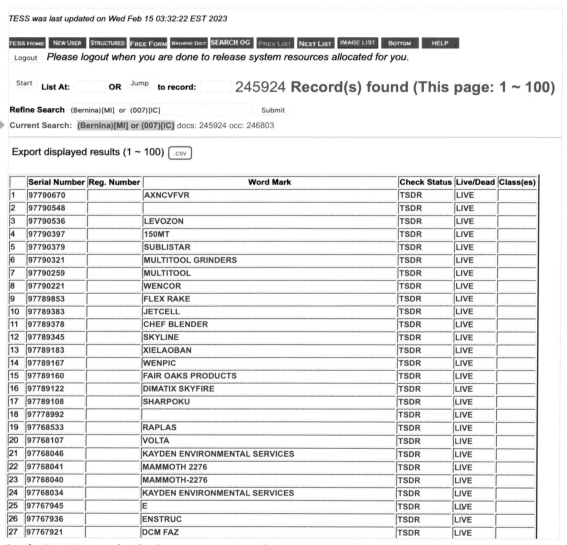

TESS was last updated on Wed Feb 15 03:32:22 EST 2023

| TESS HOME | NEW USER | STRUCTURED | FREE FORM | BROWSE DICT | SEARCH OG | PREV LIST | NEXT LIST | IMAGE LIST | BOTTOM | HELP |

Logout *Please logout when you are done to release system resources allocated for you.*

Start **List At:** **OR** Jump **to record:** **245924 Record(s) found (This page: 1 ~ 100)**

Refine Search (Bernina)[MI] or (007)[IC] Submit

Current Search: **(Bernina)[MI] or (007)[IC]** docs: 245924 occ: 246803

Export displayed results (1 ~ 100) [.csv]

	Serial Number	Reg. Number	Word Mark	Check Status	Live/Dead	Class(es)
1	97790670		AXNCVFVR	TSDR	LIVE	
2	97790548			TSDR	LIVE	
3	97790536		LEVOZON	TSDR	LIVE	
4	97790397		150MT	TSDR	LIVE	
5	97790379		SUBLISTAR	TSDR	LIVE	
6	97790321		MULTITOOL GRINDERS	TSDR	LIVE	
7	97790259		MULTITOOL	TSDR	LIVE	
8	97790221		WENCOR	TSDR	LIVE	
9	97789853		FLEX RAKE	TSDR	LIVE	
10	97789383		JETCELL	TSDR	LIVE	
11	97789378		CHEF BLENDER	TSDR	LIVE	
12	97789345		SKYLINE	TSDR	LIVE	
13	97789183		XIELAOBAN	TSDR	LIVE	
14	97789167		WENPIC	TSDR	LIVE	
15	97789160		FAIR OAKS PRODUCTS	TSDR	LIVE	
16	97789122		DIMATIX SKYFIRE	TSDR	LIVE	
17	97789108		SHARPOKU	TSDR	LIVE	
18	97778992			TSDR	LIVE	
19	97768533		RAPLAS	TSDR	LIVE	
20	97768107		VOLTA	TSDR	LIVE	
21	97768046		KAYDEN ENVIRONMENTAL SERVICES	TSDR	LIVE	
22	97768041		MAMMOTH 2276	TSDR	LIVE	
23	97768040		MAMMOTH-2276	TSDR	LIVE	
24	97768034		KAYDEN ENVIRONMENTAL SERVICES	TSDR	LIVE	
25	97767945		E	TSDR	LIVE	
26	97767936		ENSTRUC	TSDR	LIVE	
27	97767921		DCM FAZ	TSDR	LIVE	

See that? 245,924 records. That is *way* too many records.

To get useful results, you have to do one more small thing. On the right side of the Structured Search page, you'll see something that says "Operator." An operator tells the database how to combine the two terms. You have choices. Run the same search with AND as the operator. Search for BERNINA in the Mark Index AND 007 in IC. And bam! You'll get three results, all focused on Bernina's sewing machines.

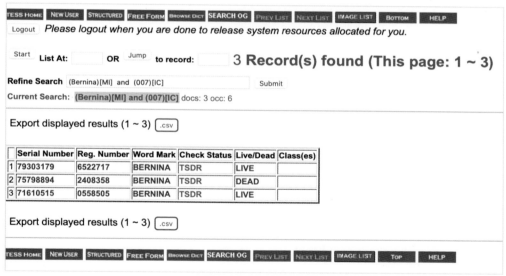

Using the operator AND targets your search.

Now, there are three results.

Each of the available operators allows you to widen your search or to drill down to find more specific results. TESS allows you to select between eight different operators, each of which has a different function.

The most helpful operators are the following:

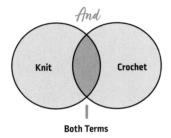

AND. Adding AND narrows your search. It specifies that both terms must be present, so you'll receive more specific results. For example, if you search for "Bernina" AND IC 007, you are specifying that the mark includes "Bernina" and must be in IC 007. You can see that you'll get three results.

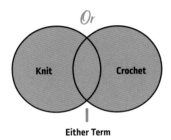

OR. Using OR broadens your search results, so you'll get all the results retrieved by both searches you enter. For example, searching for BERNINA in the mark index and 007 for the IC means that you'll get the search results for both of these searches. We've already seen that we got almost 250,000 records!

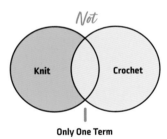

NOT. Using NOT limits your search results. Note that when you use NOT, it eliminates the search results from the second search term, so the order of your search terms is important. For example, if you search for both *cat* and *kitten* in the basic index and include the operator NOT, you'll get results that contain *cat* but won't have to wade through those that contain *kitten*. Let's use Bernina again: Search for BERNINA in the Mark Index and then 007 in the IC field with NOT. That should eliminate the sewing machine records but leave the rest.

Selecting the operator is key.

Using NOT yielded six records. That's an easy list to go through.

Those are the most common operators, but there are others if you want to get fancy, of course. You can see them in the drop-down menu, but for now, let's stick to AND, OR, and NOT.

It is important to be aware that by searching by individual International Classes, your search might get too narrow. For instance, remember that Bernina had sewing machines, but also sewing machine repair. The question is, how can you catch the related International Classes? The USPTO has come up with something called Coordinated Classes. If you choose that, the search also returns results from other related classes. Let's see how that works.

Selecting Coordinated Class instead of International Class broadens searches.

The search now picked up the Class 06 record for sewing machine parts and repair. We would have missed that if we had only searched for IC 007.

Try Your Own Structured Search

Try to do a two-field search. What do you find? Try different pairs to see what it comes up with.

Search #4: Advanced Free-Form Searches

So far, you have run a TESS dictionary search, a basic word search, and a structured search. You should be feeling pretty good about your mark. Adding an advanced free form search is the last step, and the most complicated. If you find it to be *too* complicated, we get it.

The trademark examining attorney will be conducting a similar search, so it doesn't hurt to see the results they will see. What this search tries to do is catch anything that would not come up on a "drop dead" or exact match search. Instead, it is looking for odd spellings, strange add-ons, and the like that might be seen as confusingly similar but wouldn't have come up in your previous searches.

Where in the structured search you could search two fields, here you can search as many as you want, and use the codes to do so. Once you get the hang of it, it is kind of fun!

Word and/or Design Mark Search (Free Form) is the third option on the TESS home page. You are going to build on your knowledge of searching to add a bit of flare.

Here, we introduce three new concepts:

- **Truncation.** Truncation broadens your search to include words that have different beginnings, spellings, or endings. You are using a root word, and then adding a symbol to the beginning or end.

- **Pattern matching.** Pattern matching allows you to find similar words with varied words or word parts.

- **Fields.** You've already used some fields, including International Classes, Coordinated Classes, and Mark Index. We will introduce you to a few more that you may find useful for your own free-form searches.

Remember: We are still looking for word marks. We get to design marks in the next section, Design Mark Searches (page 116).

Free-Form Strategy

The most effective way to use free-form searches is to first broaden your search with truncation and pattern matching and then narrow it to only what applies to your mark by using fields (searching logic). Let's work with a different search term, *SEW.*

Start by entering the search term *"SEW"[comb].* Putting the search term in quotes tells the database that it is the complete search. Adding [comb] tells the database to search the standard combination of databases, the ones that we were using with the Basic Word Search option. They include the Basic Index, which includes word marks and pseudo-marks; the Translation Index; and the Mark Punctuated, which includes marks with punctuation characters.

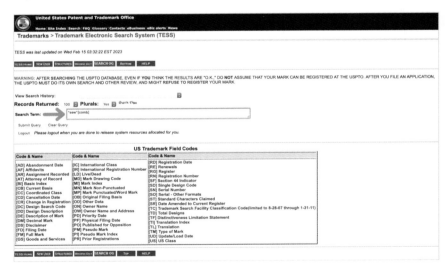

Start with a broad search.

You will get results with words in front of *sew* and words after *sew*. You may have gotten that with the other searches, too, and that's okay.

Here are some examples:

- JUST SEW CANDLE CO
- SEW SCHMETZ!
- SEW RIGHT

This is a good list to start with. When we searched, we got more than 900 word marks with *sew*.

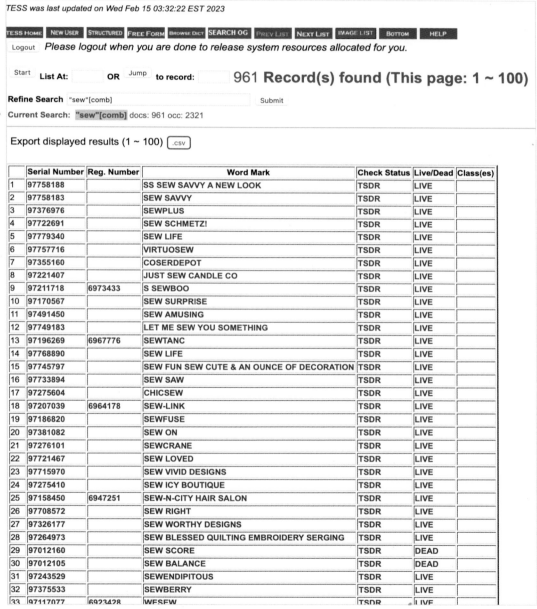

TESS was last updated on Wed Feb 15 03:32:22 EST 2023

| TESS HOME | NEW USER | STRUCTURED | FREE FORM | BROWSE DICT | SEARCH OG | PREV LIST | NEXT LIST | IMAGE LIST | BOTTOM | HELP |

Logout *Please logout when you are done to release system resources allocated for you.*

Start List At: _____ OR Jump to record: _____ **961 Record(s) found (This page: 1 ~ 100)**

Refine Search "sew"[comb] _____ Submit

Current Search: **"sew"[comb]** docs: 961 occ: 2321

Export displayed results (1 ~ 100) [.csv]

	Serial Number	Reg. Number	Word Mark	Check Status	Live/Dead	Class(es)
1	97758188		SS SEW SAVVY A NEW LOOK	TSDR	LIVE	
2	97758183		SEW SAVVY	TSDR	LIVE	
3	97376976		SEWPLUS	TSDR	LIVE	
4	97722691		SEW SCHMETZ!	TSDR	LIVE	
5	97779340		SEW LIFE	TSDR	LIVE	
6	97757716		VIRTUOSEW	TSDR	LIVE	
7	97355160		COSERDEPOT	TSDR	LIVE	
8	97221407		JUST SEW CANDLE CO	TSDR	LIVE	
9	97211718	6973433	S SEWBOO	TSDR	LIVE	
10	97170567		SEW SURPRISE	TSDR	LIVE	
11	97491450		SEW AMUSING	TSDR	LIVE	
12	97749183		LET ME SEW YOU SOMETHING	TSDR	LIVE	
13	97196269	6967776	SEWTANC	TSDR	LIVE	
14	97768890		SEW LIFE	TSDR	LIVE	
15	97745797		SEW FUN SEW CUTE & AN OUNCE OF DECORATION	TSDR	LIVE	
16	97733894		SEW SAW	TSDR	LIVE	
17	97275604		CHICSEW	TSDR	LIVE	
18	97207039	6964178	SEW-LINK	TSDR	LIVE	
19	97186820		SEWFUSE	TSDR	LIVE	
20	97381082		SEW ON	TSDR	LIVE	
21	97276101		SEWCRANE	TSDR	LIVE	
22	97721467		SEW LOVED	TSDR	LIVE	
23	97715970		SEW VIVID DESIGNS	TSDR	LIVE	
24	97275410		SEW ICY BOUTIQUE	TSDR	LIVE	
25	97158450	6947251	SEW-N-CITY HAIR SALON	TSDR	LIVE	
26	97708572		SEW RIGHT	TSDR	LIVE	
27	97326177		SEW WORTHY DESIGNS	TSDR	LIVE	
28	97264973		SEW BLESSED QUILTING EMBROIDERY SERGING	TSDR	LIVE	
29	97012160		SEW SCORE	TSDR	DEAD	
30	97012105		SEW BALANCE	TSDR	DEAD	
31	97243529		SEWENDIPITOUS	TSDR	LIVE	
32	97375533		SEWBERRY	TSDR	LIVE	
33	97117077	6923428	WESEW	TSDR	LIVE	

Some of the results for *sew* in a broad search.

That is a lot of results, but what if someone spelled it SEAUX? (We would do that in New Orleans!) Our first search wouldn't catch it. Let's see how we could.

Truncation

Truncation allows you to expand your search by additionally searching for marks that contain your mark or a portion of your mark. To do this, you include an asterisk in your search term.

By adding * on either or both sides of the search term, you can expand the search.

Try this out, using *sew* as an example:

- **Search: "SEW"[comb].** You get around 950 marks.

- **Search: *SEW[comb].** What did you get? Now around 1,000. We picked up 50 more records.

- **Search: SEW*[comb].** What did you get? We got more than 2,000 records.

- **Search: *SEW*[comb].** What did you get? We got nearly 4,000 records.

Other symbols can be used for truncation searches. You can use a question mark to allow for one different internal character and the dollar sign to search for unlimited internal characters. Try searching for S?W[comb]. We got 2,774 records, including marks that contained things like *saw* and *smw* (SAW LIFE and SMW). If you want to further expand the search, try the dollar sign instead.

Search for S$W[comb]. We got 23,514 records, including SUNBOW, SXSW, SHYKDW, and SUITREVIEW. Notice that any number of letters can be between *S* and *W*.

> **NOTE**
> Although we are covering truncation in free-form searches, it can also be used in a basic word search or a structured search.

Why do you want so many search results? You want to cast a wide net to make sure that nothing conflicts with your potential mark. You don't need to go through all the results. You will narrow these results shortly with fields.

MORE SEARCH TRICKS
If you want some additional tips and examples, visit uspto.gov/sites/default/files/documents/Trademarks-Advanced-Searching-Sept272022.pdf.

Pattern Matching

Truncation allows you to add different combinations to *the beginning, middle, or end of your word*. In contrast, pattern matching allows you to expand more precisely *within the word* you are searching, which means that you can find alternate spellings of your search term, which could be important.

To search for pattern matches, you use curly brackets { } (shift + bracket keys). Use { } to replace letters that you want to search for.

Most commonly, you would use {v} to replace a vowel with any vowel, which is helpful in finding any funny spellings. Run a search for s{v}w[comb]. It returns about 2,000 results, including SAWFISH.

If you were trying to register SEWFISH, you might want to know about that! That's why you do the substitution. Another one that would be good to know is the {c} for consonants.

PATTERN MATCHING AND OTHER ADVANCED SEARCH TECHNIQUES
For more on pattern matching and other advanced search techniques, see www.uspto.gov/trademarks/search/word-andor-design-mark-search-structured#step1.

Narrowing the Results with Field Tags

You have broadened your search to include as many terms as possible. Now, you need to narrow the results. You can do that by including other field tags and using "AND" as the operator.

In addition to the field tags you already know (the basic index [comb], International Class [ic], and Coordinated Classes [cc]), here are some of the most useful to add to your searches.

Here are some more:

[on] Owner Name. Use this to find matching owner names. If you want to find out whether a company has registered a particular mark or set of marks, you can add the name of the company or individual (for example, "Smith, John"[on] or "Quilting Army Krewe"[on]). You can also use the field code [ow] for owner and address, with a search like (Disney and Florida)[ow].

[de] Description of the Trademark. You can use this to search for applications and registrations with specific words in the description of the trademark. Use this to find examples of trade dress, only color, sound, smell, and other elements that would be part of the description (for example "scent"[de]).

[dc] Design Code. These are for trademarks with designs in them (see Using the Design Code Manual, page 116). The terms are often referenced with periods, but you need to take them out (for example, 01.02.02 becomes 010202[dc]).

[ds] Disclaimed terms. If you want to find out whether others have disclaimed a word you are using, use this field code. For instance, for JUST WANNA QUILT, we disclaimed *quilt*. You can search "quilt"[ds] and see who else has disclaimed quilt.

[ld] Live/dead. You can add "live"[ld] to get only marks that are live and not canceled or abandoned. The examining attorney often limits their search to "live" marks. For example, "quilt"[comb] and live[ld] returns around 260 results. (Note: you can use quotes or not with the word live, and get the same results). Without "live," which means that it includes canceled and abandoned marks as well, the number goes to around 803 records.

[rg] Register. You can narrow your search to see what is on the Principal, Principal-2, or Supplemental Register. Without designating a register, your search will encompass all three. Some marks that require secondary meaning can prove it during the application process, and they are designated as 2(f) registrations, after the part of the law that requires secondary meaning for merely descriptive marks (see Acquired Distinctiveness, page 35). *Principal* means that the work was registered upon application; *Principal-2* means that it was registered with acquired secondary meaning; and *Supplemental* means that it is on that register, waiting to have five years' worth of secondary meaning. To find marks with 2(f) registrations, search for **PRINCIPAL-2[rg]** or search for **SUPPLEMENTAL[rg]** for in-process merely descriptive applications that have not yet met their secondary meaning requirement.

[md] Mark Drawing Code. When you want to narrow your results just to a specific type of mark, you may want to limit your result by using a mark drawing code. There are codes for each type of mark drawing:

Code 2 for design marks only

Code 3 for designs plus words, letter, and/or numbers

Code 4 for only word marks

Code 5 for words, letters, and/or numbers in a stylized format

Code 6 for situations for which no drawing is possible (for example, sound, scent, or motion)

Every application has a mark drawing code. For example, try searching for "6."[md]

FIELD CODES IN FREE-FORM SEARCHES

If you are curious about other field codes, you can click on any of them at the bottom of the Free Form data search page, tmsearch.uspto.gov/bin/gate.exe?f=search &state=4804:z57whp.1.1, and it will take you to a description of what they are.

Now, let's put it all together. You can search by a series of terms. It looks a little bit like math. Don't freak out. What it does is give you control.

Here are a few rules for using this method of searching:

- **Pairs stay close together.** You will have a term and a field code. They cuddle. There is no space between the term and the field code.

    "Dog"[comb]: See that the term and the code are next to each other.

- **Terms can be in three basic forms:**

    Exact phrase: "dog" will return things with the word *dog*.

    Truncation: dog* will return things with dog and other terms, such as dogen, dogtie, and dog tie.

    Pattern matching: d{v}g will return dog, dag, and dug.

- **Fields always use [brackets].**

    For example, if you are looking for an International Class, you enter [ic]. It doesn't matter whether it is capitalized.

- **Use (parentheses) to keep terms together for your Boolean searches.**

    (dog and house)[comb] will return marks with both terms.

    You can also search for (dog not "doghouse") [comb] and that will exclude results with doghouse.

    ("dog house" or "doghouse")[comb] will get you results for either term.

- **If you are using design codes (you'll learn about these shortly), take out the decimal.**

    Design code 04.01.02 becomes 040102[dc]

- **Use quotes with numbers and information with field codes.** Always put information in front of the field codes.

    In quotes, when it is specific (for example, "007"[ic]

    But not design codes, which don't need anything (for example, 101012[dc]).

- **Add an operator.** Note that there is a space before and after the operator and that the operator does not need to be in quotation marks.

    "Fish"[comb] and "007"[ic]

- **Be careful: Remember, the default is OR.** Unless you tell TESS AND, it defaults to OR. So, hot dog will return results for hot or dog. (We got more than 100,000 hits.) "Hot Dog" as a phrase in quotes will give you results with that phrase together, like MCFLYS HOT DOGS. (We got around 760 results.) The phrase ("hot" and "dog") will get you hot dog but might include things like HOT DIGGITY DOG. (We got around 820 results.) Now, the last result will have both the original "hot dog" search and "hot" and "dog." To eliminate the first, you can add ("hot" and "dog" not "hot dog"). (We got 56 records.) We are looking for something that has a word between hot and dog.

You can reduce the searches one more time by using "live"[ld], so the string reads

("hot" and "dog" not "hot dog")[comb] and "live"[ld] (We got 13 results.)

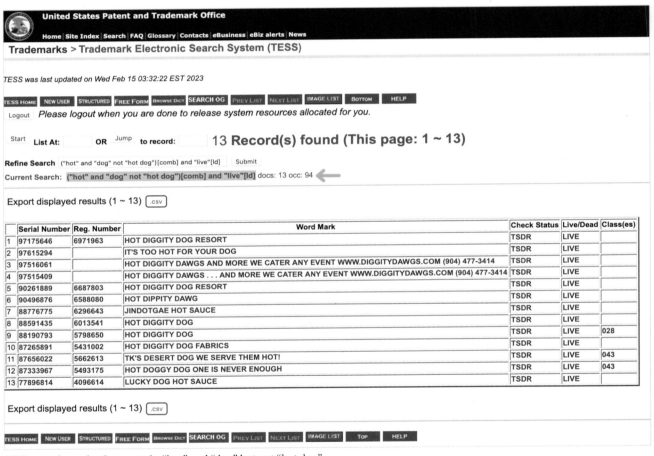

All live trademarks that contain "hot" and "dog" but not "hot dog".

TESS HELP MENU

For more tricks on searching, the TESS Help Menu is always available: tmsearch.uspto.gov/webaka/html/help.htm.

Using Field Tags

Let's look at how you can use field tags to search for many things. For example, imagine that you want to register an online handmade paper shop called The Mouse Hole. You have already searched word marks for "mouse" and "hole" and "mouse hole" and have tested all of these by using truncation and pattern matching. Lastly, you need to make sure that there is nothing out there that those searches didn't turn up.

Now, you want to see what nonword marks may be lurking. Using our example, we all know that Disney registers a lot of marks related to Mickey Mouse. You may want to search for Disney as the owner and the word mouse as part of the description [de] (search "DISNEY"[on] and "mouse"[de]). This particular search brings up 87 records, which is not that many to review to determine whether your use might be seen as a conflict.

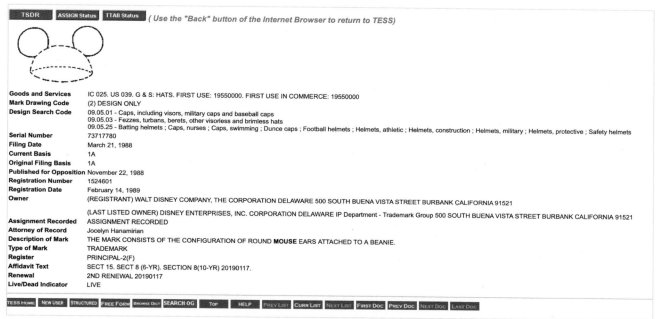

The iconic Disney mouse ears hat!

The iconic Disney mouse ears hat did not come up in a word search but did pop right up when we searched by "mouse" and description [de], along with 86 other results. Searching by [de] is extremely useful to flush out records that may not be findable by using just a word search.

You may want to run a search similar to this to make sure that a big brand is not using a motif similar to what you are hoping to register. **Keep playing with additional field tags to be sure that you won't encounter any issues after you apply.** For example, you've determined that Disney is not an issue, but what about searching for "mouse"[de] and "paper"[de], or "mouse"[de] and 016[ic], the code for paper products? Use your imagination and keep sifting to be sure that you've found everything that the trademark examiner could find.

NO RESULTS?

If your search returns no results, double-check your search writing. Simple mistakes and typos can result in a false result of zero. For example, accidentally typing 16 for the IC instead of 016 nets no results.

We can use one field tag to find out more information—say, what marks a particular company has registered. Let's look at a search example. The Warm Company produces batting for quilting. We know that it has registered the mark WARM COMPANY, but we also know that it has registered (or we think that it has) marks for individual types of batting.

How do we find out what it has registered?

   Step 1: Search for the mark WARM COMPANY[comb]

   Step 2: Look in the record (toward the bottom) and find out what the company is called—in this case, Warm Products.

   Step 3: Search for "Warm Products"[on]

And bingo! We get a search list.

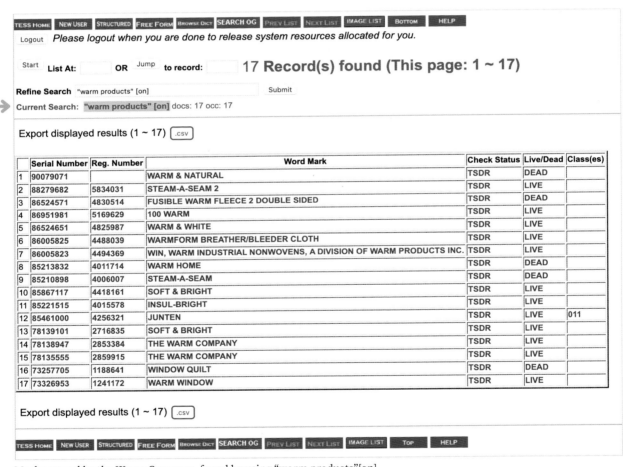

	Serial Number	Reg. Number	Word Mark	Check Status	Live/Dead	Class(es)
1	90079071		WARM & NATURAL	TSDR	DEAD	
2	88279682	5834031	STEAM-A-SEAM 2	TSDR	LIVE	
3	86524571	4830514	FUSIBLE WARM FLEECE 2 DOUBLE SIDED	TSDR	DEAD	
4	86951981	5169629	100 WARM	TSDR	LIVE	
5	86524651	4825987	WARM & WHITE	TSDR	LIVE	
6	86005825	4488039	WARMFORM BREATHER/BLEEDER CLOTH	TSDR	LIVE	
7	86005823	4494369	WIN, WARM INDUSTRIAL NONWOVENS, A DIVISION OF WARM PRODUCTS INC.	TSDR	LIVE	
8	85213832	4011714	WARM HOME	TSDR	DEAD	
9	85210898	4006007	STEAM-A-SEAM	TSDR	DEAD	
10	85867117	4418161	SOFT & BRIGHT	TSDR	LIVE	
11	85221515	4015578	INSUL-BRIGHT	TSDR	LIVE	
12	85461000	4256321	JUNTEN	TSDR	LIVE	011
13	78139101	2716835	SOFT & BRIGHT	TSDR	LIVE	
14	78138947	2853384	THE WARM COMPANY	TSDR	LIVE	
15	78135555	2859915	THE WARM COMPANY	TSDR	LIVE	
16	73257705	1188641	WINDOW QUILT	TSDR	DEAD	
17	73326953	1241172	WARM WINDOW	TSDR	LIVE	

Marks owned by the Warm Company, found by using "warm products"[on]

How Does the Trademark Examiner Search?

So, how does an examining attorney do a search? They use a program not available to the public, called xSearch. Any searches they conduct related to a mark are included in the record under the TSDR tab. Let's look at one to get a sense of what they did. How do you figure out the phonetic variants? We can see what the examining attorney searched for as part of the record.

Go to TSDR documents for any mark and then look for the XSearch Search Summary. Let's look at SEW BUTIFUL. The examining attorney ran two searches. Let's take a look:

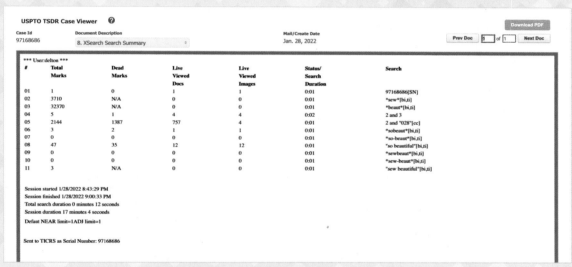

USPTO TSDR Case Viewer ❓   Download PDF

| Case Id | Document Description | | Mail/Create Date | | Prev Doc | 1 | of 1 | Next Doc |
| 97168686 | 8. XSearch Search Summary ⌄ | | Jan. 28, 2022 | | | | | |

*** User:delton ***

#	Total Marks	Dead Marks	Live Viewed Docs	Live Viewed Images	Status/ Search Duration	Search
01	1	0	1	1	0:01	97168686[SN]
02	3710	N/A	0	0	0:01	*sew*[bi,ti]
03	32370	N/A	0	0	0:01	*beaut*[bi,ti]
04	5	1	4	4	0:02	2 and 3
05	2144	1387	757	4	0:01	2 and "028"[cc]
06	3	2	1	1	0:01	*sobeaut*[bi,ti]
07	0	0	0	0	0:01	*so-beaut*[bi,ti]
08	47	35	12	12	0:01	"so beautiful"[bi,ti]
09	0	0	0	0	0:01	*sewbeaut*[bi,ti]
10	0	0	0	0	0:01	*sew-beaut*[bi,ti]
11	3	N/A	0	0	0:01	"sew beautiful"[bi,ti]

Session started 1/28/2022 8:43:29 PM
Session finished 1/28/2022 9:00:33 PM
Total search duration 0 minutes 12 seconds
Session duration 17 minutes 4 seconds
Defaut NEAR limit=1 ADJ limit=1

Sent to TICRS as Serial Number: 97168686

The XSearch summary can help find variants for your mark.

The XSearch uses some different terms—for example, [bi,ti] rather than [comb]—but reviewing the searches done for marks by your competitors or similar products/services might give you additional ideas on how to run your searches. In this case, you see that the examining attorney employed truncation by using *, and then they put together *sew* and *beaut* on the third search. They combined the searches for search 4. The fifth search was with the coordinated classes for 028. Finally, they did a few more searches for different spellings of Sew Butiful: *sobeaut*, *so-beaut*, "so beautiful," *sewbeaut*, and "sew beautiful." In a second search, they searched for *butif*. All the searching that you've been doing is to anticipate what the examining attorney is going to search. It never hurts to see the results ahead of time!

WIPO Search (International)

The World Intellectual Property Organization (WIPO) has its own database that covers marks from around the world, similar to TESS. You can use the same search terms and search language to look for potential international players that would oppose your mark for some reason, even if they have not yet filed in the United States. It is called the WIPO Global Brand Database, available at branddb.wipo.int.

To be sure that no international players might swoop in and oppose your mark, and to be sure that if/when the time comes, you can expand your mark, you should run the same types of searches in the Global Brand Database as you did in TESS. For example, we see that LIBERTY OF LONDON, a famous fabric company, has registered in Japan, the European Union, and the United Arab Emirates, with status ending in the United States, Canada, and Korea for that mark. We can double-check the results in TESS for the United States. Indeed, LIBERTY (rather than Liberty of London) is registered in the United States under IC 024. The lesson here: Keep looking to make sure.

Canadian Trademark Database

If you want to check only the Canadian trademark database, go to www.ic.gc.ca/app/opic-cipo/trdmrks/srch/home?lang=eng. The interface is different, but if you are comfortable using TESS, you should have no problems navigating the Canadian database. For instance, Olfa has registered in Canada for word and design marks. If you can read a TESS record, you now can read a Canadian one, too!

Full Clearance Searches

Now that you know the ins and outs of searching, let's talk about the available professional services for doing this. They will do a full clearance search for you, but they vary in what they do. This may be a good option for you if you have the funds to do it, you are investing in manufacturing and advertising, or you need to really, really make sure the application will have no hiccups. This includes when you are registering the mark as part of a requirement for a licensing deal. You also would likely have hired an attorney in most of these scenarios. If you are hiring an attorney, they will likely use a service like this for an additional fee, as well as the government fee for the USPTO trademark application. Check to see what is included in the attorney's fees. Some attorneys offer bundles.

Even if you do end up hiring out a full clearance search, you should still know what you are purchasing.

Here are some questions worth asking before you hire a professional organization to do a search for your mark:

- Is the service only doing a basic word search? Is it an exact, dead-on search, or is it doing more?

- Will it be doing a truncation and pattern-matching search? How far does it go?

- Will it look at more than the International Class you indicated and include coordinated classes?

- What resources is it using for the common law search?

- Which databases is it using for the state search, and, more importantly, is it *doing* a state search?

- Is it doing a global search, and, if so, which databases is ity using? This level of search usually costs extra.

Sometimes, these companies are just doing a basic dead-on word search, which often isn't enough information to make sure that your application will go through correctly. They also likely will not do an analysis of the results—you will have to hire an attorney for that. So, be sure to know what you are paying for. For more, see Resources (page 196).

Not everyone applying for a trademark needs to run a full clearance search. The USPTO is not going to run a full clearance search. Where you might run into problems is when your application is published for opposition. That's when state, international, or common law rights to the mark might appear. The biggest issue is state trademarks (see State Trademarks, page 16) and common law trademark uses (see Common Law Trademarks, page 16). These are harder to find without a comprehensive full clearance search.

Finally, Your Imagination

You have done all the searches, but before you are done, spend some time using your imagination. Play around with your chosen mark, especially with any odd spellings that tend to be used in your industry or segment. For example, if our mark contained SEW, we also might want to check the spellings we know of that are odd, like "Seaux." Use your imagination, but also your knowledge. As a sewer or quilter, you've likely seen the word *social* spelled *sewcial*, for example. You likely know that variant, but your trademark attorney might not.

What comes up when we run *Seaux*? It's a substitution for *so*, but it could also be for *sew*. Either way, we need to find out whether something could get in our way.

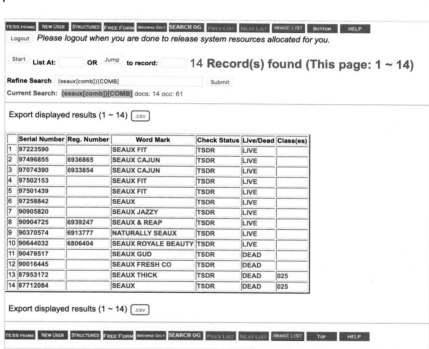

The alternative spelling *seaux* nets fourteen results to review.

Design **Mark Searches**

If you are only applying for a word mark, you can skip this section! But even if you're only applying for a word mark, you may still want to do a design search in case there is a lurking design mark that contains a word or words from your mark.

Now that you understand how to search for word marks, it is time to tackle design searches. A lot of trademark specialists treat design searches as hard or impossible, but it's just another kind of challenge. You have to think about what you are trying to accomplish: checking to find out whether the design you want to use is already being used by a product that is famous and/or is within your International Class.

When you have a design, you may have one thing, like a circle, or a number of elements to the design. We have to search to find out whether someone is already using your design mark, and that involves looking into each element of your design and then performing a likelihood of confusion analysis.

Using the Design Code Manual

Design marks are categorized by the USPTO in a three-tier system. The Design Code Manual lists each of the categories. Categories go from broad (tier 1), to more specific (tier 2), to the most detailed (tier 3). Once you figure out where your mark fits into each category, you'll end up with a six-digit number, which is your design code.

Let's look at an example. You have a logo that generally looks like a three-pointed star. Go to the Design Code Manual at tess2.uspto.gov/tmdb/dscm/index.htm. You will find a list of categories.

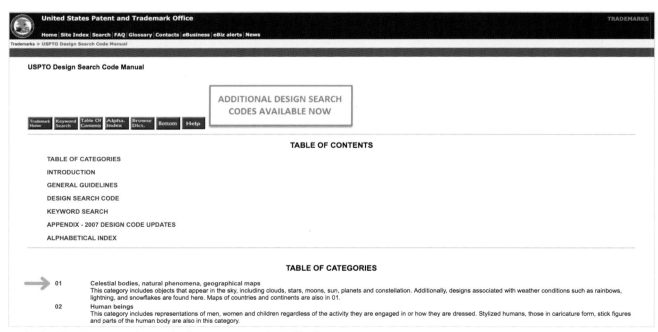

You're looking for a star. Choose the first category, celestial bodies.

The first category, 01, is for celestial bodies, natural phenomena, and geographical maps. Click on the first category. You will find additional subcategories within category 01. Scroll through the guidelines until you get to the code that best describes your mark.

Select your second level of specificity.

Under this menu of subcategories are all the sub-subcategories. Scroll through the guidelines until you get to the code that best describes your mark. In this case, it is 01.01.01 Stars with Three Points.

01.01.01   Stars with three points

Design code 01.01.01, Stars with Three Points

You now have your six-digit design code, 01.01.01. The first 01 is the first tier: Category 01: Celestial Bodies, Natural Phenomena, and Geographical Maps. The second 01 is the second tier: 01.01 Stars, Comets. The third 01 is the third tier: 01.01.01 Stars with Three Points.

When you reach the third tier, examples will be provided. They don't have to match your vision of your logo, just give you a rough frame of visual reference.

Now that you have your design code, go back and do a TESS search. You can do either a structured search, choosing Design Code as the field (see Search #3: Structured Searches, page 98), or a free-form search, using [dc] after the number so that 010101[dc] would be your search (see Search #4: Advanced Free-Form Searches, page 104). In either case, you must **remove the periods**. It is important to note that **you cannot do design searches by using Basic Word Mark Searches.**

Try running a structured search for 010101 and choose the Design Code field. You will get more than 800 search results. You can also see the search result images by clicking on the blue Image List button just above the search results.

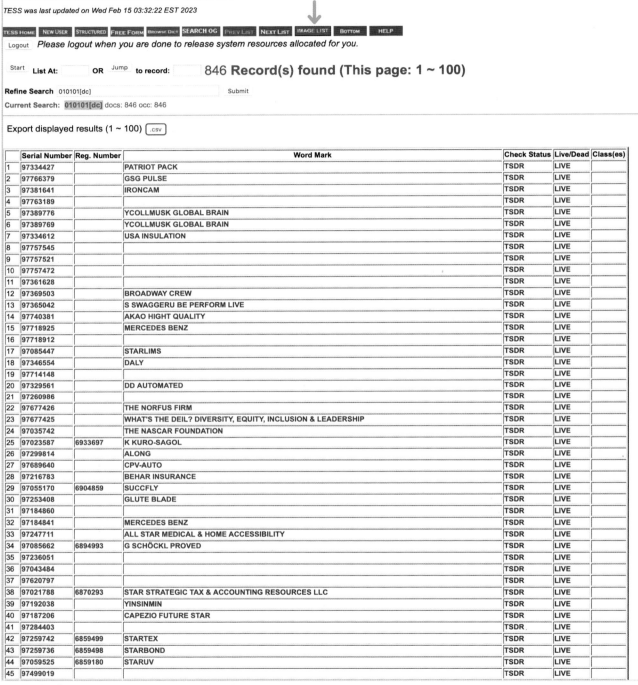

TESS was last updated on Wed Feb 15 03:32:22 EST 2023

| TESS HOME | NEW USER | STRUCTURED | FREE FORM | BROWSE DICT | SEARCH OG | PREV LIST | NEXT LIST | IMAGE LIST | BOTTOM | HELP |

Logout *Please logout when you are done to release system resources allocated for you.*

Start List At: [ ] OR Jump to record: [ ] **846 Record(s) found (This page: 1 ~ 100)**

Refine Search 010101[dc] [ ] Submit

Current Search: **010101[dc]** docs: 846 occ: 846

Export displayed results (1 ~ 100) [.csv]

	Serial Number	Reg. Number	Word Mark	Check Status	Live/Dead	Class(es)
1	97334427		PATRIOT PACK	TSDR	LIVE	
2	97766379		GSG PULSE	TSDR	LIVE	
3	97381641		IRONCAM	TSDR	LIVE	
4	97763189			TSDR	LIVE	
5	97389776		YCOLLMUSK GLOBAL BRAIN	TSDR	LIVE	
6	97389769		YCOLLMUSK GLOBAL BRAIN	TSDR	LIVE	
7	97334612		USA INSULATION	TSDR	LIVE	
8	97757545			TSDR	LIVE	
9	97757521			TSDR	LIVE	
10	97757472			TSDR	LIVE	
11	97361628			TSDR	LIVE	
12	97369503		BROADWAY CREW	TSDR	LIVE	
13	97365042		S SWAGGERU BE PERFORM LIVE	TSDR	LIVE	
14	97740381		AKAO HIGHT QUALITY	TSDR	LIVE	
15	97718925		MERCEDES BENZ	TSDR	LIVE	
16	97718912			TSDR	LIVE	
17	97085447		STARLIMS	TSDR	LIVE	
18	97346554		DALY	TSDR	LIVE	
19	97714148			TSDR	LIVE	
20	97329561		DD AUTOMATED	TSDR	LIVE	
21	97260986			TSDR	LIVE	
22	97677426		THE NORFUS FIRM	TSDR	LIVE	
23	97677425		WHAT'S THE DEIL? DIVERSITY, EQUITY, INCLUSION & LEADERSHIP	TSDR	LIVE	
24	97035742		THE NASCAR FOUNDATION	TSDR	LIVE	
25	97023587	6933697	K KURO-SAGOL	TSDR	LIVE	
26	97299814		ALONG	TSDR	LIVE	
27	97689640		CPV-AUTO	TSDR	LIVE	
28	97216783		BEHAR INSURANCE	TSDR	LIVE	
29	97055170	6904859	SUCCFLY	TSDR	LIVE	
30	97253408		GLUTE BLADE	TSDR	LIVE	
31	97184860			TSDR	LIVE	
32	97184841		MERCEDES BENZ	TSDR	LIVE	
33	97247711		ALL STAR MEDICAL & HOME ACCESSIBILITY	TSDR	LIVE	
34	97085662	6894993	G SCHÖCKL PROVED	TSDR	LIVE	
35	97236051			TSDR	LIVE	
36	97043484			TSDR	LIVE	
37	97620797			TSDR	LIVE	
38	97021788	6870293	STAR STRATEGIC TAX & ACCOUNTING RESOURCES LLC	TSDR	LIVE	
39	97192038		YINSINMIN	TSDR	LIVE	
40	97187206		CAPEZIO FUTURE STAR	TSDR	LIVE	
41	97284403			TSDR	LIVE	
42	97259742	6859499	STARTEX	TSDR	LIVE	
43	97259736	6859498	STARBOND	TSDR	LIVE	
44	97059525	6859180	STARUV	TSDR	LIVE	
45	97499019			TSDR	LIVE	

834 results for design marks with three-pointed stars

Now, it is time to sort your results. Run another structured search, this time including the IC in the second field (in this example, Class 24, Fabrics). Make sure to include the operator AND rather than OR.

You now get fewer than 20 results, which are much easier to review. To cast a slightly wider net, you might consider searching by coordinated class rather than International Class.

Now, try the same search as a free-form search. To begin, go to the main TESS page and select the option for a Free Form search. In the search field, enter 010101[dc] and "024"[ic]. Just to remind you, DC stands for the design code, and IC stands for the International Class.

Either way you search, adding a second search criteria will give you a much smaller number of results. There is no reason to do both; we just wanted you to see that you can do this search whichever way you like.

If you forget which field tag to use or what they mean when you're doing a free-form search, the field codes can all be found below the search bar, and you can click on them to find out what they mean and how to use them.

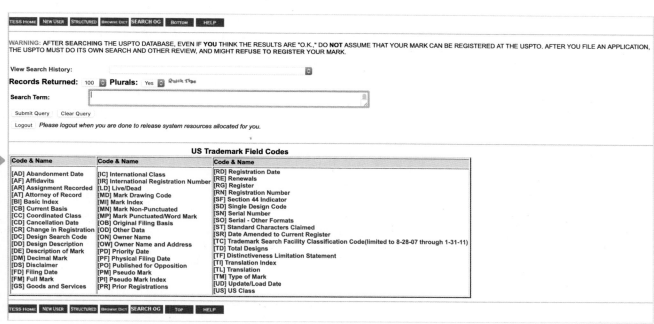

Field tags are below the search box for easy reference.

PART 2: CHECK YOUR MARK

Now that you have your search results, you can view them as an image list. As a reminder, the Image List option is one of the blue buttons along the top of your results.

There are fourteen registrations and applications for marks in Class 24, Fabric, with the design code 01.01.01. If you have a three-pointed star design mark for the source identifier/mark for fabric (and not necessarily the pattern in the fabric), and it doesn't look like any that are below, you should be starting to feel pretty good. Next, you'll want to dive in a little deeper to make sure that these would not be too close to what you are planning to use.

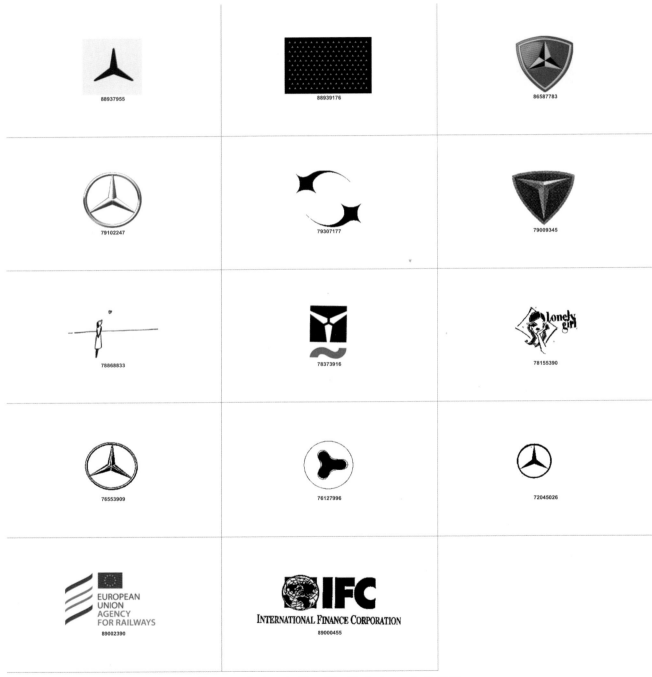

Fourteen designs in Class 24 with design code 01.01.01

Let's take a closer look at a couple of the marks.

A Marine Corp mark

This particular mark is owned by the U.S. Marine Corps. Yes, they own trademarks! This is a design mark only. In this case, the mark is registered for use on cloth flags. Then, the design search codes are listed:

01.01.01—Stars—one or more stars with three points

24.01.02—Shields or crests with figurative elements contained therein or superimposed thereon

A design mark, like word marks, has a description. It often includes information about color and other elements. Theirs reads "The color(s) red, gold and black is/are claimed as a feature of the mark. The MARK consists of a shield design, in red, with a gold strip just within the perimeter of the shield. In the center of the shield is a three-pointed star, in gold and black."

Let's look at another one.

Mercedes-Benz has registered its mark many times. It uses only two design search codes:

01.01.01—Stars—one or more stars with three points

26.01.01—Circles as carriers or as single-line borders

The description reads "Color is not claimed as a feature of the mark. The MARK consists of a three-dimensional-appearing three-pointed star design within a three-dimensional-appearing ring design. The three points of the star are connected to the inner portion of the ring."

When you dig into this mark, you can see that the owner has registered it in 35 International Classes. If I came across a mark registered in this many classes, I would know that it was a famous mark. I would keep away from this design as something I was thinking about, even if the class I wanted to use was not taken, because of how many classes the company does have registered.

DESIGN SEARCH GUIDANCE
The USPTO has created easy-to-use guidelines on design marks. You can find the link on the main page of the Design Code Manual. Click General Guidelines on the left-side menu, or simply scroll down until you get to the guidelines. Take a look at tess2.uspto.gov/tmdb/dscm/index.htm for a more in-depth understanding.

Nontraditional
Mark Searches

This chapter only applies if you are registering a nontraditional mark (color, smell, sound, trade dress, or motion). **If these do not describe your mark, skip ahead to the next chapter, Step 8: Preparing Your Specimen** (page 128).

To search for nontraditional marks, we will look at how to search for each specific kind: only color, smell, sound, trade dress, and motion.

NONTRADITIONAL MARKS ARE TRICKY!

We have suggested before that if you are using nontraditional marks, you should think about hiring an attorney. We hold true to that. However, this book gives you some tools to get prepared to see if the nontraditional mark you are considering is available, before you hire an attorney.

Only Color

If you have not reviewed Using the Design Code Manual (page 116), do so before beginning here. To search for marks using only color, you can find the design code and use the register field tag [rg] to search for the Supplemental or Principal-2 (or 2[f]) Register.

Find the Design Code

Just like design marks, color marks can be found in the USPTO Design Search Code Manual. Also similar to design marks, color marks have a three-part design code, with the first two numbers indicating the category. In the manual, color marks can be found under the category Miscellaneous, which is category 29. The second two numbers indicate the subcategory, and the final two indicate the color used.

Just as you did with design marks, you must determine which subcategory best fits your color mark:

- **29.02** Use this for a single color used for the entire good or service.

- **29.03** Pick this when a single color is used on a portion of the good or service.

- **29.04** This is for a single color used on packaging, labels, or signs.

- **29.05** This is the choice for multiple colors used on the entire good.

- **29.06** Select this one for multiple colors used on a portion of the good.

- **29.07** Choose this one for multiple colors used on packaging, labels, or signs.

OFFICIAL EXAMPLES

If you are still not sure which is the right subcategory, hop on over to the official manual to see a variety of examples: tess2.uspto.gov/tmdb/dscm/dsc_29.htm#29.

Color Codes

Lastly, you need to pick the color code, the last two digits of your design code. The color codes are:

- .01 red or pink
- .02 brown
- .03 blue
- .04 gray or silver
- .05 violet or purple
- .06 green
- .07 orange
- .08 yellow or gold
- .09 white
- .10 clear or translucent
- .11 black

A very important thing to remember when it comes to color-only marks is that the dotted line on the sample images indicates that it is the object itself and not a logo. Marks that are the whole color are indicated by a dotted line to say that it is part of the product, rather than the image being the mark.

One example in the guidelines shows the image below. The guidelines show you the codes—in this case, "a single color used on the entire surface of the goods or items used in rendering the services" and "red or pink." The code then is 29 (the category), .02 (the single color of the entire surface), and.01 (red or pink), or 29.02.01.

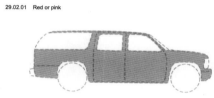

29.02.01   Red or pink

According to the manual,
the color-only design code is 29.02.01.

Color-Only Free-Form Search

Now that you are comfortable with free-form searches, use our current example, 29.02.01. For this one, you'll want to include the design code, 290201[dc], and select either the Principal Register, PRINCIPAL-2[rg], or the Supplemental Register, SUPPLEMENTAL[rg].

We suggest doing this more general search before narrowing the results by using classes. There aren't a lot of only-color marks. You may want to get a broad sense of whether your desired color is being used by a famous mark and therefore may garner even more protection through dilution.

We ran 290201 and PRINCIPAL-2[rg] and got 105 results. (If you have 24,000, you likely included OR in the search (the default) rather than AND. Click the Image List button to see the results in image form. We would likely click on each of them to see what they are, but you can also narrow by international or coordinated classes or other field tags. To narrow the results, click the Back to Hit List button at the top, add your limiting field tag, search again, and then again click the Image List button.

Nonvisual Marks

Scent and sounds are two examples for which no word mark or drawing is possible. To search for these, you add the code 6[md]. That is the mark drawing code "for situations for which no drawing is possible, such as sound." You can also include a descriptor word in the Description field, [de]. For example, "scent"[de] would bring up descriptions with the word "scent."

Try this free-form search: "scent"[de] and 6[md]. The 6[md] tells you that the mark type is a nonvisual mark, and the word *scent* in the description tells us that it is a scent mark. We found 44 records! Below is one example.

A mark for the scent of fresh oranges used with leather polish and cleaners

You can do the same thing with sound marks! For sound, this is what we searched for "Sound"[de] and 6[md]. We found 666 records. You could add a class or other field tag to narrow the search. We decided to see what was in entertainment and education, Class 41. To do so, we searched for "Sound"[de] and 6[md] and "041"[ic].

That got us to 168 records. Then, we decided to narrow it one more time to only live, not dead marks. The trademark examining attorneys only seem to look at live marks, using "not dead" as a category quite a bit. The search looked like this: "Sound"[de] and 6[md] and "041"[ic] and live[ld].

That got us to 88 records. You can go to the TSDR records. Under documents, choose "Specimen," and you can download the WMV file to listen to the sound marks if you want. Some browsers will let you listen to the specimen without any downloading, and you can access it under "Mark." Click on that and you can press a play button to hear the sound mark. A few applications were so old that no electronic file of the sound was included.

Trade Dress

You can search for trade dress by including "trade dress"[de], meaning that the term appears in the description. These are both examples of architectural registered trade dress. Architectural trade dress is the way the building looks that makes you think of the goods/services. The architecture serves as a source identifier. You can register that (or not) at the USPTO. And the USPTO protects registered and unregistered trade dress.

One result from a search for trade dress

Do you see the pink? The description tells us that the color and its shape and position are what customers would be looking for to identify that particular retail bakery shop. And in fact, Pinkbox Donuts has registered its trade dress as it has changed. It has a whole page on its website devoted to how it protects its intellectual property. In addition to trade dress, it has registered its packaging, word marks, design marks, product designs, exterior signs, and slogans. This website page even has detailed photographs of its interior trade dress in action. To see it for yourself, go to pinkboxdoughnuts.com/trademark.

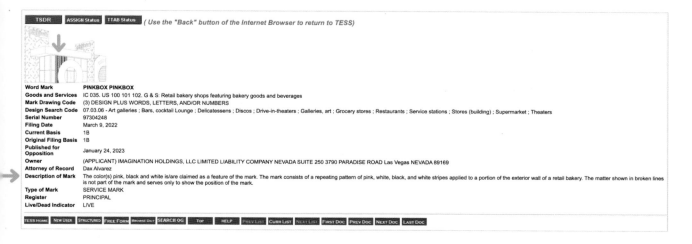

Motion

The key to searching for motion marks is to use the term "motion mark"[de]. Otherwise, you will get too many searches with just "motion." When we searched for "Motion mark"[de], we got 346 results.

What if you are looking for something in particular? You could add a field tag. Try searching by owner [on] with, for example, Disney, to find out whether it has any motion marks. Search for "Disney"[on] and "motion mark"[de]. At the time of our search, there were two results.

Let's look at *Steamboat Willie*, a film that is set to come into the public domain in 2024. Disney has now used that as a trademark for the Walt Disney Animation Studio. It uploaded a WAV file of the animation. Here is the trademark record:

Disney's registration for Steamboat Willie for entertainment services

Disney is using a portion of the *Steamboat Willie* movie as a trademark. That will not preclude other uses that are not trademark-related once the movie is in the public domain, but it will keep others from using the images for trademark purposes.

Disney has another motion mark—the castle that appears before the beginning of all Disney movies.

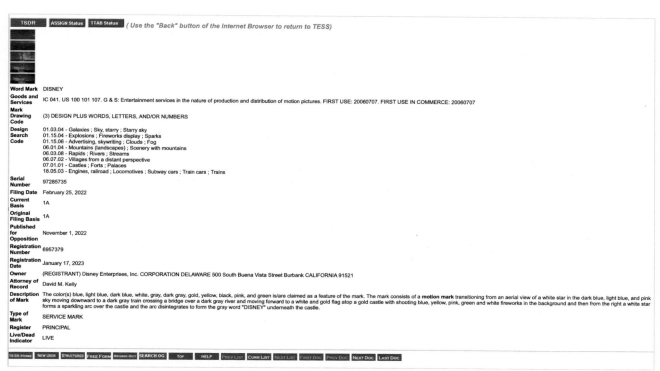

Word Mark	DISNEY
Goods and Services	IC 041. US 100 101 107. G & S: Entertainment services in the nature of production and distribution of motion pictures. FIRST USE: 20060707. FIRST USE IN COMMERCE: 20060707
Mark Drawing Code	(3) DESIGN PLUS WORDS, LETTERS, AND/OR NUMBERS
Design Search Code	01.03.04 - Galaxies ; Sky, starry ; Starry sky 01.15.04 - Explosions ; Fireworks display ; Sparks 01.15.06 - Advertising, skywriting ; Clouds ; Fog 06.01.04 - Mountains (landscapes) ; Scenery with mountains 06.03.08 - Rapids ; Rivers ; Streams 06.07.02 - Villages from a distant perspective 07.01.01 - Castles ; Forts ; Palaces 18.05.03 - Engines, railroad ; Locomotives ; Subway cars ; Train cars ; Trains
Serial Number	97285735
Filing Date	February 25, 2022
Current Basis	1A
Original Filing Basis	1A
Published for Opposition	November 1, 2022
Registration Number	6957379
Registration Date	January 17, 2023
Owner	(REGISTRANT) Disney Enterprises, Inc. CORPORATION DELAWARE 500 South Buena Vista Street Burbank CALIFORNIA 91521
Attorney of Record	David M. Kelly
Description of Mark	The color(s) blue, light blue, dark blue, white, gray, dark gray, gold, yellow, black, pink, and green is/are claimed as a feature of the mark. The mark consists of a **motion mark** transitioning from an aerial view of a white star in the dark blue, light blue, and pink sky moving downward to a dark gray train crossing a bridge over a dark gray river and moving forward to a white and gold flag atop a gold castle with shooting blue, yellow, pink, green and white fireworks in the background and then from the right a white star forms a sparkling arc over the castle and the arc disintegrates to form the gray word "DISNEY" underneath the castle.
Type of Mark	SERVICE MARK
Register	PRINCIPAL
Live/Dead Indicator	LIVE

Disney's castle animation for entertainment services

Codes Communicate Meaning

You have been using codes to search to make sure that what you want to register is available. The USPTO examining attorney will be assigning codes to your application based on your description. You can see now how you should include elements in your description that matter, such phrases as *scent, motion mark,* and so forth. You'll want to make it as easy as possible for the examining attorney to identify the codes that best describe your mark. Because you know what the design codes are, you can use that language to describe the mark—saying *three-pointed star* instead of *star,* for example.

Preparing Your *Specimen*

You need to prepare your specimen as part of the application process. Specimens are required for all use in commerce applications. If you are only filing an "intent-to-use" application, you are not yet required to submit a specimen.

A specimen shows you using your mark as a source identifier of a good or service in commerce. That is, you are selling your goods or services: You have price tags, an online cart, and a way to select the goods; you have your mark on packaging, and/ or you can see the goods being sold; or you have a display at a shop or trade show. These are just a few examples of showing your mark in commerce.

Intent-to-use is an alternative for when you are still getting everything ready but want to reserve the mark for use in commerce. You can file an intent-to-use application for the same cost as an in-use application. That gives you six months until you have to check in again and either transition to an in-use mark or extend the intent-to-use. You must

pay an extra $125 each time you extend the term (every six months) and $100 when you convert it to an in-use application.

For Just Wanna Quilt, we waited a year before filing the trademark. In part, this was because we weren't sure what we were exactly, but also because we wanted to avoid filing an intent-to-use application. But it was a risk—someone else could have seen the name and filed before us.

For other projects, such as Durationator, we filed very quickly. We had a website that offered services and a video that explained what we did, and we filed in 2008. We weren't quite ready for the public, but we were marketing the name heavily and didn't want it stolen. We likely should have filed an intent-to-use application, but we were encouraged to get sufficiently operational so that the USPTO would see us as in use. That pushed us to actually be in use, testing and getting our first customers very quickly.

Use in Commerce Requirements

To file a use in commerce application, you must provide proof that you are using the mark in commerce and that such use constitutes interstate commerce.

Showing Use in Commerce

You will have to list the first use by day, month, and year for two events:

First Use Anywhere. This can be before goods were in the marketplace, such as when you created your website, formed an LLC, and so forth. When did you start using the mark as a source identifier?

First Use in Commerce. When did you first sell the goods, offer the goods for sale, or provide services as a business while using the mark?

These dates can be the same. For example, for the Durationator, we listed 20090201, or 2009 February 1.

Interstate Requirement

The interstate requirement is a use in commerce that goes beyond your own state borders—between states, between the United States and a foreign country, or between the United States and a territory. This is what triggers federal law. It is actually very simple to demonstrate that you have met this requirement.

You can show:

- Customers from a different state
- Advertisements in a different state
- Your business uses credit cards as a method of payment
- Catalogs mailed to a different state

- Internet presence with services and goods sold nationally and internationally to individuals who use interstate telephone lines to access websites. In other words, a website counts.

In short, it is not hard to meet the interstate requirement.

Intent-to-Use Applications

Intent to use is just that: a placeholder while you get your goods/services ready for the marketplace. You must have a good faith intention of using your mark in commerce, and you don't get the registration until you do. Eventually, you'll convert your intent to use to an in-use application. You do not need specimens when you file an intent-to-use application, only an intent to create them in the future. Once you have used your mark in commerce and have a specimen, your application moves to the final stage.

You can show proof of use in commerce in three periods of time:

1. Before your application is approved for publication. You can change your application from intent to use to in use by filing an Amendment to Allege Use form.

2. Within six months of the Notice of Allowance. This is what the USPTO calls it when you are approved for an intent-to-use application. You have six months to show the mark in use.

3. Via an extension. You can request an extension up to five times. You'll pay a fee of $125 each time.

Specimens

What is a specimen? The USPTO defines *specimens* as "real-life evidence of how you are actually using your trademark in the marketplace with the goods or services in your application or registration maintenance filing. It's what consumers see when they are considering whether to purchase the goods or services you provide in connection with your trademark." For example, a specimen could be a photo of a label or tag used on your goods, a photo of outdoor signs for services provided at that location, a website where your goods can be purchased or ordered, or a website advertising your services.

THE OFFICIAL WORD ON SPECIMENS

For a more in-depth look at the USPTO guidance for specimens, visit uspto.gov/trademarks/laws/specimen-refusal-and-how-overcome-refusal

Specimen Versus Drawing

If you are applying for a design mark or a word and design mark, the design itself will be submitted as part of the application process (see Option 2: Special Form, page 142). It does not count as your specimen; it is your mark. You must still submit the use of this mark (the design) being used in commerce.

What Qualifies as a Specimen?

The point of a specimen is to demonstrate the use of your trademark in commerce, to show that your trademark is used in a way that consumers would perceive it as a source indicator for the goods or services in your application (that is, it functions as a trademark). Your specimen must meet all of these requirements, or the USPTO will refuse to accept your specimen.

Your specimen should:

- Show your trademark used in conjunction with the goods or services listed in your application.

- Depict your trademark as shown on your drawing (if you are applying for a design or word and design mark).

- Show your trademark in actual use in commerce (not a mock-up or printer's proof of how it might be used in the future or a digitally altered image that does not actually show it in use).

- Show your use of your trademark (not used by someone else, such as press releases sent exclusively to news media).

- Be the right type of specimen, based on whether you have goods or services.

- Show your trademark used in a way that directly associates the mark with the goods or services.

- Show your trademark used in a way that consumers would perceive it as a source identifier for the good or services in your application (that is, it functions as a trademark).

Acceptable Formats

You do not mail in specimens (except for scent). Specimens are submitted digitally when you submit your application. You can upload a file of each specimen as a JPG file of up to 5 megabytes or a PDF, WAV, WMV, WMA, MP3, MPG, or AVI file of up to 30 megabytes.

Number of Specimens

You will need to submit one specimen for each class in your application. You do not normally need to provide more than one specific specimen for each good or service in the class, even if the description lists more than one item.

Even though only one specimen per class is required, sometimes people include more than one specimen, all contained in one file, usually a PDF. Recently, Tula Pink applied for additional trademarks, one word mark, and several design marks for a number of goods. The specimens included a number of examples from each class that she filed in.

TULA PINK

Word Mark	TULA PINK
Goods and Services	IC 024. US 042 050. G & S: Cotton fabrics. FIRST USE: 20070101. FIRST USE IN COMMERCE: 20070101
Standard Characters Claimed	
Mark Drawing Code	(4) STANDARD CHARACTER MARK
Serial Number	87134064
Filing Date	August 10, 2016
Current Basis	1A
Original Filing Basis	1A
Published for Opposition	January 10, 2017
Registration Number	5170530
Registration Date	March 28, 2017
Owner	(REGISTRANT) MCLEAN, JENNY INDIVIDUAL UNITED STATES 3000 Sherman Ave Saint Joseph MISSOURI 64506
Attorney of Record	Sean T. Bradley
Disclaimer	NO CLAIM IS MADE TO THE EXCLUSIVE RIGHT TO USE "PINK" APART FROM THE MARK AS SHOWN
Type of Mark	TRADEMARK
Register	PRINCIPAL
Affidavit Text	SECT 15. SECT 8 (6-YR).
Live/Dead Indicator	LIVE

Word Mark	TULA PINK
Goods and Services	IC 007. US 013 019 021 023 024 031 034 035. G & S: sewing machines; sewing machine trolleys; sewing machine cases. FIRST USE: 20140317. FIRST USE IN COMMERCE: 20140317
	IC 009. US 021 023 026 036 038. G & S: sewing magnets. FIRST USE: 20210105. FIRST USE IN COMMERCE: 20210105
	IC 016. US 002 005 022 023 029 037 038 050. G & S: printed instructional and teaching materials in the field of sewing; softcover books; books containing illustrations; printed coloring books. FIRST USE: 20090930. FIRST USE IN COMMERCE: 20090930
	IC 024. US 042 050. G & S: fabrics for textile use; woven fabrics; textile fabrics for use in the manufacture of garments, bags, and apparel; textile fabrics for use in making clothing and household furnishings; furnishing and upholstery fabrics; mixed fiber fabrics; synthetic fiber fabrics; semi-synthetic fiber fabrics; cotton base mixed fabrics; acrylic fabrics; silk-cotton mixed fabrics; natural and synthetic fabrics and textiles, namely, cotton, silk, polyester and nylon fabrics. FIRST USE: 20071031. FIRST USE IN COMMERCE: 20071031
	IC 026. US 037 039 040 042 050. G & S: embroidered patches; quilt kits; sewing kits; webbing in the nature of woven fabric tape for sewing purposes; ribbons of textile materials; silk woven jacquard ribbons. FIRST USE: 20130731. FIRST USE IN COMMERCE: 20130731
	IC 028. US 022 023 038 050. G & S: playing cards. FIRST USE: 20141130. FIRST USE IN COMMERCE: 20141130
Mark Drawing Code	(3) DESIGN PLUS WORDS, LETTERS, AND/OR NUMBERS
Design Search Code	01.01.05 - Stars - one or more stars with seven or more points 26.01.21 - Circles that are totally or partially shaded. 26.01.31 - Circles - five or more ; Five or more circles
Serial Number	97484741
Filing Date	June 30, 2022
Current Basis	1A;1B
Original Filing Basis	1A;1B
Owner	(APPLICANT) Tula Pink LLC LIMITED LIABILITY COMPANY MISSOURI 3000 Sherman Ave Saint Joseph MISSOURI 64506
Attorney of Record	Sean T. Bradley
Prior Registrations	5170530
Description of Mark	The color(s) pink and white is/are claimed as a feature of the mark. The mark consists of a pink star having twenty-eight points, six pink dots set outward from and aligned with six of the points, the word Tula in white script generally centered on the star, and the word PINK in white letters positioned below the word Tula.
Type of Mark	TRADEMARK
Register	PRINCIPAL
Live/Dead Indicator	LIVE

In this case, she included examples for each part of the description, which is not necessary. For Class 7, "sewing machines, sewing machine trolleys, sewing machine cases," she included an image for each, three in total.

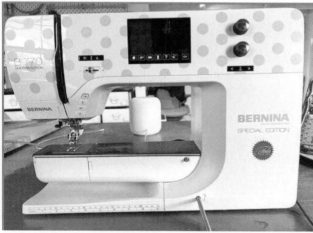

For Class 7, "sewing machines, sewing machine trolleys, sewing machine cases," they included three images and one for Class 28 for "playing cards."

Step 8: Preparing Your Specimen

Acceptable Specimens for Goods

The USPTO will not accept advertising materials as a specimen for goods. That's really important. There are two types of acceptable specimens for goods: showing your use of the mark on the goods or showing the mark as part of your display of the goods in commerce.

Viewable on the Good

Most specimens show the mark on the good, either on the packaging or on the good itself. This can also be a tag or a label on the good.

Make sure that the full label is visible in the images that you upload. If you do not have the entire mark showing, it will be rejected.

Unattached labels and tags are okay, but they have to include sufficient information to show the use of the unattached label or tag in use as a source identifier in commerce.

In a webinar on specimens, the USPTO gave two examples, one that was acceptable, and another that was not. The first was clearly in use in commerce, because it had a barcode, pricing, and in this example, a nutrition label. The other example was an unfinished mock-up that was not ready for commerce. It did not include any information, just the logo (drawing). That specimen did not show use in commerce, and it was rejected.

Display of the Good in Commerce

The other option is to show a display of your goods that demonstrates the use of your mark with your goods in commerce.

This can be accomplished through a:

Physical Display. A physical display can be at a trade show or in a shop. It can include point-of-sale materials, such as banners, window displays, menus, and other related materials. You have to show the mark directly associated with the goods within the point-of-sale environment.

Online Display. An online display can be in catalogs and electronic displays (for example, websites and shopping apps). The specimen must include the following three elements:

A picture or textual description of the identified goods

A depiction of the mark in association with the goods

A means of ordering the identified goods (for example, a way to put the goods in a shopping bag/cart and pay for them). This is important because it helps prove that the goods are in commerce and that people can purchase them.

Here is a list of examples of acceptable specimens:

- TV or radio commercials for goods or services
- Signage with the mark, such as in front of a store
- Instruction manuals or materials used in relation to the goods and/or services
- Materials used in the rendering of the goods/ service (for example, A menu at a restaurant, a photo of the band in concert with its name on the stage, or a screenshot of a website with video game services)
- Labels or tags for the goods or containers for the goods, but actually in use in commerce
- Shipping or mailing labels affixed to the goods or containers to be shipped, but not solely as a return address
- Display of the goods in a place where people can purchase them

Specimens for Components or Ingredients

When you are providing a specimen showing your mark being used as a component or ingredient, the mark must be used to identify the component or ingredient of a finished good, but it cannot be used for the full finished good. For example, think "Intel Inside" used on a computer system that might be a Dell, Lenovo, or another brand.

Another example is a mark that identifies certain fibers used rather than the finished clothing. The certification mark Wool is a good example of that. The Woolmark Company oversees this and three other certification marks for wool. They certify wool apparel, wool care products, and wool care appliances.

Acceptable Specimens for Services

When you provide specimens for services, be sure that they clearly show the mark in use and connected to the services you offer.

You must show use of the mark either:

- Used or displayed as a service mark in the sale of the services, OR

- Used or displayed to advertise the services, including marketing and promotional materials. Advertising is fine for services, but *not* for goods.

In either case, you must demonstrate a means of purchasing the services and include it in your specimen.

EVEN MORE ON SPECIMENS

For more on acceptable specimens, see uspto. gov/about-us/events/trademark-specimens-overview-experienced-filers.

Advertisements as Specimens for Goods Versus Services

The USPTO will **not** take advertisements as specimens for goods; they will only accept advertisements if they include sales displays. Other items that are **not acceptable** include advertising circulars, brochures, press releases, business cards, and invoices. The office wants to see the good itself being sold.

In contrast, the USPTO will take advertisements for specimens for services. This can include their use or display as a brochure at a point of sale. Can you see why? If you want to purchase the services of the Geek Squad, a company offering computer-related repair and services, how would you know what they were? They offer no goods, per se. The advertising must be used to identify the services specified on your application.

Unacceptable Specimens

Here are some reasons a specimen may be rejected:

- The specimen doesn't show the trademark!

- The specimen doesn't show the trademark on applicable goods and/or services, or in the right IC.

- The specimen is not actually in use.

- The specimen doesn't demonstrate that the use is in commerce. An example is a web page for downloadable software, with no way to download the software.

- The specimen is unreadable or illegible.

- The specimen is merely advertising for goods and not showing the goods themselves.

- The specimen is a photocopy of the design mark or word and design mark.

- The specimen is part of an online catalog, but there is no pricing or ordering information (thus, it is not in commerce).

- The specimen is digitally created, a mock-up, or altered. These are no-goes. The USPTO will not be fooled. Fake specimens are bad and considered to be fraud!

- The specimen appears on a website that does not show the URL or date/time accessed.

And, of course, if you don't submit a specimen with an in-use application, that's a big problem.

Websites and Podcasts

Websites can be acceptable specimens if they clearly show what the good or service is and that it is for sale. To use a screenshot of a website as a specimen, the mark has to be recognized as a mark on the website, it must include the URL and the date/time of the screenshot, and it needs to show a price and how to purchase the goods and/or services (for example, shopping cart, pricing, and so forth). If your screenshot does not show those things, then it does not show use in commerce and will be disqualified by the USPTO examining attorney.

The USPTO requires you to **include the URL bar and the date**. The url bar allows the trademark examining attorneys to confirm that the website actually exists and that the goods/services are advertised on that website. To do this, be sure to take a screenshot of your computer screen that captures the URL and the time/date you accessed the page.

Sometimes you register a work in something that you don't sell, like a podcast. What do you do then? You can take a snapshot of episodes on your website or at a podcast platform, along with the date and time you snapped it. For example, The Reprise: A Young Artists of America Podcast.

Not an Ornamental Use

If your specimen shows the mark being used as an ornament rather than as a source identifier, the examining attorney may ask for a substitute specimen showing the mark being used as a source identifier. A merely ornamental use fails to function as a mark.

Digitally Created Specimens and Mockups

It is important to restate that mock-ups of any sort will not work as specimens. If it looks like it doesn't really exist, the USPTO will not register it. That goes for digitally created labels as well. Genuine labels on the product can work, but if you digitally alter a specimen to put your mark on someone else's existing product, that is very, very bad.

The Big Trademark
Application List

On the next two pages you will find the Big Trademark Application List to help you get ready to file your application. Once you complete the steps, you'll have all of your information ready when it is time to file your application.

Download the Form

You can download the Big Trademark Application List too! Scribble on it. Fill it in. If you find you need to start over or you decide to file a second application, you can print a fresh copy.

To access the forms through the tiny url, type the web address provided into your browser window.

To access the list through the QR code, open the camera app on your phone, aim the camera at the QR code, and click the link that pops up on the screen.

tinyurl.com/11564-patterns-download

The Big *Trademark* Application List

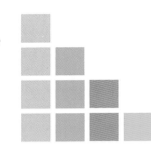

Write or Sketch Your Mark!

Start Here

Describe Your Mark!

My mark is a....

SMELL, ONLY COLOR, MOTION, OR SOUND MARK.

WORD, DESIGN, OR WORD/DESIGN MARK.

My mark identifies a....

- ☐ Collective Mark
- ☐ House Mark
- ☐ Certification Mark
- ☐ Trade Dress

☐ **Good**
(See Step 2 + 5)
IC: _____
Manual ID Description:
_____
_____
_____
_____

☐ **Service**
(See Step 2 + 5)
IC: _____
Manual ID Description:
_____
_____
_____

Sugestive or merely descriptive? If it's suggestive, it has a leap. If it's merely descriptive, it needs seconday meaning.

Checkpoint 1:
Strength of the Mark
[See Step 3]

THE MARK MAY BE STRONG BECAUSE...

THE MARK iS STRONG BECAUSE...

THE MARK ISN'T STRONG BECAUSE...

☐ It's generic!

- ☐ It's fanciful!
- ☐ It's arbitrary!
- ☐ It's suggestive (with a leap)!

I'm ready to start my application.

Specimen Requirements
- ☐ Shows actual use in commerce.
- ☐ Is likely perceived as a source identifier.
- ☐ Mark in the specimen matches the mark in the application.
- ☐ If image of website, include url and date of search.
- ☐ At least one specimen per class.

I INTEND TO USE THE MARK (SOON).

Stop and Summarize!
- ☐ **Word Mark:** _____
- ☐ **Design Mark:**
  Drawing in .jpg format, 300-350 DPI.
  In color or black/white?

IC: _____

Owner: _____

Preparing the Application
(See Part III)

THE MARK IS IN USE.

The first date my mark was used in commerece was....

_____

What I Found Out!
_____
_____
_____
_____
_____

Secondary Meaning Required
- ☐ Geographic Term
- ☐ Merely a Surname
- ☐ Only Color
- ☐ Merely Descriptive

Out-in-the-World Check
- ☐ Domain Name
- ☐ USPTO TESS Search
- ☐ Google Search
- ☐ Dictionary Search
- ☐ Be Creative

Secondary meaning:
There has been substantially exclusive and continuous use for at least five years?
- ☐ Yes
- ☐ In Progress

Checkpoint 2:
Not Off Limits
(See Step 4)

Checkpoint 3:
Can You Use this Mark?
(See Step 5)

Start over with new mark

This word/design is not off Limits by Statute.

FALSE   TRUE

PART III
Your Application

You have chosen a mark, and you've checked to make sure that no one else is using it in a way that might be conflicting or potentially keep your use from being registrable. You are now ready to start the application process.

In this part, we walk you through the process, including:

- **The application.** We will walk through the basic elements of the application, found on the USPTO website.

- **Specialty applications.** Get tips for filling out applications for less common kinds of marks, including certification and collective membership marks, scent and motion marks, and trade dress.

- **Office Actions.** Learn about basic types of Office Actions you may encounter from the USPTO's trademark examining attorney.

- **Published for Opposition.** Once the examining attorney has determined that your mark is registerable, it is published for opposition to make sure no one else objects to the USPTO granting your application.

- **State trademark applications.** If you choose to register your mark at the state level, we explain how that works.

- **Filing outside the United States.** We will introduce you to the larger global system of trademarks, including the Madrid Protocol and a little bit about Canada.

The *Application,* Step by Step

You will file your application using the Trademark Electronic Application System (TEAS). Unless you have already applied for a trademark, you will need to set up an account before you begin. This is free, and you can't get to the application without an account. Setting up an account takes a few steps, so allow time to do this. Access TEAS and register for an account at uspto.gov/trademarks/apply.

The TEAS application system is not pretty. The USPTO is redesigning it, but the exact date of the new version's release is uncertain. Regardless of the current interface, this section walks you through the basic elements that come up in the application. We address each part of the application in the order in which it appears in version 8.1. Once you have an account, you can go directly to my.uspto.gov/home to log in and apply.

> *Unless you have already applied for a trademark, you will need to set up an account before you begin.*

VIDEO APPLICATION HELP

The USPTO has a YouTube channel, USPTOvideo (youtube.com/@USPTOvideo), that hosts a series of videos to assist with your application. Its Trademark Information Network videos cover a variety of subjects, so if something has you stumped, jump over to find out whether a help video is available.

You don't have to pay a fee to fill out the application form, so you can take some time to practice if you want. You are only charged a fee when you submit the application. **Warning: The TEAS system will log you out after 30 minutes of inactivity.** Allow yourself enough time to fill out the application from beginning to end to ensure that you do not lose your work.

Filing Options

You have two filing options to choose from: TEAS Plus or TEAS Standard. TEAS Plus is the USPTO's preferred filing method.

TEAS Plus

This is the least expensive and most streamlined application form. TEAS Plus moves faster through the system. **It costs $250 per International Class.** You can include as many classes as you want for the mark you are applying for, but you'll pay this fee for each class.

In the TEAS Plus system:

- You must complete the application in full, and you must file electronically, with correspondence by email. This includes additional relevant statements (see Additional Statements About the Mark, page 145).

- You have to complete all mandatory fields.

- You have to choose a description from the USPTO's Trademark ID Manual. If you do not find what you are looking for, you have to email the USPTO to have your description added, or you can switch to the TEAS Standard application, see Choosing Your Description (page 67).

- You have to pay the fee at the time of filing. If your application is not complete, it is converted to a TEAS Standard application, and you are required to pay the additional difference in fees.

TEAS Standard

With the TEAS standard option, you don't have to file a complete application, and you can correspond in person, over the phone, or electronically by email. You pay an initial application fee, but pay the rest of the fee later. You can also write the description of your goods and services yourself and are not limited to the Trademark ID Manual.

We walk you through the TEAS Plus application, but the TEAS Standard application is similar so you can still follow along.

TEAS PLUS VERSUS TEAS STANDARD

If you need additional help choosing between these two options, more information and a video are on the USPTO site at uspto.gov/trademarks-application-process/filing-online/initial-application-forms#Chart%20Application%20requirements.

Is an Attorney Filing This Application?

This is a simple "yes" or "no" question. The USPTO is used to nonlawyers filling out the application, and so when the trademark examining attorney sends you an Office Action (see Office Actions, page 155), they recognize that you are not a lawyer and they seem to be more gentle and kind in dealing with you. That's just anecdotal.

To file without a lawyer, you must have a current domicile address in the U.S.

FOREIGN-DOMICILED APPLICANTS

If you are a foreign-domiciled applicant, including Canadian trademark filers, you must be represented by a U.S.-licensed attorney. For more, see uspto.gov/trademarks/laws/trademark-rule-requires-foreign-applicants-and-registrants-have-us.

Optional: Access Previously Saved Data

Skip this. This allows you to access previously saved data, which you likely do not have.

◆ ◆ ◆

Applicant Information

On this screen, you fill in basic information about who the applicant is. None of the questions on this screen is very difficult. However, if you are unsure of any of the answers, clicking on the highlighted terms will get you a pop-up help screen with additional information.

The questions on this screen ask you to provide the following information:

Owner of the Mark. This is tremendously important. Make sure that you accurately identify the correct owner of the mark. Ask yourself: Who controls the trademark? Is it a company or an individual? We have often hear that if you get this wrong (put down the wrong owner and want to change it later) that this may be a fatal flaw to your application. Is it your company that controls the decision making related to the goods/services and the mark, or is it an individual? Carefully determine who controls and owns the mark.

DBA, AKA, TA, Formerly. These stand for "doing business as," "also known as," "trading as," and "formerly known as." Fill in this field if you are currently going by a name other than the owner's name.

Entity Type. You will notice that as you choose the entity type, the form changes, requiring different information from different types of filers. Make sure to select the option that accurately describes your filing status. Some things to keep in mind:

If you have formed an entity, choose it. If you haven't formed an entity, and it is just you, select "individual."

You can also register the mark under an individual's name and transfer it to a company later.

If you choose "individual," you will be asked for your country of citizenship.

If you choose a corporation (LLC or other entity), you will be asked for the state where the organization is legally organized or, if non-U.S., the country.

If you are a tax-exempt corporation, choose "corporation." You will later include information about your nonprofit status.

If you are hoping to create an LLC or corporation but haven't yet, apply as an individual. To choose that category you must have created your LLC before applying.

Internal Address. If your address includes a room, suite, or similar, include it here. Not everyone will have an internal address.

Mailing Address. Your address will be part of the official information about your trademark. **Your address will be listed in the database and even on the certificate.** If the public nature of this information troubles you, you may want to list a business address instead of your home address. You are not allowed to include a P.O. box or a "care of" address.

Phone Number. This is important because the examining attorney may call you to amend something on your application.

Fax Number. This is not required.

Email Address. This is key. Make sure to list an email account that you check often. Note: If you are using a U.S.-licensed attorney, include their email here, as they will be the ones corresponding with the USPTO as your representative.

Website Address. This is not required.

At the bottom of this page, you have the option to go back, continue, or add another owner. You can add more than one owner, but if you do so, you must include all the information listed above for each owner.

Mark Information

You can enter only one mark for each application. This means that if you want to register a word mark and a separate design mark, you must submit two different applications.

You have three choices of which type of mark to apply for. Choose carefully! You cannot revise your application once you pay your fee and submit it.

Option 1: Standard Characters (Word Mark)

With this option, you are not claiming a particular font, style, size, and/or color. With this choice, you type your mark in the box provided. You can preview it by clicking the "Preview USPTO-Generated Image" button to confirm that it is accurate. Check the spelling a thousand times! This is the mark you are submitting.

As a reminder, a lot of marks are registered as standard characters because it gives flexibility in the use of your mark, so you can change the font or look without reregistering. By the time you file, the look of this screen may change, but it will still ask you for the same information.

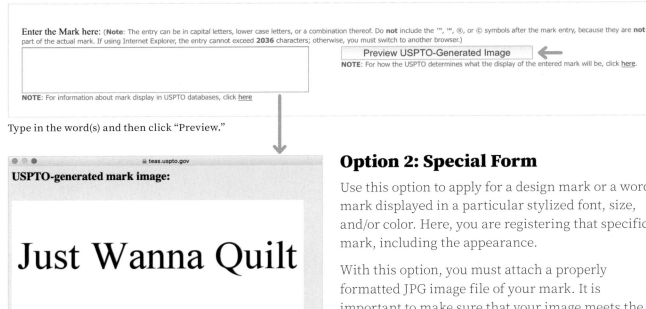

Type in the word(s) and then click "Preview."

Make sure to check spelling and spacing!

Option 2: Special Form

Use this option to apply for a design mark or a word mark displayed in a particular stylized font, size, and/or color. Here, you are registering that specific mark, including the appearance.

With this option, you must attach a properly formatted JPG image file of your mark. It is important to make sure that your image meets the USPTO specifications.

JPG Requirements

You must have a properly sized JPG image file of your mark. Make sure that your image:

- Is no fewer than 300 dots per inch (dpi) and no more than 350 dpi.

- Is the proper dimensions. It should have a length and width of no fewer than 250 pixels and no more than 944 pixels (for instance, a pixel dimension of 640 × 480 pixels).

- Is in color if you are claiming color; if you are not claiming color, the image must be in true black and white or in grayscale.

Elements of a Special Form

Work your way through this page of the application and address the applicable fields and questions, including:

Attaching the JPG file. Click "Choose File," select the correct file, and then click "Attach." A thumbnail version of the mark will be displayed in the application form and will also appear in the USPTO's Trademark Electronic Search System (TESS) database.

Literal Elements. For any image that includes word(s), letter(s), punctuation, and/or number(s), enter them into the provided textbox. Only enter the words, numbers, and punctuation that are part of the mark, and nothing else.

Let's use the Just Wanna Quilt logo as an example. The literal element would be "Just Wanna Quilt Community Copyright Creativity."

Color Choice. If you are claiming color as part of the mark, include that in the next text box, including black and white if they are used as actual colors within the mark (such as red, white, and blue). Colors should be written in **lowercase**. If your mark is only black and white and you are not claiming color, check the box next to "Check this box if you are NOT claiming color as a feature of the mark."

Click on the "Browse/Choose File" button to select a properly-sized JPG image file (the only accepted format) from your local drive. This image should show the mark exactly as you would wish the mark to appear on your registration certificate, if the mark registers. If you are claiming color, you **must** submit a color image; otherwise, the image must be clear black and white. After the file name appears in the window, click on the "Attach" button to upload the file into the application. A "thumbnail" version of the image will then display directly within the form.

NOTE: The image files for, respectively, the mark and the specimen (if filing under Section 1(a), use in commerce, and showing actual use in commerce of the mark at the time of this filing) should **NOT** be the same files (or, even if different files, should **not** display essentially the exact same thing). The mark image file should **ONLY** show the mark by itself, and **not** a representation of how the mark is used on the overall packaging for the goods or within an advertisement for services, for example. On the other hand, an image file that shows the complete package for the goods or a full advertisement for the services, with the mark clearly displayed thereon or within, would be an appropriate attachment for a specimen in the later "basis" section of the form (which only appears where a Section 1(a) filing basis is being claimed).

| Choose File | no file selected | | Attach |

For any image that also includes a word(s), letter(s), punctuation, and/or number(s), enter the LITERAL ELEMENT only of the mark here:

NOTE: Do **NOT** enter any word(s), letter(s), punctuation, and/or number(s) that do not appear in the attached image file. Leave this space blank if your mark consists only of design elements. The image file **must** include **all** elements of the mark; *i.e.*, if your mark consists of a design and word(s), letter(s), punctuation, and/or number(s), the image file must include all of these elements. Any entry in the literal element field that is not found in the attached image file will **not** be considered part of the mark.

* If claiming color as a feature of the mark, list the colors below, including black and/or white if actual "colors" within the mark (*e.g.*, enter red, white, and blue). Begin the entry with a lower-case, **NOT** an upper-case, letter. (Entry required for color marks only.)

The color(s) [   ] is/are claimed as a feature of the mark.

☐ Check this box if you are **NOT** claiming color as a feature of the mark. NOTE: Check *only* if you believe your image is black and white, yet you received after clicking the "CONTINUE" button a WARNING about color within the mark (perhaps because the image consists of too much grayscale); otherwise, do **not** check this box, because the attached image was automatically accepted as black and white.

* **Enter a complete and accurate description of the entire mark below, being sure to include ALL literal elements and/or design elements that are found in the attached mark image, but NOT including any element not appearing in the image. If a color mark, you must specify the color(s) that are part of the mark, including black and white, and also state the location thereof in the mark image.**
The mark consists of: (do NOT repeat this language)

[   ] . (end period is automatic)

NOTE: A description of the mark is required for **ALL** marks that are in a special form or a sound/motion mark (i.e., for any mark not in standard characters). You must to enter a description even if what the mark represents is immediately clear, *e.g.*, "the letter C." Also, for any color mark, the description of the mark must include the nature and location of the color; i.e., you must specifically state where each color is located within the mark, *e.g.*, "a bird with a red body, blue wings, and yellow beak."
NOTE: Do **NOT** include as part of the description either the words "The mark consists of" or a final period, because that introductory wording and the punctuation will automatically be added after validation; otherwise, the overall description will have improper repetitions. Also, begin the entry with a lower-case, **NOT** an upper-case, letter.

List the colors you are claiming.

Complete and Accurate Description of the Mark. Enter the description you've created as you worked through this book. It must include the literal elements, plus the design elements, plus the color elements. **Do not capitalize the first word or include a period in the last sentence.** And, because you have done your homework, you can add words from the design code manual that will alert the examining attorney to which design code to use, but do not include the codes themselves. If you are applying to register a nontraditional mark, include that as part of the description: Include the word "scent," for example, and then the description (see Less Common Applications, page 151). The examining attorney may alter this description, but they will ask you before they do, as part of an Office Action or a phone call to you (see Office Actions, page 155).

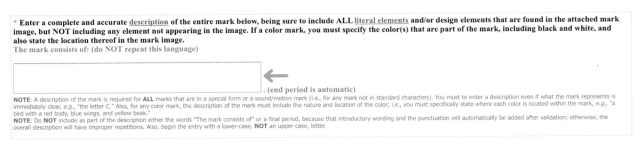

Enter your description, being careful to follow the instructions.

For Just Wanna Quilt, we wrote this: "The color(s) blue, green, pink, orange, black, white is/are claimed as a feature of the mark. The mark consists of the phrase JUST WANNA QUILT on the left-hand side, with JUST and QUILT stylized in cursive, with WANNA in basic font, with to the right four blue squares stacked on top of each other, with three green squares stacked on top of each other, with two pink squares stacked on top of each other, with one orange square, and at the bottom three words, each capitalized with a blue dot between them: COMMUNITY, COPYRIGHT, CREATIVITY."

Here is the version from the USPTO, after the examining attorney made suggested changes: "The color(s) blue, green, pink, orange, black, white is/are claimed as a feature of the mark. The mark consists of the phrase JUST WANNA QUILT on the left-hand side, with JUST and QUILT stylized in cursive, with WANNA in basic font, with to the right four blue squares stacked on top of each other, with three green squares stacked on top of each other, with two pink squares stacked on top of each other, with one orange square, and at the bottom three words, each capitalized with a blue dot between them: COMMUNITY, COPYRIGHT, CREATIVITY."

Nonvisual Sound Mark

To apply for nonvisual sound marks, you have to upload a sound/motion file as a WAV, WMV, WMA, MP3, MPG, or AVI file. This should only be the sound itself (the sample) and not how the mark is used (the specimen). And that's it!

Additional Statements About the Mark

At the bottom of the page for all three of the previous options is a box that allows you to provide additional statements about your mark. Not every application requires additional statements, but some might. Check the box to see the full listing of additional statements and decide whether any apply. If they don't, uncheck the box and select "Continue."

The additional statement box has a small button to click.

ADDITIONAL RESOURCES FOR COMPLETING THE APPLICATION

If this section is confusing, check out the USPTO video on providing additional statements at uspto. gov/learning-and-resources/uspto-videos/teas-nuts-and-bolts-additional-statements.

If you do need to provide additional statements, everything with a red * is mandatory to complete, with the caveat that if it doesn't apply to your application, you don't have to fill it out. However, if you do not fill out mandatory fields that the examining attorney later determines do apply to your application, your application will be converted to a TEAS Standard, and the USPTO will make you pay an additional $100 per IC.

The USPTO does not want you to overfill the additional statements. It even says in one of its videos, "If in doubt, leave it out."

Several possible additional statements may apply, including:

Disclaimer. Fill this in if you are disclaiming a word, meaning you recognize that even though the word is part of your mark, you do not claim exclusive use of that word. We did not check this for our mark, but we got a letter from the examining attorney requiring us to disclaim "Quilt." We have seen this a lot—that you don't have to add disclaimers during the application, but you may be asked to do so later by the examining attorney.

As a reminder, a disclaimer is necessary when you are using:

- Merely descriptive terms

- Laudatory words (e.g. greatest, ultimate, best)

- Generic words

- Geographic words

- Business designations (e.g. corporation)

- Informational words (e.g. the year the business was established)

- Well-known symbols

If you are disclaiming a word, just put it in the text box without quotes. You can disclaim more than one word. For instance, Angie Wood Creations, a family business in Canada that makes wooden watches, disclaimed "wood" and "creations" as required by an Office Action. They too, waited to see what the trademark examining attorney wanted disclaimed.

Active Prior Registration(s). If you are the owner of an active prior U.S. registration for the same or a similar mark, or if you have other registrations related to the mark, you can add it here. This is important because it lets the examining attorney know that anything they find that might seem confusing with the same mark may actually be yours.

Translation. If your mark is or contains a foreign word, provide the translation. If the word is not a foreign word, you can include that in the "additional statement" box or wait until you are asked by the examining attorney to confirm that it is not a foreign word.

Transliteration. If the mark includes script or non-Latin characters that need translating, add that script here.

Meaning or significance of wording, letter(s) or numeral(s). If there is any trade or industry significance related to a particular word, lettering, or numerals, you must alert the USPTO as part of your application.

Indicate the nature of the 2(f) claim of acquired distinctiveness. Use this section when your mark is merely descriptive and you have to provide information/evidence that it has acquired distinctiveness. You must first decide whether "Whole" or "In Part" is the correct choice for your mark. You must then click the box next to the item that best describes how your mark has acquired distinctiveness; for a refresher, see

Acquired Distinctiveness (page 37). **These choices are:**

- *Based on 5 or more years of use.* You see the "substantially exclusive and continuous use" language.

- *Based on active prior registration for the same mark.* You include the registration numbers.

- *Based on evidence.* You attach the evidence as a PDF.

Name(s), portrait(s), signature(s) of individual(s): If you are using a name, portrait, drawing, or signature of an individual, you have to identify the person, and then attach a letter of consent. You can also check that the mark *does not* identify a particular living individual.

Use of the Mark in Another Form. This is where you can add that the mark was used, and in commerce, in a different form from earlier dates. This would include prior registrations and common-law uses of an older version of the mark.

Concurrent Use. If this statement applies to your mark, stop and consult an attorney. This is a more complicated situation and requires a professional.

Miscellaneous Statement. You can provide additional information that is not entered elsewhere, but the USPTO warns to not include anything that might derail the application.

Goods/Services Information

On this page of the application, you indicate which International Class(es) you are applying for and add the appropriate description. Click the "Add Goods/Services" button.

> Add Goods/Services

The USPTO has additional resources within the application, including videos.

A new page with a search box will appear. Your goal is to find the closest definition that has already been filed.

You can perform the search in a number of ways:

- **Enter a noun.** Choose a word that describes what you are doing: podcast, book, fabric, or other.

- **Put in the International Class number.** Enter the IC number you already selected in the search box. Be sure that it has a zero (for example, 024 or 001), or it won't work. Then, browse what others have already filed.

- **Use a combination of IC numbers and nouns.** For example, 024 cotton would bring back results of descriptions for fabrics that are cotton.

Once you have found a description you like, check it, and then click the "Insert Checked Entries" button.

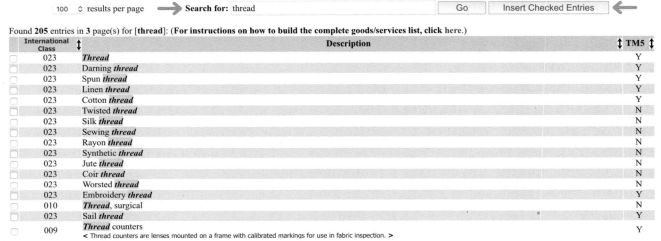

International Class	Description	TM5
023	*Thread*	Y
023	Darning *thread*	Y
023	Spun *thread*	Y
023	Linen *thread*	Y
023	Cotton *thread*	Y
023	Twisted *thread*	N
023	Silk *thread*	N
023	Sewing *thread*	N
023	Rayon *thread*	N
023	Synthetic *thread*	N
023	Jute *thread*	N
023	Coir *thread*	N
023	Worsted *thread*	N
023	Embroidery *thread*	Y
010	*Thread*, surgical	N
023	Sail *thread*	Y
009	*Thread* counters < Thread counters are lenses mounted on a frame with calibrated markings for use in fabric inspection. >	Y

100 ◇ results per page → Search for: thread — Go — Insert Checked Entries ←

Found **205** entries in **3** page(s) for [thread]: (For instructions on how to build the complete goods/services list, click **here**.)

Once you choose and click the "Insert Checked Entries" button, you are taken to the next screen.

The goods/services that you added on the previous screen show up here. Each International Class costs $250 in TEAS Plus or $350 in TEAS Standard.

Trademark/Service Mark Application, Principal Register
TEAS Plus Application (Version 8.1)

Goods/Services Information

Instructions:
Step 1: Click on the "Add Goods/Services by Searching IDManual" button below to select goods/services from the *Manual of Trademark Acceptable Identifications of Goods & Services* (IDManual).
Step 2: After creating the complete list of goods/services for this application, you will then be able in the next section of the form to designate the filing basis (or bases) appropriate for each listed item.

NOTE:
1. Your selection of goods/services from the IDManual must accurately identify your goods/services. For additional information, see TMEP Chapter 1400. If you do not find a listing that accurately identifies your goods/services, you may email TMIDSUGGEST@uspto.gov to request that your identification be considered for addition to the IDManual. Visit the USPTO's website for information on IDManual suggestions. If your request is approved, you must wait until the approved identification is added to the IDManual. If your request is not approved or you wish to file immediately, you must use the TEAS Standard form.
2. The TEAS Plus version of the IDManual intentionally does not include the following: (1) items classified in Classes A, B, or 200, because those marks are not eligible for filing under TEAS Plus; (2) any listings that appear in the "regular" manual under "000," because correct classification is required under TEAS Plus, and classification for these listings varies according to the additional information provided within the listing; and (3) the Class 25 listing of "Clothing, namely, ...", because this entry is too open-ended, and could result in items being listed that do not truly fall within this class. Instead, search for and select the specific clothing items you wish to include in your application.
3. Some entries include instructional language beneath the actual entry, within < > symbols. This language is only to assist in the proper selection of an entry, and will NOT be included as part of the actual identification after the checked entry is inserted into the form.
4. If you cannot access the IDManual through the "Add Goods/Services by Searching IDManual" button, try switching to another browser. If after changing browsers you still cannot access the IDManual through the "Add Goods/Services by Searching IDManual" button, please contact TEAS@uspto.gov.
TIMEOUT WARNING: You're required to log back in after 30 minutes of inactivity. This ensures the USPTO complies with mandatory federal information security standards and protects user information. After 25 minutes of inactivity, you will be prompted to continue your session. If you do not continue within 5 minutes, the session will end, you will be logged out of your USPTO.gov account, and you will lose any unsaved data in the form. Please have all of your information ready before you start.

NOTE - INSTRUCTIONAL VIDEOS AVAILABLE REGARDING GOODS/SERVICES:
Watch the TMIN Goods and Services video explaining what is meant by "identification of goods and services," and watch the TEAS Nuts and Bolts: Goods and Services video for instructions on filling out the Goods/Services page in this application.

→ | Add Goods/Services | Remove Checked Goods/Services

NOTE: Clicking "Go Back" will take you directly back to the MARK section of the form.
Go Back

See the button "Add goods/services"? That's what you are looking for. And then, once you choose the International Class and description, you can remove it if you make a mistake.

If you choose an International Class and description that requires additional detail, a new box will appear so you can provide it. You'll see a blank description field where you indicate the field, subject, components, or other requested information.

Please specify the required information below:
NOTE: Do not use any of the following wording in the listing(s), as it may make the identification "indefinite" for purposes of registration: "including," "comprising," "such as," "and the like," "and similar goods," "concepts," "like services," etc. The terms "namely" and "consisting of" are proper substitutes. Also, do not include any html or other programming code or language that may create links in the listing of goods and/or recitation of services, nor any abbreviations.
Remove | Add | 041 Entertainment services, namely, providing *podcasts* in the field of quilting ←

If you choose a description that allows you to fill in more, you do it in the yellow box.

Add the requested information. Be sure to follow the do's and don'ts in the related note above the blank when entering your information. If approved, what you enter here is what your trademark will be—the property right the USPTO is giving you. For us, it was the use of the mark for Class 41, entertainment—namely, podcasts in the field of copyright and crafting.

Basis for Filing

Next, you'll be asked to choose your basis for filing. If you are filing an application from the United States, you'll need to select either Section 1(a) or Section 1(b). If you are a foreign filer, you'll need to choose 44(d) or 44(e):

Section 1(a) In Use. This indicates that you are already using your mark in commerce. You must provide proof that you are using the mark in commerce (see Step 8: Preparing Your Specimen, page 128). When you choose Section 1(a), you are taken to a subset of questions:

- **Attach Specimen.** Upload your specimen. Remember, this is different than the design mark itself (if you have chosen a design mark). It is evidence that you are using the mark in commerce. (See Specimens, page 129)

- **Description of Specimen.** Describe what is included in the specimen (for example, tags, instructional manuals, the front page of a catalog, and so forth).

- **Date of First Use of Mark Anywhere.** This date may be before the goods or services were in the marketplace, such as when you created a website, formed an LLC, or undertook any other activity to prepare for using the mark. This question really wants to know when you first started using the mark as a source identifier.

- **Date of First Use of Mark in Commerce.** This is the date when you first sold or offered for sale the goods or services with the mark.

Section 1(b) Intent to Use. This choice means that you are preparing to use your mark in commerce but are not yet doing so. You will later need to provide proof the mark is actually being used in commerce; it will cost you an additional $100 to file a "Statement of Use," but sometimes that is well worth it. When you file the intent-to-use application, you need to state what the mark will be used for. For instance, in 2000, FreeSpirit Fabrics, a fabric company, filed an intent-to-use application for "Fabric used in the making of handmade quilts, dolls, and other craft projects." It explained in the application that the mark will be "affixed to goods, labels and used in advertisements in connection with the goods." Then, on October 16, 2001, it submitted its Statement of Use, listing the first use anywhere as well as the first use in commerce as November 1, 2000, along with the additional $100 filing fee.

To file an intent-to-use application, you must check a box confirming that you have a bona fide intention to use the mark in commerce or in connection with goods/services. Be sure to read the statement carefully before checking the box.

Section 44(d) Foreign application. This option is for foreign applicants that also have a foreign trademark application in process for the same mark and the same goods/services in the same IC(s). Choose this basis if you are filing the U.S. application within six months of filing the first foreign application. To do this, you must have your foreign application number and the date of foreign filing. Remember, to file as a foreign application, you must obtain a U.S. attorney. Filing with this status establishes a right of priority, meaning that you get the application date of your original foreign application, as long as it is the same mark and for the same IC(s). If no foreign application filing already exists (that is, you do not have an application pending in a trademark office outside the USPTO), do not claim this basis. This filing basis is not appropriate if you are merely doing business or intend to do business outside the United States and do not actually have a foreign application.

SECTION 1 VERSUS SECTION 44

An attorney can help you decide whether to rely on your foreign application as the basis for your application or to file a section 1(a) or section 1(b) application. If your foreign application fails, so will your U.S. application.

Section 44(e) Foreign registration. This option is for foreign applicants that already have a foreign trademark for the same mark and the same goods/services in the same IC(s). You will be asked to include the information from your foreign registration, which includes attaching a copy of the registration certificate. **Remember, to file as a foreign application, you must obtain a U.S. attorney.**

Correspondence Information

This page is where you enter your basic contact information. You can add a docket or reference number for your own records. Attorneys use this page to include client docket information. You are free to add references, too, but it is not necessary.

Fee Information

This page displays a summary of the number of classes being applied for and which class(es). It also shows the fee per class and the amount due. The USPTO does not refund your money, even if your application is not successful; you pay regardless of whether it is accepted.

Electronic Signature

You next have to sign the form; read and agree to a declaration; and sign, date, and add your position, name, and signatory's phone number (in case the signer is not the applicant). First, choose your signature method. If you are filing your own application, select the first option, "Sign Directly."

Next, carefully read and check each of the statements in the declaration. Finally, sign the application. There are two fields to fill in:

- **Signature and Date Signed.** Just as it sounds, you need to add your signature and enter the current date. One very important thing to note is that the signature has to include two forward slashes, one on each side of the name (for example, /charla smith/).

Finally, there is a payment screen. Pay and then submit! That's it! You've done it. It's time for you to go eat some cake. Cake eating is the *most important* part of submitting a trademark application.

Waiting Period

Once your application is submitted, it's time for the hardest part—waiting. You are now waiting to see whether you'll get an Office Action from the trademark examiner. We address those in Office Actions (page 155). Some problems are merely technical, such as spelling errors, and some are more substantial, such as addressing issues like merely descriptive, merely a surname, or likelihood of confusion.

A word of warning. When you file your application, you may find yourself inundated with emails and postal mail containing semi-official-looking letters or notices from attorneys/services telling you that you must "do things" to your application to scare or intice you to send them money or hire them. **These are scams.** Once you file your application, your information is now public, and anyone can see that you have filed a trademark application. **Ignore all of these.** When the flood comes in, go directly to your MyUSPTO account to see whether anything is pending. Don't trust strangers telling you anything about your trademark or trademark application. The USPTO also posts this warning on their website.

Less *Common* Applications

If you plan to register a collective or a certification mark, there are different forms. In this section, we go through the specific differences between these two kinds of marks. We also look at any additional steps that you need to take when applying for other less common types of marks, such as scent, motion, trade dress, or house marks. All of these marks are complicated and should not be filed without an experienced attorney.

SEEK THE RIGHT ATTORNEY

Please, please, *please* find an experienced attorney for the kind of less common mark you are filing. To do this, you can search Free Form for the type of mark and/or use [de] with the particular kind of mark, such as "scent" or "motion," to see who has successfully registered these before.

Collective Membership Marks

Collective membership marks require additional information as part of the application.

Method of Control. The USPTO explains, "The applicant must specify how it controls or, if filing under Section 1(b), intends to control the use of the MARK by members. If the applicant's bylaws or other written provisions specify the manner of control, or intended manner of control, applicant may simply state that."

To have a collective membership mark, you have to have bylaws or other rules for your members. Explain that in the text box.

Basis for Filing. The International Class is automatically filled in: 200. Fill in the description of the Collective Membership Mark.

Certification Marks

When you are applying for a certification mark, a screen requires you to enter the common commercial name for the specific goods/services associated with your mark. Here is the USPTO's explanation:

Enter only the common commercial name for the specific goods and/or services associated with the mark; e.g., "computer software for accounting purposes;" or "shirts, pants, and shoes." While you may be able to amend the listing during prosecution of your application to clarify a broad recitation, if the initial listing is too ambiguous, you will not receive a filing date and no amendment will be permitted (i.e., even though the electronic form would transmit and you would be assigned a serial number, after initial review at the USPTO, it may be determined that assignment of a filing date was not warranted, and your application would be returned, along with the filing fee). Also, you can never expand the listing beyond the scope of what has been presented in the original filing; the addition of goods and/or services would require a new application filing.

The USPTO suggests consulting the U.S. Acceptable Identification of Goods and Services Manual (ID Manual), but it is not required.

And, finally, you have to include a certification statement. The USPTO explains, "Applicant must enter a statement of the characteristic, standard, or other feature that is certified or intended to be certified by the mark, e.g., a particular regional origin of the goods, a characteristic of the goods or services, or that labor was performed by a particular group."

It suggests starting with this statement: "The certification mark, as used or intended to be used by persons authorized by the certifier, certifies or is intended to certify that the goods/services provided have [specify]."

Once you complete that, the screens return to the correspondence, review, payment, and so on.

Special Procedures for Applications for Scents

Applications for scents always require secondary meaning—that is, at least five years of use where the public identifies that scent with the product or good. The scent must function as a mark and cannot be functional to the goods or services. Scent applications are very rare. If you are doing this, make sure to find an attorney who has experience registering scent trademarks.

Scents are one area where you have to mail in your specimen, which makes sense. Applicants should indicate that the mark is a "NON-VISUAL MARK." In the standard character section (Option 1), you should type "SCENT MARK" in the standard field. Drawing code 6 will be entered by the examining attorney.

You have to use the TEAS Standard application, which costs $100 more. You also have to mail in a sample of the scent as part of your application to the following address:

Commissioner for Trademarks
P.O. Box 1451
Alexandria, Virginia 22313–1451

MAILING TIPS

For more on mailing requirements, see tmep.uspto.gov/RDMS/TMEP/print?version=current&href=TMEP-300d1e459.html.

ATTORNEY FOR SCENT APPLICATIONS

If you are thinking about registering a certification mark, please again think of finding an experienced attorney, not just with trademark applications, but certification trademark applications.

Registering a Motion Mark

Registering a motion mark is the same as applying for other marks, with a few small changes. For the drawing of the mark, include a depiction of a single point in the movement, with up to five freeze frames of the movement as a square drawing. Write a detailed description of the mark. For the specimen, you can upload the actual motion mark. Motion files can be WMV, WMA, MP3, or AVI and must be smaller than 30 MB for video files. Motion marks are merely that: motion. If you want to register a sound, that would be a sound mark.

Registering Trade Dress

We've discussed trade dress before. Trade dress protects the look and feel of a product or service. It's special because trade dress can be registered and unregistered and still have protection under the Trademark Act. Trade dress is considered a "symbol" or "device" under the U.S. Trademark Act that serves as a source identifier.

Anything that conveys meaning and serves as identifying a source or origin of the product can count as trade dress. One key element is that the trade dress you are registering (for example, the design or color) cannot be functional. Trade dress is considered a nontraditional mark. Restaurants are big users of trade dress registration. McDonald's Happy Meal is one example of a registered trade dress. Sometimes, even how a restaurant plates food can be protected by trade dress.

Trade dress includes:

- Product packaging, including interiors of stores and restaurants

- Dressing

- Product design

- The layout and look of a shop

- Uniforms that employees wear

- Exterior and interior of architecture that serves as a source identifier

- Décor and interior floor plan

- Shape

- Color

Drawing and specimen of a McDonald's Happy Meal submitted to the USPTO.

DECIDING WHETHER TO REGISTER TRADE DRESS?

If you are thinking of registering trade dress, this can get complicated, as you have to make sure that you meet the nonfunctional requirements and the distinctiveness requirements. You should also decide whether it is best to register or not register your trade dress, which is, again, a legal choice. So, in short, it's a lot. You know what we are going to write next: If you are considering registering trade dress, consult with an attorney with trade dress experience.

Unregistered Trade Dress

Not all trade dress is registered with the USPTO. Unregistered trade dress is protected by Section 43(a) of the Lanham Act (a trademark law):

> Any person who shall affix, apply, or annex, or use in connection with any goods or services, or any container or containers for goods, a false designation of origin, or any false description or representation, including words or other symbols tending falsely to describe or represent the same, and shall cause such goods or services to enter into commerce, and any person who shall with knowledge of the falsity of such designation of origin or description or representation cause or procure the same to be transported or used in commerce or deliver the same to any carrier to be transported or used, shall be liable to a civil action by any person doing business in the locality falsely indicated as that of origin or in the region in which said locality is situated, or by any person who believes that he is or is likely to be damaged by the use of any such false description or representation.

A case about tacos (yes!) helps us understand unregistered trade dress. In this case, Taco Cabana, a chain of fast-food restaurants that serves Mexican food, operated in Texas. The restaurant had a specific look and feel, with bright colors, paintings and murals, and an interior patio. Two Pesos, a competing taco store, opened in Houston and adopted a motif very similar to Taco Cabana's trade dress, making the restaurants look very much alike. The U.S. Supreme Court ruled that unregistered trade dress could be inherently distinctive and protectable under Section 43(a). That means that trade dress that met the arbitrary, fanciful, or suggestive line and was not merely descriptive could be protected without secondary meaning. The first to use unregistered trade dress has priority. Again, trade dress is the overall appearance, including the wrappers, packaging, and the atmosphere or interior decor of a restaurant. It's all about the look and feel.

Registering House Marks

House marks are unusual and difficult to get through the USPTO trademark application process. Consult with an attorney with house mark experience.

Office **Actions**

You have submitted your application. Now, a trademark examining attorney will review it. It will take several months (possibly eight or more) before you hear back from them. Three steps remain: Review and respond to any Office Actions, get published for opposition, and, if you survive both, receive notice that your mark is registered.

When the attorney reviews your application, they are looking for any likelihood of confusion or dilution with another mark, checking to make sure that your mark is not functional, and, in short, reviewing all the things we've been checking throughout this book.

When the examining attorney sends you an Office Action, that means that there's a problem with your application. It may be something small, such as a typo, or it could be more significant. In either case, it is important to address any Office Action right away.

Some applications will sail through, without office actions. For instance, the Quilted Twins had no problems at all when they registered QUILTED TWINS. You can tell because when you look at their Trademark Status & Document Retrieval (TSDR) documents, there is no listing for an outgoing Office Action.

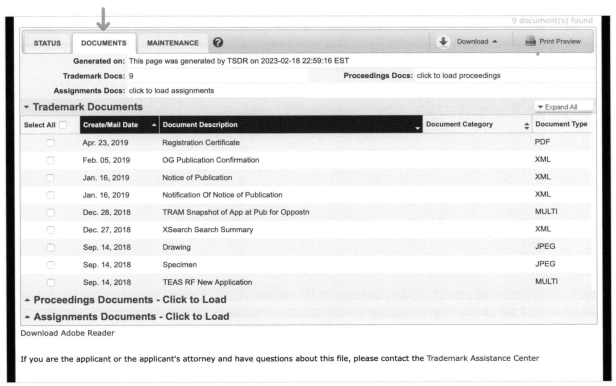

The Quilted Twins' word mark sailed through the process.

Social Justice Sewing Academy had the same experience when it registered SOCIAL JUSTICE SEWING ACADEMY. The TSDR files show that they had an examiner's amendment. That means that a trademark examining attorney called to clarify something with them and then made the adjustment. Click on it, and you can read for yourself!

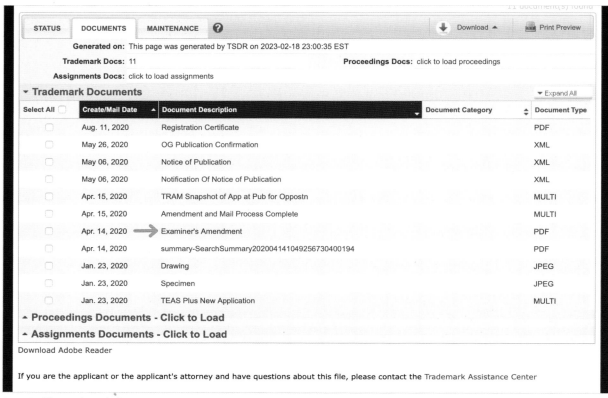

Sara Trail's word mark for SOCIAL JUSTICE SEWING ACADEMY also sailed through.

Sara had to disclaim *sewing academy*. That was descriptive, and she wasn't claiming it as something others couldn't use if they had their own sewing academy. Tula Pink had the same thing happen, an examiner's amendment in which she was asked to disclaim *Pink*. Not a big deal.

About 45 percent of TEAS Plus applications are approved without any further action needed by the applicant. This means that 55 percent of applications have something that is called an Office Action. As we've mentioned, an Office Action is a communication between the USPTO trademark examining attorney and yourself. If you have selected the TEAS Plus application, you will be communicating through email and the online system. Sometimes, an examining attorney will also give you a call for clarification or to make a suggestion on your application. If you had an attorney file your application, the USPTO will correspond with your lawyer.

If you get an Office Action, don't panic. Let's find out more about them and how to address any questions that the trademark examining attorney may have about your application.

Respond Promptly

As of December 3, 2022, the time allowed to respond to Office Actions was shortened from six months to three. You can extend the response time for another three months for $125, but you have to file for the extension within the first three months.

It is always best to respond promptly, but if you miss a deadline, you can file a petition to revive your application. You can either hire an attorney or work through the steps provided by the USPTO. The petition to revive an application is an online form, and you will pay a $150 fee.

WHEN YOU MISS A DEADLINE

So, you missed a deadline. Start with the information at the USPTO, and if you feel like that doesn't answer your questions, you have two options: Talk with an attorney and see if there any way to fix the missed deadline, or start the application again. People and companies do that all the time to restart the clock. For more about reviving abandoned applications, see uspto.gov > Trademarks > Abandoned Applications.

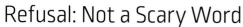

Refusal: Not a Scary Word

You may get something back from the USPTO that includes the word *refusal*. This means that the application as it is now has a problem. Some problems are easy to fix. For example, a misspelling needs to be fixed, or you forgot to let them know that you already had a prior trademark using the same mark (which could make it look like the new one is confusingly similar to the old one, but you are the owner of the old one!). These are easy, fixable mistakes. Others are more serious, such as the likelihood of confusion, the mark being generic, or the mark being seen as merely descriptive. Those may require more work, and if you haven't already, you may want to consult an attorney at this point. Sometimes, sadly, there may be no fixing the problem.

What are the most common bases for refusal?

- Likelihood of confusion

- Merely descriptive (either requiring a disclaimer or proof of secondary meaning)

- Geographically descriptive of the origin of the goods/services

- Specimen not supporting use for listed items

- Mark being used in an ornamental manner (not functioning as a mark)

What Does an Office Action Look Like?

You can go through your MyUSPTO account to see and respond to Office Actions. You can also view Office Actions for any application for any mark through the TESS database, but you have to sign in to your account to respond to them. Go to the record for the mark in question and click the "TSDR" button to see all associated documents, including the Office Actions. To view an Office Action, click on "Outgoing Office Action." We're going to use some of the marks we registered as part of this project as examples.

JUST WANNA QUILT was a mark we registered for the podcast called *Just Wanna Quilt.* We put in the application on May 8, 2019, just before the original law students who worked on the project were about to graduate, and we got an Office Action on August 9, 2019. A record of that Office Action is below.

An Office Action is a form letter, which you can also download (upper-right-hand corner). The attachments at the top are the examples the examining attorney provided for whatever the issue was that they found.

You can see that at the top, the Office Action is addressed to Elizabeth, and it lists the trademark application by its serial number and the word mark. You can see that there are attachments. These relate to the findings of the examining attorney.

The Office Action has two main parts:

- Whether the examining attorney's search turned up any problems or conflicting marks

- Whether there are other issues you must address. These will be written in a formal way and will include citations to the law. Don't be afraid of these comments. Just read carefully and use your trademark knowledge. If you believe that it is more than a trivial problem, you might hire an attorney.

In the example to the left, you see the word *nonfinal*. Let's go through the two types of Office Actions: nonfinal (the first letter from the examining attorney) and final (the second one).

Nonfinal Office Action

The first letter about any legal problem with your application will be a nonfinal Office Action. You have three months to respond, but we encourage you to do it immediately so you don't forget. If the examining attorney is satisfied with your answer, you are good to go, and your application will go to the next phase of registration: publication for opposition. If it doesn't, you will be sent a final Office Action.

NONFINAL OFFICE ACTION

The USPTO must receive applicant's response to this letter within <u>six months</u> of the issue date below or the application will be <u>abandoned</u>. Respond using the Trademark Electronic Application System (TEAS). A link to the appropriate TEAS response form appears at the end of this Office action.

Issue date: August 02, 2019

The referenced application has been reviewed by the assigned trademark examining attorney. Applicant must respond timely and completely to the issue(s) below. 15 U.S.C. §1062(b); 37 C.F.R. §§2.62(a), 2.65(a); TMEP §§711, 718.03.

SEARCH RESULTS

The trademark examining attorney has searched the Office's database of registered and pending marks and has found no conflicting marks that would bar registration under Trademark Act Section 2(d). TMEP §704.02; *see* 15 U.S.C. §1052(d).

SUMMARY OF ISSUES:
- Clarification of the Identification of Services
- Disclaimer Required

Example of a nonfinal Office Action

You also see in all caps *SEARCH RESULTS*.

In this case, the trademark examining attorney has "searched the Office's database of registered and pending marks and has found no conflicting marks that would bar registration under Trademark Act Section 2(d)." What does that mean? The trademark examining attorney has searched the internal USPTO database (similar to TESS), along with the other searches we discussed, including the Internet, dictionary, and so forth, and has not found any issues. Note: They have not searched state trademark records. If there was a conflict, that would only come up if someone objected *during the registration or publication process* (see Office Actions Based on a Letter of Protest, page 171).

In this case, there were no conflicting marks that would bar registration. (Second 2[d] refers to the likelihood of confusion in trademark law talk.)

The next part is a summary of any problems the examining attorney found. In this case, they found two issues.

Let's look at what might come up in Office Actions.

Clarification of the Identification of Goods or Services

This relates to the description you choose/wrote in the application. The examining attorney may want modifications. Often, they provide what they want you to substitute and how to do so. Let's take a look at the JUST WANNA QUILT application:

I. CLARIFICATION OF THE IDENTIFICATION OF SERVICES

As filed, the identification of services appears as follows:

- *International Class 041*: **Educational and entertainment services, namely, a continuing program about copyright, community, quilting, hitory, entrepreneurship and crafting accessible by means of podcasts, training resources, cultural activities, publications, and online resources.**; Entertainment services, namely, providing podcasts in the field of copyright and quilting

The above-bolded wording in the identification of services is indefinite and must be clarified because the fill-in section following ". . . accessible by means of . . ." in the TEAS Plus identification does not properly specify the telecommunications means through which the continuing program is made available, such as by television, radio, satellite, audio, video, web-based applications, mobile phone applications, and global computer networks. *See* 37 C.F.R. §2.32(a)(6); TMEP §1402.01. Additionally, "history" appears to be misspelled as "hitory" in the portion of the segment describing the subject matter of the continuing program. Applicant may substitute the following wording, if accurate:

- *International Class 041*: **Educational and entertainment services, namely, a continuing program about copyright, community, quilting, history, entrepreneurship and crafting accessible by means of audio, video, web-based applications, mobile phone applications, and global computer networks;** Entertainment services, namely, providing podcasts in the field of copyright and quilting; **Providing a website featuring online training resources, namely, non-downloadable publications in the nature of {specify, e.g., training manuals, books, magazines} in the field of copyright, community, quilting, history, entrepreneurship and crafting; Providing on-line non-downloadable directory publications in the field of copyright, community, quilting, history, entrepreneurship and crafting**

Applicant's goods and/or services may be clarified or limited, but may not be expanded beyond those originally itemized in the application or as acceptably amended. *See* 37 C.F.R. §2.71(a); TMEP §1402.06. Applicant may clarify or limit the identification by inserting qualifying language or deleting items to result in a more specific identification; however, applicant may not substitute different goods and/or services or add goods and/or services not found or encompassed by those in the original application or as acceptably amended. *See* TMEP §1402.06(a)-(b). The scope of the goods and/or services sets the outer limit for any changes to the identification and is generally determined by the ordinary meaning of the wording in the identification. TMEP §§1402.06(b), 1402.07(a)-(b). Any acceptable changes to the goods and/or services will further limit scope, and once goods and/or services are deleted, they are not permitted to be reinserted. TMEP §1402.07(e).

For assistance with identifying and classifying goods and services in trademark applications, please see the USPTO's online searchable *U.S. Acceptable Identification of Goods and Services Manual*. *See* TMEP §1402.04.

An example of how the examining attorney communicates. There are lots of legal citations to show why, but you can follow the reasoning by skipping them.

You can see that they want more specificity and that we misspelled *history*. They want that fixed. It is important to note that if there is a modification to the description, it must be more narrow and cannot broaden the description from the original application. What is interesting is that the description was pretty limited when we chose it from the list in the application. The trademark examining attorney is adding more nuance than we might have been able to at the time of the application. That is totally okay.

You will need to paste the examining attorney's description into your response.

Disclaimer Requirement

Sometimes, the examining attorney will require you to disclaim a portion of your mark, which is usually a generic term. You are disclaiming exclusive use over that particular term. In the case of JUST WANNA QUILT, we had to disclaim *quilt*. Let's see what that looks like:

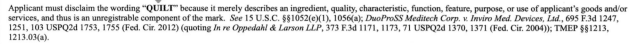

> **II.   DISCLAIMER REQUIRED**
>
> Applicant must disclaim the wording "**QUILT**" because it merely describes an ingredient, quality, characteristic, function, feature, purpose, or use of applicant's goods and/or services, and thus is an unregistrable component of the mark. *See* 15 U.S.C. §§1052(e)(1), 1056(a); *DuoProSS Meditech Corp. v. Inviro Med. Devices, Ltd.*, 695 F.3d 1247, 1251, 103 USPQ2d 1753, 1755 (Fed. Cir. 2012) (quoting *In re Oppedahl & Larson LLP*, 373 F.3d 1171, 1173, 71 USPQ2d 1370, 1371 (Fed. Cir. 2004)); TMEP §§1213, 1213.03(a).
>
> The attached evidence from Dictionary.com shows this wording means "to make quilts or quilted work." Applicant's identification of services explicitly includes a continuing program about, among other things, quilting and includes an ongoing program the subject matter of which includes quilting. Therefore, the wording merely describes a feature and/or characteristic of applicant's services, namely, the making of quilts, which is a subject matter to which applicant's services pertain.
>
> An applicant may not claim exclusive rights to terms that others may need to use to describe their goods and/or services in the marketplace. *See Dena Corp. v. Belvedere Int'l, Inc.*, 950 F.2d 1555, 1560, 21 USPQ2d 1047, 1051 (Fed. Cir. 1991); *In re Aug. Storck KG*, 218 USPQ 823, 825 (TTAB 1983). A disclaimer of unregistrable matter does not affect the appearance of the mark; that is, a disclaimer does not physically remove the disclaimed matter from the mark. *See Schwarzkopf v. John H. Breck, Inc.*, 340 F.2d 978, 978, 144 USPQ 433, 433 (C.C.P.A. 1965); TMEP §1213.
>
> If applicant does not provide the required disclaimer, the USPTO may refuse to register the entire mark. *See In re Stereotaxis Inc.*, 429 F.3d 1039, 1040-41, 77 USPQ2d 1087, 1088-89 (Fed. Cir. 2005); TMEP §1213.01(b).
>
> Applicant should submit a disclaimer in the following standardized format:
>
> **No claim is made to the exclusive right to use "QUILT" apart from the mark as shown.**
>
> For an overview of disclaimers and instructions on how to satisfy this disclaimer requirement online using the Trademark Electronic Application System (TEAS) form, please go to http://www.uspto.gov/trademarks/law/disclaimer.jsp.

Example of "disclaimer required"

Now, sometimes people disclaim words in the application. Others wait to see what the examining attorney wants them to disclaim. It can be one word or a number of them. You will need to paste the examining attorney's disclaimer into your response.

DEEPER LOOK AT DISCLAIMERS

For more on disclaimers as part of an Office Action, see uspto.gov/trademarks/laws/how-satisfy-disclaimer-requirement#heading-4.

Likelihood of Confusion Refusal

The Office Action will explain the problem. You are encouraged to talk with an attorney, but what they are looking at are the du Pont factors (see Likelihood of Confusion or Dilution, page 73). The examining attorney will include information about what mark may be confusing. Let's take a look at one that we had with one of our trademarks for this project. You will respond (or your attorney will respond) to the Section 2(d) likelihood of confusion in a response to Office Action. Section 2(d) refers to the part of the trademark law related to likelihood of confusion, see Resources (page 196).

How should you and/or your attorney approach a 2(d) refusal? Make specific, fact-based points about:

- Why your trademark is not similar to the registered trademark in appearance, meaning, sound, or overall commercial impression

- How your goods or services are different, unrelated, or travel in different trademark channels from those the trademark examining attorney has suggested pose a likelihood of confusion

- How others besides the marks found by the examining attorney also use the same elements at issue

- The sophistication of the purchasers, explaining and giving proof that they will know the difference and that no likelihood of confusion exists.

- Amending your goods or services to narrow the description so that it doesn't conflict

- Plans to contact the owners of the conflicting mark to find out whether they will sign a "consent agreement" that they do not see a likelihood of confusion and are okay with you using it

- The status of the "confusing" mark: If it is "dead," let the examining attorney know

For our design mark for JUST WANNA QUILT, we had two issues. We had to disclaim *quilt*, which you saw in the previous section. In addition, the examining attorney brought up the likelihood of confusion. Fortunately, the mark that caused potential confusion was just our previous mark that we hadn't added to our application as a prior registration. We amended that, and we were good to go.

Descriptiveness Refusal

If the mark describes at least one significant function, attribute, or property of the goods or service, it may be found to be merely descriptive. Respond with fact-based points of why it is not merely descriptive. Or, you can change your application to a Section 2(f) claim: merely descriptive with secondary meaning.

In your response to the examining attorney, you can make an argument as to why your trademark is not merely descriptive. Be specific and fact-based in your argument.

Electric Quilt, a software company for designing quilts, received a descriptive refusal notice: "Here, the term at issue is merely descriptive because it describes the fact that the computer software is able to help you make an 'electric quilt' thereby describing the very goods that can or will be produced."

Electric Quilt overcame this issue by establishing that it had acquired distinctiveness. We look at this in more depth shortly.

Amend Your Application to Add a Section 2(f) Claim or to List It in the Supplemental Register

This response means that you will be required to establish secondary meaning for a merely descriptive mark (more than five years of use) or, alternatively, that you want it put on the Supplemental Register until that happens. To address this concern, see Responding to Office Actions (page 164).

Merely a Surname Refusal

We know that there is a test for whether something is merely a surname (see Merely a Surname, page 43). But now you have an Office Action that claims that your mark is merely a surname.

What do you do?

- If it is a rare surname, point that out. Using census data to show that it is not a common surname might help in your response to the Office Action.

- Search for other applications that use that surname to find out whether they got through.

- Include a design or other element to make it more than merely a surname.

- Consider having your mark put on the Supplemental Register until you can prove secondary meaning.

PART 3: YOUR APPLICATION

Specimen Refusal

Your specimen should have shown your mark on goods and/or services being used in commerce (see Step 8: Preparing Your Specimen, page 128), but something about it is not satisfying the requirements:

- The trademark does not appear on the specimen.

- The drawing of the mark and the mark on the specimen do not match.

- The mark is not associated with the goods and/or services.

- The specimen is a mockup, printer's proof, or digitally altered image.

- The specimen does not match the International Class.

- The specimen does not show the mark functioning as a mark or source identifier.

- The mark is merely ornamental.

- The specimen shows the mark as the title of a single creative work.

- The specimen indicates that the mark is the name of a process or system, rather than the source identifier for goods or services.

- The specimen is a web page and does not include the URL and date/time it was taken.

- The specimen is advertising for goods (not acceptable). (Advertising is okay for services.)

Note: Not all specimen issues are allowed to be fixed. The USPTO gives an example of a beer bottle label for a trademark application for wine.

What happens if you get a specimen refusal? You can make your case as to why the examining attorney is mistaken, or you can "substitute" a new specimen, which can include more than one example. You can also explain how the mark is used on the specimen in commerce and when it was on sale.

Generic, Commonly Used Phrase or Failure to Function as a Mark Refusal

This refusal encompasses a number of things. The examining attorney may believe that your mark is generic, is a commonly used phrase, warrants a merely geographic refusal or other geographic refusal, or is not actually functioning as a mark. It may also get flagged as "ornamental." The Office Action will provide guidance on what to do next, or you can take it to an attorney.

In addition to the reasons listed above, a few more reasons why you could have received this type of refusal include:

- It is or contains the flag or insignia of a nation, state, or municipality.

- It is or contains statutory words that are off limits.

- It is or contains the name, portrait, or signature of a living individual, and permission has not been obtained or submitted (the attorney will give you a chance to correct this).

- It is a widely used phrase, religious text, or popular meme.

The above list is not comprehensive.

> **HIRE AN ATTORNEY**
> These situations can be complex, and having an attorney who is experienced in addressing substantive rejections can make all the difference. If you find yourself in this position, you really should consider hiring a professional.

Other Kinds of Office Actions

In addition to nonfinal and final Office Actions, several other types of Office Actions may occur, including:

- **Examiner's Amendment.** This is something that was agreed to by phone or email that is added to your application by the examiner. Usually, you don't have to respond to these.

- **Suspension Letter.** Your application is put on hold because of something happening on your end, such as waiting for a foreign application to be issued or transferring ownership of the mark.

- **Notice of Incomplete Response.** You haven't signed the application. Often, law firms registering a mark for a client leave the signature blank until the signature is requested.

Responding to Office Actions

Go to your MyUSPTO home page, accessed through the same account you used to file your application. The column second from the left, "Trademark Docket," lists all of your correspondence, including applications and Office Actions. Select "Respond to correspondence from the USPTO." A lot of information is available on this home page. Forms are available in the far-left column, and additional help and information are located throughout. Just as you did for the original application form, find the related topic and supply the necessary information. The examining attorney may have explained exactly what to do; if so, be sure to use the text or information the examiner requested. In some instances, you may have a long response (for example, to a likelihood of confusion issue) for which you may need to upload a PDF.

Some issues may require some time to prepare a proper response. Do not leave addressing Office Actions until the last minute. This is equally true if you engage an attorney to help you address an Office Action. Allow enough time to prepare a thoughtful and complete response.

Response To Office Action
TEAS - Version 8.1

GENERAL FORM INFORMATION:
- **TIMEOUT WARNING:** You're required to log back in after 30 minutes of inactivity. This ensures the USPTO complies with mandatory federal information security standards and protects user information. After 25 minutes of inactivity, you will be prompted to continue your session. If you do not continue within 5 minutes, the session will end, you will be logged out of your USPTO.gov account, and you will lose any unsaved data in the form. Please have all of your information ready before you start.
- **DO NOT USE YOUR BROWSER BACK/FORWARD BUTTONS:** Use only the navigation buttons at the bottom of each page.
- **TIPS ON USING THIS FORM MOST EFFECTIVELY:** Click on any underlined (hyperlinked) terms for additional information.
- **REQUIRED FIELDS:** All have an ASTERISK (*), and the form will not validate if these fields are not filled-out.
- **EXTENSION OF TIME TO RESPOND:** One extension request per Office action can be made using the Request for Extension of Time to File a Response form **prior to filing a response**. Do **not** use this response form to request an extension of time to respond to the issued Office action.

TO ACCESS THE RESPONSE FORM:

STEP 1: CHECK STATUS.
To use this form, the "Current Status" of your application must be "A Non-final Action has been mailed." Use the Trademark Status & Document Retrieval (TSDR) to confirm the status before proceeding. If the application is not in the correct status, you must wait until the status is updated (usually 48-72 hours after receiving an email notice that an Office action has issued). Otherwise, you will receive an error message when you click the "Continue" button at the bottom of the page.

STEP 2: ENTER APPLICATION SERIAL NUMBER BELOW OR ACCESS PREVIOUSLY FILLED-OUT/SAVED FORM.

* Serial Number: → [   ] *(Do not enter serial number if you are accessing your saved form.)*

OR

To upload a previously saved form file, first review the TEAS Help instructions for accessing previously saved data and then use the "Browse..." button below to access the form file saved on your computer. WARNING: Failure to follow the TEAS Help instructions will result in the inability to edit your data.

> Do **NOT** upload or attach any other file(s) (for example, a specimen or foreign registration certificate) using the button below. You must upload other attachments within the proper section of the actual form, after answering "Yes" to the appropriate wizard question(s) on the next page.

[Choose File] No file chosen

[Continue]

Response to Office Action online form

You can see that you put in the serial number (step 2). The form contains detailed instructions, and the USPTO has released a video to help guide you: YouTube > USPTOvideo > TMIN News 14: Response to office action.

Filling out the form is a two-step process:

1. Answer the questions on the form to know what you need to fill in. This will correspond to the summary of issues list that you received in your Office Action.

Answer all the questions and/or provide the requested additional information, and then click "submit."

2. You will then get a second form that allows you to submit the information requested to resolve the Office Action.

Let's take another look at the Electric Quilt application. The examining attorney did not think that the design mark using Electric Quilt matched the specimen showing Electric Quilt 5:

> The drawing displays the mark as Electric Quilt. However, this differs from the display of the mark on the specimen, where it appears as Electric Quilt 5. The applicant cannot amend the drawing to conform to the display on the specimen because the character of the mark would be materially altered. 37 C.F.R. §2.72(a); TMEP §§807.14, 807.14(a) and 807.14(a)(i). Therefore, the applicant must submit a substitute specimen that shows use of the mark as it appears on the drawing. 37 C.F.R. §2.51; TMEP §807.14. The applicant must verify, with an affidavit or a declaration under 37 C.F.R. §2.20, that the substitute specimen was in use in commerce at least as early as the filing date of the application. 37 C.F.R. §§2.59(a) and 2.72(a); TMEP §904.09.

Don't be scared of the citations—TMEP and the like. These tell you where the examining attorney got the requirement. The TMEP is the Trademark Manual of Examining Procedure (see The Trademark Manual of Examining Procedure [TMEP], page 196). If you need further information, you can look up the legal citation and see what the problem is, and it may give you insight into how to solve it. In this case, the examining attorney's issue was easy enough to understand, and no digging was necessary.

The examining attorney also thought that the mark was merely descriptive. Let's see how Electric Quilt responded. You can find that under Response to Office Action.

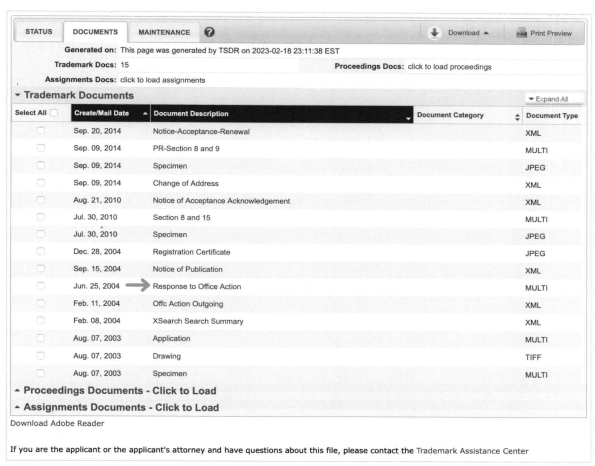

STATUS	DOCUMENTS	MAINTENANCE ❓		⬇ Download ▲	🖨 Print Preview

Generated on: This page was generated by TSDR on 2023-02-18 23:11:38 EST

Trademark Docs: 15

Proceedings Docs: click to load proceedings

Assignments Docs: click to load assignments

▼ Trademark Documents

▼ Expand All

Select All ☐	Create/Mail Date ▲	Document Description	Document Category	Document Type
☐	Sep. 20, 2014	Notice-Acceptance-Renewal		XML
☐	Sep. 09, 2014	PR-Section 8 and 9		MULTI
☐	Sep. 09, 2014	Specimen		JPEG
☐	Sep. 09, 2014	Change of Address		XML
☐	Aug. 21, 2010	Notice of Acceptance Acknowledgement		XML
☐	Jul. 30, 2010	Section 8 and 15		MULTI
☐	Jul. 30, 2010	Specimen		JPEG
☐	Dec. 28, 2004	Registration Certificate		JPEG
☐	Sep. 15, 2004	Notice of Publication		XML
☐	Jun. 25, 2004	➡ Response to Office Action		MULTI
☐	Feb. 11, 2004	Offc Action Outgoing		XML
☐	Feb. 08, 2004	XSearch Search Summary		XML
☐	Aug. 07, 2003	Application		MULTI
☐	Aug. 07, 2003	Drawing		TIFF
☐	Aug. 07, 2003	Specimen		MULTI

▲ Proceedings Documents - Click to Load
▲ Assignments Documents - Click to Load

Download Adobe Reader

If you are the applicant or the applicant's attorney and have questions about this file, please contact the Trademark Assistance Center

The TSDR document list for Electric Quilt's word mark application

Electric Quilt responded that it had acquired distinctiveness. Remember, merely descriptive with secondary meaning = acquired distinctiveness? That's what it said in its response, below. It also provided a supplemental specimen to support this claim.

The examining attorney refused registration based on 15 U.S.C. §1052(e)(1). The applicant wishes to meet this claim by verifying the acquired distinctiveness of the mark in question under 15 U.S.C. §1052(f) and 37 C.F.R. §2.20.

The mark has become distinctive of the goods through the applicant's substantially exclusive and continuous use in commerce for at least the five years immediately before the date of this statement.

The mark cannot be refused registration under 15 U.S.C. §1052(e)(1) because the mark has acquired distinctiveness in use in interstate commerce for at least ten years and is not excluded under 15 U.S.C. §§1052(a), (b), (c), (d), (e)(3), or (e)(5).

The applicant understands that the statement of distinctiveness above is sufficient only if it meets the provisions of TMEP §1212.05(a). Thus, the applicant asserts that the statement of distinctiveness above is sufficient in and of itself to establish acquired distinctiveness because the degree to which the mark is merely descriptive is relatively small. The mark only tangentially describes the purpose of the good, i.e. to assist the software user in creating designs for creative crafts. Specifically, the product facilitates the creative stitching of fabric into pieced and appliquéd crafts. Because the purpose of the good is described by "electric quilt" only in the abstract sense that a computerized process is at work within the general process of designing quilted crafts, the mark is only descriptive to a small degree. However, the mark does differentiate itself from the generic sense of "quilt" by signaling with "electric" that a technological, electronic, or computerized process is involved in the quilt designing process.

The applicant is also submitting a substitute specimen that shows use of the mark as it appears on the drawing because the original specimen differed from the drawing. The applicant verifies that the substitute specimen was in use in commerce at least as early as the filing date of the application. 37 CFR §2.59.

Response to establish secondary meaning

Take a closer look at Electric Quilt's acquired distinctiveness/merely descriptive with secondary meaning argument:

The examining attorney refused registration based on 15 U.S.C. §1052(e)(1). The applicant wishes to meet this claim by verifying the acquired distinctiveness of the mark in question under 15 U.S.C. §1052(f) and 37 C.F.R. §2.20. The examining attorney thought it was merely descriptive of the product, and so was requesting secondary meaning.

The mark has become distinctive of the goods through the applicant's substantially exclusive and continuous use in commerce for at least the five years immediately before the date of this statement. Notice the language "exclusive and continuous use for at least five years"? That's providing secondary meaning, which is required if a mark is considered merely descriptive.

The mark cannot be refused registration under 15 U.S.C. §1052(e)(1) because the mark has acquired distinctiveness in use in interstate commerce for at least ten years and is not excluded under 15 U.S.C. §§1052(a), (b), (c), (d), (e)(3), or (e)(5). Again the attorney is arguing that it has been in use across states (the requirement of the Commerce Clause) for more than the period required.

The applicant understands the statement of distinctiveness above... In this paragraph the attorney is stating that the substitute specimen makes it clearer what the mark is and what it is not.

CLAIMING ACQUIRED DISTINCTIVENESS
The USPTO gives you guidance on how to claim acquired distinctiveness under Section 2(f); see uspto.gov/trademarks/laws/how-claim-acquired-distinctiveness-under-section-2f-0.

But there's more. Electric Quilt also addressed the comment that *electric quilt* is merely descriptive of when "you make an 'electric quilt' thereby describing the very goods that can or will be produced." Here is the response:

> The applicant understands that the statement of distinctiveness above is sufficient only if it meets the provisions of TMEP §1212.05(a). Thus, the applicant asserts that the statement of distinctiveness above is sufficient in and of itself to establish acquired distinctiveness because the degree to which the mark is merely descriptive is relatively small. The mark only tangentially describes the purpose of the good, i.e. to assist the software user in creating designs for creative crafts. Specifically, the product facilitates the creative stitching of fabric into pieced and appliquéd crafts. Because the purpose of the good is described by "electric quilt" only in the abstract sense that a computerized process is at work within the general process of designing quilted crafts, the mark is only descriptive to a small degree. However, the mark does differentiate itself from the generic sense of "quilt" by signaling with "electric" that a technological, electronic, or computerized process is involved in the quilt-designing process.

In short, it explained that its product did not create "electric quilts" and therefore was only slightly descriptive.

Lastly, it submitted a substitute specimen to match the drawing (the mark applied for). Remember, the examining attorney had a problem with "Electric Quilt 5" being different from the design mark "Electric Quilt." Let's look at the substitute specimen.

The revised specimen separated the version number from the mark, making it clear what the mark is. Here, the application was for a word mark, ELECTRIC QUILT, but the original specimen did not match. The revised specimen did. See how in the original one, *5* looked like part of the mark? Now, it didn't.

Electric Quilt's original specimen

Electric Quilt's replacement specimen shows the name and version number separated.

Final Office Action

Final Office Actions are your second chance to fix an issue and the last time the issue will be addressed by the USPTO. Don't panic—just address the problem(s). If you do not, the application will be considered abandoned. You can also take it to the next step and file a timely appeal if you do not like the response of the examining attorney. If this is the case, you really do need an attorney, and this will cost time and money, without any guarantee of success.

OFFICE ACTIONS

Office Actions can seem scary. If you feel like you don't want to do this on your own, now is a good time to hire an attorney.

USPTO HELP FOR OFFICE ACTIONS

The USPTO has information you may find helpful regarding responding to Office Actions. Go to uspto.gov > Trademarks > Responding to Office actions.

The Trademark Trial and Appeal Board

If you have received a final rejection that you think is unfair, you can appeal the decision to the Trademark Trial and Appeal Board (TTAB). The TTAB is the review arm of the USPTO, made up of 27 judges appointed by the commerce secretary. Half are former trademark examiners. They consider around 600 cases each year and rarely reverse the examining attorney's decision. The TTAB is a specialty unto itself. If you feel like your final Office Action rejection is not fair and you want to pursue having it reviewed, this is definitely time to consult with an attorney for their advice and expertise. But also recognize that doing so will cost money, and the likelihood of your succeeding in reversing the rejection is low. A better path would be to talk to an attorney about why the rejection occurred and make alternative plans for protecting your brand and/or mark (for example, with design mark instead of a word mark because it was a generic term).

Office Actions Based on a Letter of Protest

Before the opposition period, someone can get wind that you are trying to register a mark and may file a *letter of protest* (LOP) during your application process. The USPTO allows third parties to file information that they think the agency should know about a particular application as part of the application process.

A third party might file a LOP for several reasons, including:

The likelihood of confusion with a pending or registered mark

The trademark is merely descriptive, generic, or misdescriptive or should have an element disclaimed on that basis. You don't want your competitor locking up a word you also want to use.

False association with a person, institution, belief, or national symbol. You think that this is just wrong or, worse, that it will falsely skew the competition in their favor.

The mark fails to function as a source identifier (for example, is a widely used slogan). Somehow the examining attorney is not aware that the mark describes something functional to your industry and is a widely used term. This can also run into the problem of something being generic but not caught by the examining attorney. For example, SEWCIAL was registered when it shouldn't have been, as it is not a source identifier for a business and is used by many people.

Not federally lawful use in commerce (for example, fabricated or digitally altered specimen). Fake trademarks are a big problem right now. Digitally altering something is a big problem. You don't want your products being used to obtain a fake trademark.

The mark is involved in pending litigation. You and your former business partner are now fighting about ownership of intellectual property, and your former partner tries to register the mark.

These are just a few examples. Note, common-law prior-use rights are not an appropriate reason to file a letter of protest. When a letter of protest is filed, it goes to a special part of the USPTO for review, where it is either filed for reference or passed on to the examining attorney to review and consider. LOPs are ideally filed before publication, at which time the examining attorney will review any LOP forwarded to them. But LOPs may also be filed during the "published for opposition" period, and this changes the stakes (see Published for Opposition, page 172). If a LOP is filed after publication, the evidence has to establish a case for refusal of the mark, and an Office Action will be issued.

MORE ON LETTERS OF PROTEST

For more on letters of protest, both filing them (when you have your trademark certificate and see others' marks that you oppose) and dealing with one filed against your mark, visit uspto.gov/trademarks/trademark-updates-and-announcements/letter-protest-practice-tip

Published for *Opposition*

You are getting very close to having an official trademark, but there is one more important step.

Once the Office Actions have been satisfied, the trademark examining attorney approves the mark for publication in the *Official Gazette*, published weekly by the USPTO at uspto. gov > learning and resources > official gazette. After your mark appears in the *Gazette*, any party that believes it may be damaged by the registration of your mark has 30 days from the publication date to file its opposition to the registration or request an extension of an additional 90 days to prepare its opposition. If someone objects to the registration of your mark, they pay a $600 fee per class and file a Notice of Opposition with the TTAB. The TTAB then begins a legal proceeding about the mark. If someone opposes your mark, a three-judge panel will make a decision after both sides present the evidence and make arguments in a legal brief before the TTAB.

HELP FOR OPPOSITION

If someone opposes your mark, it is time to get an attorney. This has become something greater than a DIY application.

If no one opposes your mark, it is likely now registered. If there had been a problem with its being generic or merely descriptive, those issues would have come up during the Office Action process.

Filing a *State* Trademark Application

In the Introduction, we mentioned that one option was to apply for a state trademark. This is a cheaper and often faster alternative to registering federally.

You might also elect to pursue a state trademark registration because:

- It can be a bridge while waiting for a federal trademark to be completed.

- It puts others on notice that you are using the mark, even if just at the state level.

- You have no plans to operate outside your state, even with tourists, or a website.

- You want to go to state court or have the opportunity to do so.

You may not use a registered symbol (®) with a state trademark, only a federal trademark. For a state trademark, use the trademark symbol (™) for goods or the service mark (℠) for services. You can have a federal and a state trademark.

What is interesting is that the application for each state mimics the federal trademark system in many ways!

The Illinois form is a good example (to view the form for yourself, jump to ilsos.gov/publications/pdf_publications/tmsm15.pdf).

It requires the same basic information as the federal application, including:

- Registrant's contact information and type (individual or other)

- Name, type, and description of the mark

- The specific goods or services provided by the mark

- Classification number (which turns out to be the ICs you already know!)

- How the trademark or service mark is used

- Date of first use

- Acknowledgment of any previous owners or users of the mark

STATE TRADEMARK SYSTEMS

To find more information about applying for a trademark in a particular state, the USPTO has created a database of links. Go to uspto.gov/trademarks/basics/state-trademark-information-links.

Trademarks *Outside* the United States

Trademark is considered a property right, and with property rights, the space of protection is based on the territory of a particular country. A U.S. trademark application only applies to the United States. There's no such thing as an international trademark. We will look at how you register works in other countires, and we also look at something called the Madrid Protocol, which makes it easier to apply for trademarks around the world.

Since trademark rights are territorial, a U.S. trademark registration only protects a mark in this country. There are several strategies and mechanisms for registering a mark overseas, but each is distinct.

The most straightforward way is to file national applications outside the U.S. on a country-by-country basis. There is also a process by which you can file an application for an International Registration under a trademark treaty to which the U.S. belongs, called the Madrid Protocol.

> *Since trademark rights are territorial, a U.S. trademark registration only protects a mark in the United States.*

Under the Madrid Protocol, you can seek to extend the protection of that International Registration to other countries that are also members of the Protocol.

However, for the first five years after registration your International Registration, and all the extensions to other countries, are "dependent" on your US registration. If something goes wrong with your U.S. trademark, your foreign marks are potentially also in jeopardy.

Lastly, there's the Paris Convention, a different trademark treaty to which the U.S. belongs, which allows a U.S. applicant to get a favorable filing date for their overseas application, so long as the foreign application is filed within six months of the corresponding U.S. application for the same mark. This is called a Paris Convention "priority claim" and it simply gives your foreign application an early effective date.

Applications in Other Countries

You can get a trademark for a specific country or sometimes a set of countries. For instance, you can get a trademark in Germany, and you can also apply for a European Union (EU) trademark because the EU has created a *community mark*, a special trademark that can be used across all EU countries. This chapter introduces you to the application process for trademarks around the world, particularly once you have filed a trademark in the United States. You'll want to register for a foreign trademark when you are doing business in a foreign country, and you want your trademark protected. Weighing the cost or time it takes is a business decision. Trademarks are territorial, meaning that your U.S. trademark only protects you in the United States. If you are doing substantial business or feel

the need to protect your mark in another country, you must file a trademark application for that country.

BEYOND THE UNITED STATES

If you are thinking about trademarks outside the United States, you should think about hiring an attorney with international experience or experience in the country where you are seeking registration. They can take care of all of the searching, the application, and other steps.

The Madrid Protocol

If you are considering filing on your own or just want to get the lay of the land, you will like the *Madrid Protocol*, an international system for obtaining trademark protection in up to 122 countries and/or regions by using a single application (for a fee for each, of course). The idea of filing a trademark in a foreign country may seem daunting, but the Madrid Protocol can make it more manageable. You can use this system if you have already filed a U.S. trademark application. Madrid then sends your U.S. application to your chosen countries, where it is processed under the same information you provided to the USPTO.

MORE ON THE MADRID PROTOCOL

Not every country has joined this treaty. Which countries are included? Here is a list: wipo.int/treaties/en/ShowResults.jsp?lang=en&treaty_id=8. You also can find out more about rates and other requirements. Each country requires a fee, and the USPTO also charges a fee. It can get expensive, so talk with an expert about which countries you actually need to apply in and make smart business choices.

Timing

You must file your trademark application in the United States before filing in other countries. If you file with the Madrid Protocol within six months of your U.S. application, you can use the filing date from your U.S. application. This will give you a competitive advantage because it is an earlier priority date, which may come in handy if you are trying to be the senior mark and there is competition for that position with your mark.

One way of doing this is to pay for a country-by-country search with a professional company. The most widely used professional services are CompuMark and Markify. Professional searches can be expensive, but they are thorough, and you'll have a report from a third party.

Bundled Countries

Under the Madrid Protocol, a number of marks include more than one country:

- **Benelux (BX)** covers Belgium, Luxembourg, and the Netherlands.
- **EM** includes the 28 EU member states, often called a community mark.
- **African Intellectual Property Organization (OA)** covers 17 member states.

More on the EU Community Mark

You can register your mark as a community mark, giving you protection in all EU countries. The hitch is that your mark has to be accepted in all of them to gain the mark. If Poland, for example, rejects your mark, you will not gain the community mark. Instead, you will then have to file in each country where you would like a mark. It's a gamble but can save you money if your mark goes through. If you do a professional search of the EU beforehand to make sure that your mark is available, you likely will have better luck getting through the process.

With the United Kingdom (UK) leaving the EU system, it is no longer included in the EU Community mark. Even when the UK was part of the EU, it was considered wise to file through Madrid in each country we really cared about, along with the community mark. So, we filed for an EU community mark as well as a mark in the UK and a few other countries.

Canada and Trademark

Canada recently joined the Madrid Protocol, making it easy to file an application. Before, you had to find a Canadian trademark attorney and then go through this country's unique process, which was a bit expensive.

However, you can still file directly with Canada and not use Madrid, but you will have to hire a Canadian attorney. Your choice may come down to the cost. Filing a Madrid application will cost at least $900 for the application alone, along with any fee for the individual country you choose. You'll need to weigh the cost of using the Madrid Protocol system against the cost of hiring local counsel in Canada. It still might be less expensive to file directly with a Canadian lawyer.

And if you are Canadian? You can file in Canada. The system looks much the same. You can also file in the United States, either through the Madrid Protocol (through the Canadian trademark office) or directly. If you file directly, you will need a U.S. attorney.

CANADIAN RESOURCES

You can search the records and find out more about trademarks in Canada here: ic.gc.ca/eic/site/cipointernet-internetopic.nsf/eng/h_wr00002.html. Canadians who want to file a trademark can get started at canada.ca/en/services/business/ip.html.

How Much Does It Cost to File a Madrid Protocol Application?

The Madrid Protocol offers a fee calculator at wipo.int/madrid/en/fees/calculator.jsp. It's fun to play with. But note that you must pay a fee for each country or bundle of countries, and there is an additional application fee for the USPTO.

You choose the type of transaction (new application), your office of origin (your home country), the number of classes covered by your mark, whether it is a collective or certification mark, and whether it is in color.

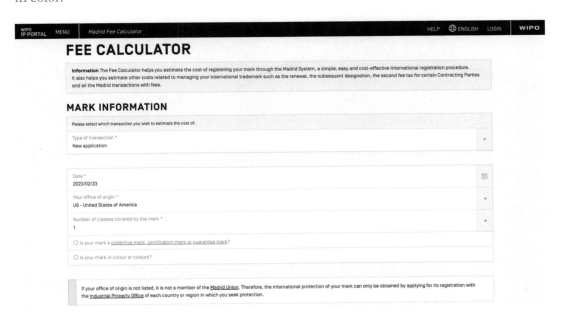

Then, you can choose as many countries as you want. For this example, we chose Estonia.

Click "calculate," and the tool estimates your cost. The total is in Swiss francs, so be sure to look at the exchange rate, which you can do using an online calculator.

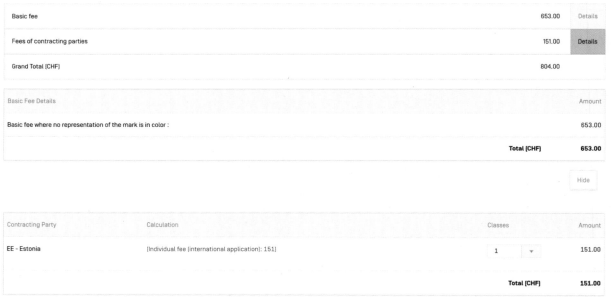

In addition to the fees for the Madrid Protocol, an additional $100 per class is paid to the USPTO. Because you file through the USPTO, it requires a processing fee. For U.S. applicants, the USPTO has the TEASi form, available at uspto. gov/trademarks-application-process/filing-online/trademark-electronic-application-system-teasi-online.

BEWARE OF SCAMS!

Again, just like when you file with the USPTO, once you file with the Madrid Protocol, you will start receiving all kinds of materials in the mail that are not official **but look official.** Do not be fooled. If in doubt, you can contact madridlegal@wipo. int and ask for verification. These fake notices often are styled to look as though they come from the country in which you have filed. The scams are nasty and often seek more money.

We have seen these fraudulent notices at the application and at the renewal stages. When something comes in the mail, email the address above to check whether it is legitimate. **Always.**

BAD PARABLE

PART IV
Your Trademark: What's Next?

You have registered your trademark. You have received a certificate. Now what? Part IV takes you quickly through life after you have completed the application stage and are the proud owner of a U.S. trademark.

In this part, we discuss a few of the elements to think about once you have been awarded a mark from the USPTO, including:

- **Your certificate.** What you can do now that you have a trademark certificate, besides print it out and frame it.

- **Maintaining your mark.** What you need to do so that you do not lose your mark, including policing your mark and renewing it.

- **Your trademark out in the world.** Learn what others can and cannot do with your mark and what you can do about unlawful use.

- **Licensing your trademark.** Get a quick overview of the elements of licensing your trademark for use by a third party.

- **Changing or expanding your trademark.** You may find your goods and/or services expanding, or you want to change the look of your logo. We give you pointers to be sure that your trademarks keep up.

This book gets you started, and Part IV helps point you in the direction of the next adventures with your trademark and brand. What excitement lies ahead!

Your *Certificate*

Once your trademark is officially registered, you will receive an electronic version of your certificate.

When you do, a few things are now true:

- Your trademark is listed in the federal database so that everyone can see that you own it and in which class(es). This is super-important.

- There is now a legal presumption that you own the trademark and have the right to use it.

- You can use this registration as the basis for foreign applications (see Trademarks Outside the United States, page 174).

- You can bring a trademark lawsuit in federal court.

- You can now use ® with your trademark (see Using the Registered Symbol, page 182).

- You can now record your registration with U.S. Customs and Borders Protection to prevent the unauthorized importation of goods with an infringing mark.

The Power of Registration

In Part I, we talk about the power of registration. Let's do it again! What do you get for all of your work in getting the application through?

Let's see whether this makes more sense now:

- **Rule the world.** Well, okay, you claim ownership of a trademark in a specific class nationwide, except where someone was previously using it locally or in a particular state, where they can continue to use it.

- **Give notice to everyone that you own the mark.** You can let the world know by including a registered mark ® on your products, services, and/or company. That tells the world that the trademark has been registered with the USPTO.

- **Strengthen your position.** After five years, your trademark becomes stronger, "incontestable," so if someone challenges your use, you are in a better position to win.

- **Claim ownership.** A trademark gives you the legal presumption that you are the owner.

- **Gain priority.** Promptly file an application for the same trademark in other countries through the Madrid Protocol system, and you'll get to use your earlier U.S. application date (see Trademarks Outside the United States, page 174).

- **Keep imposters out.** Register your registered trademark with the U.S. Customs Office to keep infringing works out of the country.

- **Collect larger damages.** In a trademark lawsuit, you are more likely to collect larger damages if your mark is federally registered.

- **Better defend your trademark.** If someone starts using your trademark, and you send a cease-and-desist letter, it has more strength and substance, and the other party is more likely to stop infringing because you have a federal trademark. This includes the ability to file a notice and takedown with social media platforms if someone is infringing on your trademark. Some platforms require registration numbers to do so.

Using the Registered Symbol

Now that you have been granted your mark, you can use the ® registered symbol for goods and services. You can place the ® symbol anywhere near the trademark, but most place it in the upper-right-hand corner of your goods or services. Using the registered symbol alerts the world that it is a registered trademark.

If you use the registered mark and someone infringes, they cannot claim to be an innocent infringer. The damages you might receive in a lawsuit would be higher because the other party would be considered a willful infringer. If there is a dispute, you'll forfeit lost profits and actual money damages unless you can prove that the defendant had actual knowledge that your mark is registered because there was no notice.

Do I Have to Use It Every Time?

It is not necessary to use the registered symbol every time you use your mark. That is true of a TM mark as well. You should include the ® or TM at least once on the product or service to alert people that it is a registered mark.

For example, Mattel, a toy company, trademarks the names of the characters in their fashion line dolls MONSTER HIGH. So, characters like DRACULAURA, a fictional vampire teenager, often have the TM next to their names, despite having a registered mark on the name. But these dolls come with small diaries where the gimmick is the characters have written about their lives and their friends. It would be weird if inside these diaries they included the TM next to every registered character name.

Monster High doll packaging versus the product diary

Maintaining Your Mark

As a trademark owner, you have a number of maintenance obligations. They don't come up very often, and you should receive advance notice from the USPTO. These obligations are the key to keeping and strengthening your mark.

> *If you don't properly maintain your mark, it could be canceled or tagged as abandoned.*

Maintain Your Information

The USPTO contacts you through email, so be sure to keep that up to date. Also, if you receive anything in the mail from someone *other than the USPTO*, go to your USPTO account to find out whether you need to do something. When there is an Office Action or renewal date, you will suddenly get tons of mail from third parties. Receiving these third-party notices may indicate that you have something to address. Go to your account to check.

When do you need to contact the USPTO? When your address changes, when you transfer ownership of the mark, when you change your attorney, when you change your email address, and so forth.

Use It or Lose It

Make sure to continuously use your trademark. If there is no activity for more than three years, the USPTO may consider it abandoned, and you could lose it. Having goods available for sale is enough. You will have to show the mark in use periodically, and you could get randomly audited during a renewal period.

Don't Become Generic

Make sure that your mark does not become generic. As a reminder, that is when people are using your mark to describe the general goods during that time (see Generic, page 40). This happened to both ESCALATOR and ASPIRIN. We worried about this problem with our DURATIONATOR copyright system. Someone in Israel ran into me and said, "We have our own Durationator now." I quickly corrected her, explaining that Durationator was a brand name, not a thing. That's what you want to make sure you are expressing and policing. Google is a search engine, but not all search engines are Google.

Police Your Mark

You *must* police your mark. If others start to use your mark without your permission and you do not stop them, you can see how your mark won't actually reflect the goodwill that you are providing. You can sign up for services that help you do this. Put a Google alert on uses of your mark or pay for a trademark watch service, which will let you know if others are using your mark to apply for their own. But, most importantly, know your community and make sure that people are not using your mark as a noun or a verb. The mark has to stand for something, and if others start to use it without your permission, your mark loses meaning.

License Your Mark

You can license your mark if you want to or give permission for its use—just make sure that you keep the branding consistent. Again, make sure to police the licensees, or your mark could be classified as naked or blanket (meaning that it has no meaning and doesn't indicate that it is a source identifier), and then it will lose its significance as representing goodwill for your products or services, which puts you in jeopardy of losing the mark (see Licensing Your Trademark, page 191).

Your Fifth Year

Once you have had your mark for five years, you must file two forms with the USPTO, which you can do online through your MyUSPTO account. You will get a notice by mail from the USPTO when it's time. **Make sure to file on time, between the fifth and sixth years.** This is super-important. Don't be late. You will need to file two forms:

Section 8 declaration. This declaration states that you are still using the mark. If you do not file this declaration on time, the mark will be canceled, and you won't be able to get incontestable status for another five years!

Section 15 declaration. This declaration confirms that you have been using the mark continuously in the same manner with the same kinds of goods for five years. When you file your Section 15 declaration, your mark becomes **incontestable**, meaning that it is stronger and safer from attack. Someone might sue you for trademark infringement, but the courts will look at your incontestability status as pointing in your favor. It's like leveling up.

Go to your MyUSPTO account and look for a notice that you need to renew. The notice will provide instructions for filing Section 8 and Section 15 declarations. As of 2023, the fee is $425 per class for the on-time filing of the combined Sections 8 and 15 declarations. For an additional fee of $100, you can have a filing extension of six months. Failure to file these forms at that time will result in the cancellation of the registration.

Renew Every Ten Years

Your trademark must be renewed every ten years. Go to your MyUSPTO account to look for a notice that you need to renew. Again, you will fill out a Section 8 declaration, this time along with a Section 9 renewal application. As of 2023, the fee is $525 per class for the on-time filing of the combined Sections 8 and 9 declarations. All of this is done online, just like the forms at the five-year mark. Failure to file these forms will result in the cancellation of the registration.

Post-Registration Audit Program

In 2017, the USPTO began the Post-Registration Audit Program, wherein it randomly audits trademarks for use in commerce. If you are audited, you will be required to prove use of your mark. If you cannot show use, you must pay a $250 deletion fee per class and potentially a $100 deficiency charge, or your registration may be canceled. About half of the marks audited are canceled, but not all marks are audited. To be audited, you must fall into one of two categories: you have one class with four or more goods or services and you timely filed Section 9 or 71 declarations of use; or your registration has two classes with two or more goods. Most of us do not fall into this category, so this is not something to worry about. Moreover, the audit period happens when you are renewing your trademark, not in the immediate years after registration. Audits are performed by audit examiners using a random algorithm. If selected, you must show proof of use in commerce, the same way you would prepare a specimen for an application (see Step 8: Preparing Your Specimen, page 128).

Monitor Published for Opposition Applications

We discussed the possibility that someone could issue a letter of protest during the application or published for opposition stage against your mark (see Office Actions Based on a Letter of Protest, page 171). You can/should do that too! Some people don't monitor their marks, while others are obsessed.

If you find an application for a mark that you believe infringes on yours, you can file a LOP during that party's application stage or during the published for opposition stage. There is a $50 filing fee for a LOP. If you file a LOP during the examination (application) period, you are providing evidence that is relevant to possible refusal of the registration. That information may or may not be passed along to the examining attorney.

The bar of required evidence is set higher once the mark has been published for opposition, as what you suggest will lead to an Office Action during that stage. If you file your LOP within the 30-day period after the mark in question was published for opposition, the evidence must establish a prima facie case for refusal of registration. What is a prima facie case? That means that it is legally sufficient to establish a fact or cause to issue an Office Action.

To file a letter of protest, log in to your USPTO account and follow the directions supplied at teas.uspto.gov/ccr/lop/.

Your *Trademark* Out in the World

Your trademark

power is not

absolute.

This chapter is about the balance between what others can and cannot do with your mark.

You have received your certificate. You are on top of the world, until suddenly people are using your trademark in ways that you didn't expect or want. In this chapter, we explain which things people can do with your trademark and what to do if you believe that they are infringing. Again, this book is just the beginning. Consult more books or an attorney if you have further questions or concerns.

Permissible Uses

You do not have absolute control over your mark: Like children or pets, it interacts with the world in a variety of ways. Some public uses of your mark are allowed, even without your permission.

First Sale Doctrine

Once someone purchases your goods, they own that object. This means that they can give it away, sell it, burn it, destroy it, and even possilby turn it into art. You don't control the object any longer. That does not mean that the purchaser has any rights related to the trademark or other underlying intellectual property. There are questions about how far someone can go in making art with the objects they buy, and particularly in selling them. It gets complicated fast. If a piece of art is commenting and criticizing (copyright terms), you are likely to find a fair use (another copyright term). There is an intersection of copyright and trademark, but that, my friend, is for another book.

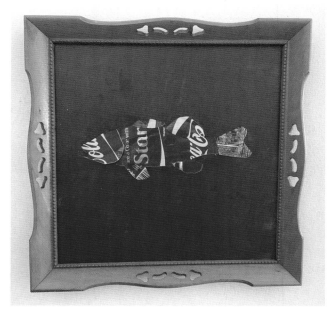

Fish Lake by Keira Cerda is an example of using found objects, in this case a Coke can, to create art work. The trademark is distinct from the object, the coke can, and in this case, now the fish!

Nominative Use

People can use your mark to discuss your mark. You have to name things. Elizabeth is a Professor at Tulane University (a registered trademark), and Sid is an undergraduate at the School of the Art Institute of Chicago (also a registered trademark). In both instances, we must use the trademark to name our affiliations. One famous case on this very issue is about a former Playboy Playmate of the Year. The court found that she could use the designation Playboy Playmate of the Year, but she went too far and plastered the phrase all over her website. Although she could use it to cite her affiliation, she could not use it over and over as a decoration. You can name the trademark, but you can't decorate with it.

Another classic case on nominative use regards a quiz about the band New Kids on the Block: The court said that the quiz could name the boys to allow readers to choose which was their favorite. All nominative use means is that you have to be able to name the thing you are talking or writing about.

This is also the part of the law that allows you to compare products, such as Crest toothpaste versus Colgate. Nominative use allows you to comment or criticize a brand *using their mark*. How else would you understand the politically charged problems of Nike if the company couldn't be named?

So, if you say, "Amazon has become the largest bookseller in the world," that's nominative use. No one would think that Amazon has endorsed your product based on that statement. We employ nominative use all the time.

Descriptive Fair Use

Descriptive fair use allows someone else to use your trademark when your trademark is merely descriptive. Remember all of that? (See Acquired Distinctiveness, page 37). If you have used something that stands as your source identifier but is also descriptive of the product, others may use the term to describe their product, as long as it is not in a way that would be confusing to the public. They are using it not as a source identifier but as a description of a good or service. These usually apply to marks that were merely descriptive but have acquired a secondary meaning. PARK 'N FLY has acquired distinctiveness after five years. Another company at the airport could describe its business as "Park and fly here." That would not infringe on PARK 'N FLY because the second use is not a source identifier but descriptive of the product. See why a mark that is merely descriptive with secondary meaning is not as strong?

First Amendment and Fair Use

Someone can use your mark to comment or criticize your original mark. This goes one step further than just naming the mark. It means that others can use your mark in their art, in some situations, without your permission. A good example is *Mattel, Inc., v. MCA Records, Inc.,* regarding the Aqua song "Barbie World." Mattel objected to the use of its BARBIE trademark in the song and song title, but the court upheld that the use constituted free speech because the song was commenting on and criticizing the lifestyle of Barbie. It goes further than nominative use (naming) to provide the ability for all of us to comment on, and criticize, the world around us.

Can artists use trademarks within their work? One court decided that an artist could depict trademarks in paintings, but they couldn't sell merchandise with that trademark based on those paintings. *University of Alabama v. Moore* was a battle over First Amendment rights and the university's trademark rights. The court, in that case, turned to *Rogers v. Grimaldi*, a case wherein Ginger Rogers sued a filmmaker for using her name in a film's title, *Ginger and Fred*, claiming false endorsement of the film. The court ruled that no one would think that Ginger Rogers was endorsing the film, so the film title was a protected use of her name. The court in the *Moore* case concluded that it had to "weigh the public interest in free expression against the public interest in avoiding consumer confusion." So, if an artist uses a trademark, the Lanham Act (trademark law) is not violated, "unless the use of the mark has no artistic relevance to the underlying work whatsoever, or if it has some artistic relevance unless it explicitly misleads as to the source or content of the work." So, Moore was allowed to use the University of Alabama uniforms in a realistic picture without a license because it had artistic relevance, and he was not misleading

as to the source. However, if he sold mugs with the painting, the public might believe that the University was the source (a licensing deal). As of 2023, the U.S. Supreme Court has taken up the boundaries of trademark and the First Amendment, and so we await the outcome.

In conclusion, the First Amendment and fair use are both big topics, beyond the scope of this book. But recognize that people can comment or criticize, and even parody your mark. We want that in a democracy. Think *Saturday Night Live*.

Infringing Use

If you find someone else's use of your mark that you suspect is infringing, consider whether their use of the mark is likely to cause confusion. To do so, you can use the same test you did on your own mark when preparing to file your application (see Likelihood of Confusion or Dilution, page 73). But note that the actual test is slightly different, depending on which circuit you are in. Those differences often matter.

Although trademark is federal law, the different circuits rule and make up tests that are slightly different. When your application is examined, the USPTO uses the *Du Pont* factors because the federal circuit (where the USPTO is) uses those as the likelihood-of-confusion test for trademarks. However, the evaluation of your application may be different than the court's test in the event of a lawsuit. It might be best to consult an attorney.

Geographic Boundaries
of United States Courts of Appeals and United States District Courts

The circuit jurisdictions in the United States—which circuit do you live in?

At right is a map of the U.S. circuits. Each circuit court has its own specific test, with its own specific name, for the likelihood of confusion. It can be quite complex.

TESTS BY STATE

For more on the different circuit tests for the likelihood of confusion, see thebillinglife.com/blog/likelihoodofconfusiontestsbycircuit.

You can do a few things to stop infringing behavior.

Cease and Desist

You can write the offending party a letter. Lawyers are good for this! You need to let the other party know that you have a registered trademark and that they are infringing. There are many options for writing a cease and desist: threatening, offering a license to them, or even extending kindness. By this point in the book, you are probably able to guess what comes next: Writing these letters is an art, and you need legal advice—hire an attorney.

Communicate

You might try just reaching out to see what they say. Again, you might ask an attorney first.

LAWYER TIME

This book focuses on applying for a trademark. Someone can infringe upon your mark in several other ways. If you suspect that this has happened, it may be time to consult an attorney.

Notice and Take Down

If the infringing use is on a social media platform, such as Facebook, you can sometimes file a notice-and-takedown request. Let's take a look at the notice and takedown mechanism at Facebook, available at facebook.com/help/contact/634636770043106. You'll choose whether the issue is related to copyright or trademark.

You will also provide the following information:

- Your relationship to the trademark
- Your contact information
- Name of the rights owner (make sure that this matches the registration)
- A link to the rights owner's official online presence
- Information about the trademark, including which country it is registered in, the registration number, and a link to the trademark registration
- To attach a copy of the trademark registration certificate or screenshot of the registration on the USPTO website

Then, you'll report the content and why you believe it is infringing, with a link to the infringing work.

You'll also electronically sign a declaration statement: "By submitting this notice, you state that you have a good faith belief that the reported use described above, in the manner you have complained of, is not authorized by the intellectual property rights owner, its agent, or the law; that the information contained in this notice is accurate; and, under penalty of perjury, that you are authorized to act on behalf of the owner of the intellectual property rights at issue."

Trademark Report Form

A trademark is a word, slogan, symbol or design (for example: a brand name or logo) that a person or company uses to distinguish their products or services from those offered by others. This form is to be used only for reporting alleged infringements of your trademark rights. Abuse of this form may result in the termination of your account.

- ⦿ Continue with my trademark report
- ◯ I found content that I believe offers counterfeit goods

Describe your relationship to the rights owner.

- ⦿ I am the rights owner.
- ◯ I am reporting on behalf of my organization or client.
- ◯ I am reporting on behalf of someone else.

Your Contact Information

Note that we regularly provide the rights owner's name, your email address and the nature of your report to the person who posted the content you are reporting. This person may use the information you provide to contact you. For this reason, you may wish to provide a valid generic business or professional email address.

Your full name

Mailing address

Email address

Please provide a valid email address that can be used to contact you. This may be a professional or business email address. Keep in mind the reported party may use this email to contact you.

Confirm your email address

Name of the rights owner

This may be your full name or the name of the organization for whom you are the authorized representative.

Please provide a link to the rights owner's official online presence.

(Ex: website, Facebook Page, etc.)

http://

What is the trademark?

Please provide information for one trademark at a time. You will have an opportunity to list additional trademarks at the end of this section.

Where is the trademark registered (if applicable)?

--Select an option--

What is the trademark registration number (if applicable)?

If possible, also provide a link (URL) leading directly to the trademark registration.

Attachment

If possible, please provide a scanned copy of your trademark registration certificate(s) or screenshot of your registration on the website or database of the applicable national or community intellectual property office(s). Please note that we only support the following file formats: JPG, GIF, PNG, TIFF and PDF.

Choose Files   no files selected

- ☐ I have additional trademarks.

Content You Want to Report

Why do you believe this content infringes rights owner's trademark rights?

- ☐ This photo, video, post or story uses rights owner's trademark.
- ☐ This ad is using rights owner's trademark.
- ☐ Rights owner's trademark is used in the username.
- ☐ Other

Facebook's notice-and-takedown form

Other social media platforms have similar processes. Notice that the Facebook form asked, "Where is your mark registered?" in addition to the registration number and the category of goods/services covered by your registration. This is why registration is so important!

TAKEDOWNS MAY NEED AN ATTORNEY

If you report infringing or counterfeit behavior, the platform takes down the post, site, or other infringing content.

However, the infringer can make an argument that their use is permissible (for example, they have a license, it constitutes fair use, or it is in the public domain). If this happens, then the infringing behavior may resume.

As the trademark owner, you have 14 days to file a complaint in federal court. If you do not, the behavior can continue. You have to decide how serious you are about complaining, and then if you are, you must pursue legal action **very quickly**. If you are in this situation, it is time to consult and hire a lawyer. These are the requirements for copyright notice and takedown by law, and many platforms have adopted them also for trademarks.

Licensing Your Trademark

One of the benefits of having a federal registration is clear proof that you, indeed, have the right to use the mark. This is particularly useful when you are licensing the use of the mark to third parties.

A license allows a third party to use your mark on products and services. You can also license your right of publicity—your look, name, likeness, and so forth. Right of publicity is about you; the mark is about your products and services. Ideally, you would create a licensing contract (rather than merely a handshake deal). Why? Because it will help both parties understand the parameters of the relationship and also provide a roadmap of what happens if something goes wrong or when it is time to end the relationship.

The Licensing Agreement

In a licensing agreement, key elements need to be defined. Most importantly, which marks are being licensed? This should be made clear. You should include the registered and unregistered marks that are part of the agreement. You should include whether there are certain requirements for use of the trademark and whether you require the licensee to use it as a word, design, or word/design mark. You should include a description of the goods and services of the license.

A trademark license agreement can be in the form of a letter or a contract to authorize a third party to use your trademark in specific circumstances.

In either form, the agreement should include:

- The parties. Who owns the mark (licensor) and who is licensing the mark (licensee)?

- Allowed use of the trademark (this can be set forth in an attached document called an appendix or schedule A). This would include information about the marks being licensed and the agreed-upon use.

- Terms and conditions of the license, including:

    Purpose of the use

    Term of the contract and whether it is renewable

    Any limitations or restrictions

- Whether the licensee must get the licensor's approval on any products or service where the mark appears.

- Whether the license is exclusive (only the licensee can use it) or nonexclusive (the licensor can license the use of the mark to others).

- What the license includes: manufacture, promotion, distribution, sale, and/or advertising?

- How to use the mark. Does the licensor require the use of a registered mark, and, if so, where should it be placed? What should the trademark notice include?

    Example: "Made by _ under a license from _. [mark] is a registered trademark of."

- Where the licensed goods/services can be sold. Is there a territory limitation? Only retail or also wholesale? On the Internet or in person?

- A statement that the licensor cannot use the mark in any way that would denigrate, disparage, tarnish, present in a false light, or otherwise reflect negatively on the mark or the licensor.

- How the licensee is to pay the licensor for use of the mark. Include the type of payment: Is it a lump sum, a percentage of the sale, or another arrangement? How does the payment occur?

- Warranty and indemnifications.

- Ownership. The licensor states that they own the trademark. Include the registration number and in which countries the registration has been secured.

- Term of the license and whether it is renewable.

- Whether the licensor has the right to sub-license the trademark.

- Which state's laws govern the agreement.

- A statement that the letter constitutes the entire agreement, not anything said outside the agreement.

- How the license can be revoked or terminated and the required timing (for example, if notice of revoking it is given, is there a 30-day waiting period?).

- Whether there is a sell-off period once the agreement has terminated (for example, the licensor can sell the remaining inventory for six months). What happens during that time?

- Any marketing and sales requirements of either the licensor or licensee.

These are just a few examples of the terms you could find in a trademark license agreement. And you know what we are going to write next...

LAWYER FOR LICENSING DEALS

If you are entering into a license agreement, it is a good time to have a lawyer do a contract review. You can make a list of the things that matter to you, and your attorney can look it over for general issues and for what you care about. You can also have a lawyer involved in the negotiations, but many times, craft entrepreneurs are handling these kinds of things themselves. If you are going to invest in an attorney, reviewing your contract is a great time to do it.

Do You Need to Have Your Trademark Registered to License It?

You do not necessarily have to have a registered trademark to license it. You can still license your goods and services without a trademark, but you won't get the same federal protection for the mark. It can be much more difficult to successfully file notices and takedowns and stop infringing goods at the border. Someone else might use it or even register it, and then you may not have recourse. What if your rival registered instead of you? However, we see many examples of companies licensing their mark to third parties without having a trademark in place.

Changing or *Expanding* Your Trademark

Building Your Brand

As you build your business, you may find yourself wanting to expand your trademarks to add additional registered marks. You can do this at any time—just go through the application steps again, with one key difference: You must let the USPTO know that you have previously filed a trademark. You will have the option in the application to list the serial numbers of any related trademarks. That way, the trademark examiner doesn't end up sending an Office Action.

If you forget to include the previous registration on your subsequent application, all is not lost. For instance, when we first filed for JUST WANNA QUILT, it was a word mark. A few years later, we filed for a design mark for the logo. As part of the second mark, we had to include in our application, "The applicant claims ownership of active prior U.S. Registration Number(s) 8842132." In this case, we did it by amendment after we were asked to do so in an Office Action. The trademark examining attorney asked whether we were also the owner of the first mark. So, you have two bites at the apple: on the application itself and on a potential Office Action from the USPTO. In our case, we confirmed that we were the same party, and all was resolved.

Abandoning a Mark

You can also stop using a mark. You may have closed one business, or maybe you have a different logo, or you have put in a new application for an updated mark. We see this all the time. For any number of reasons, you may decide not to continue with the old mark. In these cases, you can abandon it.

Transferring Ownership of a Mark

You can also transfer ownership of the mark, but you need to record the reassignment with the USPTO. You can change ownership through the Electronic Trademark Assignment System (ETAS) at etas.uspto. gov. There, you'll create a cover sheet by completing an online form and attaching the supporting legal documents.

You will be asked:

- For the conveyance type—how are you transferring ownership?

- Whether multiple properties are being transferred

- For your correspondence information (your contact information)

- For information about the conveying party (where does the ownership begin) and whether it is an individual or a company

- For information about the receiving party (who is the new owner?)

- For the serial number for each property being transferred

- To attach the legal document showing the change in ownership

- To complete the signature and validations screens

- To submit payment

TRADEMARK CHANGES OF OWNERSHIP (ASSIGNMENTS)

For more help on trademark assignments, see etas.uspto.gov/etas/help.html.

Conclusion

Well, as Grover would say, we got to the "end of the book." (*The Monster at the End of This Book* was, and still is, one of our favorites.) See, trademarks aren't scary! Filing a trademark application is just a step-by-step process. Understanding what happens once you have the certificate—maintaining, policing, and keeping your mark from becoming generic—is not onerous. And what types of use by others are permitted is not hard to grasp.

This is a great beginning. Even if you still think, "I just want to hire an attorney to do this," that's fine! This book has given you the vocabulary to have a constructive conversation with your lawyer. So, that's it! You've completed the book. Go file a trademark! Read more things! Play! Invent! Create! What if you need more assistance? Visit our website and listen to our podcast at www.justwannaquilt.com.

Resources

If you have worked your way through this book, you've learned a lot. If you are hungry for more knowledge or just want more in-depth information on a specific topic, the resources in this section will help. Here are our favorite additional resources.

USPTO Resources

USPTO Homepage

www.upsto.gov

This is one of our favorite resources. Over the years, the USPTO has developed helpful resources, including videos. Numerous articles, FAQs, and videos help you understand and work through the trademark process.

The Trademark Manual of Examining Procedure (TMEP)

tmep.uspto.gov

This is the manual that the trademark examining attorneys use, and it is searchable! You can find more information on any aspect of trademarks in the manual. The TMEP provides the guidelines and procedures for examining attorneys and can be cited in your responses to Office Actions. The TMEP is updated regularly to reflect changes.

Example search of the TMEP. You can search and understand what these records say, now that you have read this book.

Enter your search term, and you can see the results. In this case, we searched for *smell*. We found that specimens for scents cannot be submitted electronically and that you must send a sample of the actual scent for the trademark examining attorney to review. How cool is that?

One search result for smell. Now that you've read the book, you can read and understand it!

This is a valuable resource because the law changes. You may also want to search for anything specifically related to your mark. The manual just gives you more access to knowledge. *Just Wanna Trademark for Makers* is the starting point. Now, take this knowledge to learn more!

Trademark Electronic Search System (TESS)

tess2.uspto.gov

We've been using this throughout the book to conduct searches.

Trademark ID Manual of Goods and Services

idm-tmng.uspto.gov/id-master-list-public.html

You've seen this before too. This is where to find potential descriptions for the International Class you choose.

Design Search Code Manual

tess2.uspto.gov/tmdb/dscm/index.htm

This is the resource you use to look up the six-digit code for designs and logos.

Professional Search Resources

Markify

markify.com

Markify provides comprehensive trademark searching for under $200. This includes federal trademark records (TESS), state trademarks, Internet searches, domain names, and, for an additional fee, a worldwide search (using the WIPO database). You can also order a full image search and subscribe to trademark watch services, among other products. If you do a good deal of trademark searching, you can purchase a subscription. In full disclosure, we have a subscription to Markify and we have also used their comprehensive search service to double check our work for this book.

Alt Legal

altlegal.com/blog

One of our new favorite sites is the Alt Legal blog. This is a company trying to sell trademark resources to attorneys, but it has an amazing (and searchable) blog. It offers insight to attorneys on how to counsel clients. It's like peeking behind the curtain.

Trademarkia

trademarkia.com

This is a wonderful free search engine for all things trademark, and it has licensed attorneys to help you register your mark. It is the largest registerer of trademarks each year. Trademarkia's search engine is powerful, so explore this space. But don't forget that your own research is key. Remember, with knowledge of the specific field, ENGLISH PAPER PIECING would not have been registered for English Paper Piecing. Your knowledge and understanding of trademark is important, even when you are in dialogue with an attorney.

Clarivate CompuMark Comprehensive Searches

clarivate.com/products/compumark-family

CompuMark is a leading provider of comprehensive trademark searches. It is more expensive than Markify and offers many product options.

U.S. Trademark Law

The Constitution

Federal trademark law comes from a small clause in the U.S. Constitution: Article 1, Section 8, Clause 3, or I.8.3, which gives Congress the power "to regulate commerce with foreign nations, and among the several states, and with the Indian tribes."

Trademark requires goods or services to be in interstate commerce. For more on the commerce clause and trademark, see www.law.cornell.edu/constitution-conan/article-1/section-8/clause-8/federal-power-over-trademarks.

Cornell's Legal Information Institute

law.cornell.edu/uscode/text/15/1051

We've been discussing trademark law for many pages, but sometimes it is useful to read and review the actual law. If you want to review the full text, Cornell Law School's Legal Information Institute has a public version of the Lanham Act, the current trademark law in the United States. The numbering starts with "1051" and continues. Remember, you may encounter 2(f), but that means in the law "1052(f)."

You will see where everything in this book comes from. It all starts with the law.

Key Sections of the Law

We've included a few parts of the law on the upcoming pages. The trademark law starts at 15 U.S.C. Code Section 1051.

The first number identifies the code where trademark law is, in this case 15 (for copyright, it is 17). The second four-digit number identifies a particular section of the law, like Section 1052. You will sometimes see four-digit numbers. That's U.S. law. Sometimes, you will see something like 2(d). That's the numbering from when it was a bill, and for some reason, that number just stuck. So, you'll see "Section 2(d) refusals" in Office Actions and other places. That is actually 15 U.S.C. Section 1052(d). The *2* corresponds to the last number in the law, so 1052 is Section 2. Sorry that it is so confusing!

15 U.S. Code § 1051—Application for registration; verification

(a) Application for use of trademark

(1) The owner of a trademark used in commerce may request registration of its trademark on the principal register hereby established by paying the prescribed fee and filing in the Patent and Trademark Office an application and a verified statement, in such form as may be prescribed by the Director, and such number of specimens or facsimiles of the mark as used as may be required by the Director.

(2) The application shall include specification of the applicant's domicile and citizenship, the date of the applicant's first use of the mark, the date of the applicant's first use of the mark in commerce, the goods in connection with which the mark is used, and a drawing of the mark.

(3) The statement shall be verified by the applicant and specify that—

(A) the person making the verification believes that he or she, or the juristic person in whose behalf he or she makes the verification, to be the owner of the mark sought to be registered;

(B) to the best of the verifier's knowledge and belief, the facts recited in the application are accurate;

(C) the mark is in use in commerce; and

(D) to the best of the verifier's knowledge and belief, no other person has the right to use such mark in commerce either in the identical form thereof or in such near resemblance thereto as to be likely, when used on or in connection with the goods of such other person, to cause confusion, or to cause mistake, or to deceive, except that, in the case of every application claiming concurrent use, the applicant shall—

(i) state exceptions to the claim of exclusive use; and

(ii) shall specify, to the extent of the verifier's knowledge—

(I) any concurrent use by others;

(II) the goods on or in connection with which and the areas in which each concurrent use exists;

(III) the periods of each use; and

(IV) the goods and area for which the applicant desires registration.

[omitted material]

(b) Application for bona fide intention to use trademark

(1) A person who has a bona fide intention, under circumstances showing the good faith of such person, to use a trademark in commerce may request registration of its trademark on the principal register hereby established by paying the prescribed fee and filing in the Patent and Trademark Office an application and a verified statement, in such form as may be prescribed by the Director.

[omitted material]

(c) Amendment of application under subsection (B) to conform to requirements of subsection (A)

At any time during examination of an application filed under subsection (b), an applicant who has made use of the mark in commerce may claim the benefits of such use for purposes of this chapter, by amending his or her application to bring it into conformity with the requirements of subsection (a).

[omitted material]

15 U.S. Code § 1052—Trademarks registrable on principal register; concurrent registration

No trademark by which the goods of the applicant may be distinguished from the goods of others shall be refused registration on the principal register on account of its nature unless it—

(a) Consists of or comprises immoral, deceptive, or scandalous matter; or matter which may disparage or falsely suggest a connection with persons, living or dead, institutions, beliefs, or national symbols, or bring them into contempt, or disrepute; or a geographical indication which, when used on or in connection with wines or spirits, identifies a place other than the origin of the goods and is first used on or in connection with wines or spirits by the applicant on or after one year after the date on which the WTO Agreement (as defined in section 3501(9) of title 19) enters into force with respect to the United States.

(b) Consists of or comprises the flag or coat of arms or other insignia of the United States, or of any State or municipality, or of any foreign nation, or any simulation thereof.

(c) Consists of or comprises a name, portrait, or signature identifying a particular living individual except by his written consent, or the name, signature, or portrait of a deceased President of the United States during the life of his widow, if any, except by the written consent of the widow.

(d) Consists of or comprises a mark which so resembles a mark registered in the Patent and Trademark Office, or a mark or trade name previously used in the United States by another and not abandoned, as to be likely, when used on or in connection with the goods of the applicant, to cause confusion, or to cause mistake, or to deceive.

[omitted materials]

(e) Consists of a mark which (1) when used on or in connection with the goods of the applicant is merely descriptive or deceptively misdescriptive of them, (2) when used on or in connection with the goods of the applicant is primarily geographically descriptive of them, except as indications of regional origin may be registrable under section 1054 of this title, (3) when used on or in connection with the goods of the applicant is primarily geographically deceptively misdescriptive of them, (4) is primarily merely a surname, or (5) comprises any matter that, as a whole, is functional.

(f) Except as expressly excluded in subsections (a), (b), (c), (d), (e)(3), and (e)(5) of this section, nothing in this chapter shall prevent the registration of a mark used by the applicant which has become distinctive of the applicant's goods in commerce. The Director may accept as prima facie evidence that the mark has become distinctive, as used on or in connection with the applicant's goods in commerce, proof of substantially exclusive and continuous use thereof as a mark by the applicant in commerce for the five years before the date on which the claim of distinctiveness is made. Nothing in this section shall prevent the registration of a mark which, when used on or in connection with the goods of the applicant, is primarily geographically deceptively misdescriptive of them, and which became distinctive of the applicant's goods in commerce before December 8, 1993.

A mark which would be likely to cause dilution by blurring or dilution by tarnishment under section 1125(c) of this title, may be refused registration only pursuant to a proceeding brought under section 1063 of this title. A registration for a mark which would be likely to cause dilution by blurring or dilution by tarnishment under section 1125(c) of this title, may be canceled pursuant to a proceeding brought under either section 1064 of this title or section 1092 of this title.

15 U.S. Code § 1053—Service marks registrable

Subject to the provisions relating to the registration of trademarks, so far as they are applicable, service marks shall be registrable, in the same manner and with the same effect as are trademarks, and when registered they shall be entitled to the protection provided in this chapter in the case of trademarks. Applications and procedure under this section shall conform as nearly as practicable to those prescribed for the registration of trademarks.

15 U.S. Code § 1054—Collective marks and certification marks registrable

Subject to the provisions relating to the registration of trademarks, so far as they are applicable, collective and certification marks, including indications of regional origin, shall be registrable under this chapter, in the same manner and with the same effect as are trademarks, by persons, and nations, States, municipalities, and the like, exercising legitimate control over the use of the marks sought to be registered, even though not possessing an industrial or commercial establishment, and when registered they shall be entitled to the protection provided in this chapter in the case of trademarks, except in the case of certification marks when used so as to represent falsely that the owner or a user thereof makes or sells the goods or performs the services on or in connection with which such mark is used. Applications and procedure under this section shall conform as nearly as practicable to those prescribed for the registration of trademarks.

[omitted materials]

15 U.S. Code § 1056—Disclaimer of unregistrable matter

(a) Compulsory and voluntary disclaimers

The Director may require the applicant to disclaim an unregistrable component of a mark otherwise registrable. An applicant may voluntarily disclaim a component of a mark sought to be registered.

(b) Prejudice of rights

No disclaimer, including those made under subsection (e) of section 1057 of this title, shall prejudice or affect the applicant's or registrant's rights then existing or thereafter arising in the disclaimed matter, or his right of registration on another application if the disclaimed matter be or shall have become distinctive of his goods or services.

Index

About the *Authors*

Sid and Elizabeth co-wrote this book to bridge the discourse between the legal world and those whose art and craft depend on understanding the law. It has been an awesome project to work on together.

Sidne K. Gard (they/them) has told stories from the beginning. Currently, an undergraduate at the School of the Art Institute of Chicago, they study writing, fiber arts, comics, and time-based storytelling. Sid also works as Managing Editor and Entertainment Editor of F Newsmagazine, where they also write an entertainment column, "Loving the Monster," and a comic strip, "Luma's World." Previously, they attended and received a Certificate of Artistry in Creative Writing from the New Orleans Center for the Creative Arts. Already, they have won writing awards in high school and college, and they have been published for their photography, writing, and experimental work in literary and art journals. When not writing about law-related topics, their work focuses on identity-based storytelling. For more, go to sidnekgard.com.

Elizabeth Townsend Gard (she/her) is the John E. Koerner Endowed Professor of Law at Tulane University, where she teaches intellectual property, art law, entrepreneurship, and social media. She has received numerous fellowships; been cited by the U.S. Supreme Court in Golan v. Holder (2012); and writes for law journals, magazines, blogs, and books. Elizabeth has focused her career on the question of the role of law in creativity, in great part because of Sid's involvement with art and craft from an early age. Elizabeth earned a Ph.D. from UCLA, a J.D., and an LL.M. from the University of Arizona, and was awarded a Leverhulme Postdoctoral Fellowship at the London School of Economics. She also just wants to quilt.

She is the host of the *Just Wanna Quilt*s podcast, which explores the intersection of quilting, craft, community, and of course, intellectual property. For more, see Dr. Townsend Gard's bio at Tulane Law School, law.tulane.edu/faculty/full-time/elizabeth-townsend-gard.

Sid and Elizabeth began the Just Wanna journey in 2017, with a six-week trip across the United States where they explored the meaning of quilting and crafting, which led to the *Just Wanna Quilt* podcast, numerous adventures at quilt shows, and presentations about the role of law in creativity in many venues. Sid lives it; Elizabeth researches it. Together, they have come to understand the role of law in creativity from many viewpoints. This duo brings a fresh and different perspective, both practical and thoughtful, to the intersection of craft, art, and the law. For more, go to justwannaquilt.com.

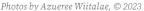

Photos by Azueree Wiitalae, © 2023

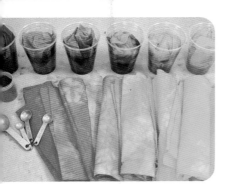

CREATIVE SPARK
ONLINE LEARNING

Crafty courses to become an expert maker

From their studio to yours, Creative Spark instructors are teaching you how to create and become a master of your craft. So not only do you get a look inside their creative space, you also get to be a part of engaging courses that would typically be a one or multi-day workshop from the comfort of your home.

Creative Spark is not your one-size-fits-all online learning experience. We welcome you to be who you are, share, create, and belong.

Scan for a gift from